Bestiary of Souls

—

Sean Lause

FUTURECYCLE PRESS

Mineral Bluff, Georgia

Published by FutureCycle Press
Mineral Bluff, Georgia, USA

ISBN 978-1-938853-24-1

Contents

For my son, Christopher, with love

Heaven of fireflies

Each night it appeared, the heaven
of fireflies, in that lucid summer
of nearing storms. The air shivered a sliver-
moon, wink of a cat's eye, then a wind sluiced
down, and the stars glided, descended into
hushed fields that looked back at my longing,
daring me to capture the light of these
gods of wheat, weeds, glades and hollows.

Intricate crickets designed the darkness,
then a firefly, here, there, then a whole line,
suturing the night, allowing just a glimpse,
brushing the far fields with glimmers.
But if you grew proud, lunged with greedy palm,
they would whirr, fade, slip through the velvet
seam between silence and eternity,
that haven where all wonder returns.

I plunged down the hills with my glass jar,
scooping the airy gold, and never surrendered
until I became a lamp of bottled lightning,
weaving a path through the mystery,
or, snatching only one, bend him to a ring,
a glow, a covert pulse, wedding me to the stars.
At dawn I would free them, ask their pardon
for disturbing their calm with beauty.

I knew a world once deeply in its wounds

A candle, a sail, a vigil,
I kept the hours gently and well.
Honey bees festooned the breeze,
and I was the strength and faith of days.

Then one morning, I blindly waved a wand
of dandelion seeds. They tumbled down a wind,
drunken, each suddenly lost, alone,
and time awoke, wound up the sun.

The air gasped like a smothered candle.
Treetops grasped at fleeing angels.
Something came accusing the rose,
and the afternoon sighed with butterflies.

I plunged deep in the trees and gardens
and pulled out webs and roots of wounds.
Everything bled tears or dreams or words,
and the cricket's call shivered through the stars.

I followed a child's cry and found it was my own.
Still, I remember how that final sparrow
sank deep within the November winds
with the purity of all beaten wings.

The dragonfly's response

I watched a dragonfly
rest on the quicksand
like a praying mantis
on a bed of Queen Anne's Lace.

"It's the wings,"
said the scientist.
"They maintain its equilibrium."

"It's the mass,"
said the physicist,
"its relation to gravity."

"It's its brain,"
said the cynic.
"It's too stupid to know better."

"Wrong," whispered
the dragonfly.
"This is what I do."

The door

A monarch butterfly,
freshly unwoven,
glitters with uncertainty,
clings to my front door handle,
shivers, pulses, watches
me with its needle eyes.
If I open the door,
it may tumble and scatter
like burning paper.

And it is burning,
burning with time
and possibility, and so
I keep the door closed,
waiting for this presence to
turn from the green of all imagining
to the blood of all ascent,
thrust into oneness like a heart,
wounding the air with its wings.

We both know how much this means.
Compared to it, the crucifixion needs
explaining. Yet it is as beyond me
as flight. I am no citizen of gardens
or bowers. Two wanderers then.
One seeks home, the other
its rightful kingdom of winds.
And so I wait as long as is given
an everyday miracle to suffice.

The exiled menagerie

God is a gunpowder behind the eyes,
shot through the core of a desperate paradise.
When you catch the bullet in your teeth you will know
you are no longer lost in the circus.

Now you guess the bearded lady's cue.
The gypsy will bless your midnight dreams with wolves.
You will recite extraterrestrial alphabets
to the rhythm of the knife's near-miss.

All the whipped and tortured beasts
will guide your graceful taunts of gravity
as you watch your feet dare each other
across the wire—netless, terrified, home.

You, prince of the circle of wounds.
You, priest of the exiled menagerie.

Night vision

Driving home late on ice-bitten road,
my headlights probing like a blind man's fingers,
the night trembling with snow, my boy
blissfully asleep in his magic chair...

They appeared from the abyss
as if projected by the moon,
their legs flowing silently through the snow,
a herd of deer, fleeing remembered guns.

Leaping in plumes of electricity,
embracing us in soft brown flesh,
implicating me in my own breaths
and every snow that falls unseen.

Their eyes seemed to know me from long ago,
their leafy heads nodding as if in prayer.
We swung in one motion, relentless, pure,
then they curved beneath the night and disappeared.

When my son stirred, I could not tell
who had dreamed and who had been awake.
I only knew we were safe and blessed,
and I had never lived and would never die.

Scrambling device

There is a scrambling device
between you and the sky
that prevents you from hearing the stars.
There is a small box
stuck in each of your eyes
that keeps your vision
from getting out.

I, deaf and blind for years,
was taught this
by a small red fox
while he was cheating at cards.

This absence is the control.
With it, we breed money.
Without it, we might find
satori in Wal-Mart.

As he departed,
between my sight and hearing,
slipping between stars, the fox
said: "What if it's all a path?"

Twelve triumphs over the material world

— 1.

Cat in freezing rain—
First its breath,
then its cry.

— 2.

The rubbish heap
releasing
crows.

— 3.

After the rain
the ladybug
shines.

— 4.

Geese flying home
and the sky seems
less alone.

— 5.

Lilies in the field
considering
Christ.

— 6.

Long Spring grass.
Here, there,
Easter eggs.

— 7.

Still pond.
A carp's breath
quivers the sky.

— 8.

The wind tonight.
The stars go out
like candles.

— 9.

Night sky—
Nouns, verbs,
adjectives.

— 10.

Burned-down church.
Inside the remains,
sparrow nests.

— 11.

Sunlight-
enlightened
dragonfly.

— 12.

Watching you,
she blows out one candle,
then the other.

Bird lights

Inside each bird is a light.
The light is singing.
It sings of distances
between breath and silence.
At night it perches,
wondering back at what it sang by day.
And only then are its distances achieved,
its fear folded in the sleep of wings,
and its loneliness cast to a million galaxies.

What the cockatiel sees

Awake,
the cockatiel can see
neither before nor behind,
future nor history, illusions.
Yet she sees—both sides at once,
double vision, the present complete.
What we could call schizophrenia,
to her is all unity.

Frightened,
she presses her beak to the wall.
There she weaves magic,
inventing her own prison and freedom
at once. Her enemy gone,
she sees nothing but wall,
a world, a universe of wall.

Asleep,
she turns into a question mark,
the question composed, unanswered,
gentle eyes closed, sunk in soft feathers.
Curled to the curve of earth and time,
she dreams a heaven of cockatiels
clattering up their cages to the sun.

Spiders of equilibrium

They balance on hunger
and spin their eggs from suns,
strung between doom and deathless faith,
tracing the signatures of butterflies.

Their legs flutter
like a child's eyelashes,
and they are the patience the grass keeps.
They weave the veins of winds, and stars
guard the fleece of their imaginings
as they dream a tender communion of flies.

A view from the white whale

I thought I recognized him,
the whale-line man, when he
pricked that pin in me,
my ancient wounds maskless,
that barbaric white leg
carved from my brother.

Yet I could not understand
what he was saying. His voice,
small and far away. I must have pulled
him down with me to my
wall-less depths. Even his cannibal ship
was a sigh in the round infinite.

I returned to the vortex,
my home, the eternal silence,
sole answer to his doubloon words.
Perhaps now, wrapt in the
mingled threads of the ocean floor,
his bones will see more clearly.

Kafka lived

Kafka did not die
in that coughing
sanatorium.
That was a cover story
issued in duplicate
by the control authorities
with so much to hide.

He became what he imagined,
a waiter
in Palestine.
He arrived incognito
though everybody knew.

The Kafka Restaurant,
where, oddly, there is no waiting,
except for K.,
who waits and waits, and waits,
at last at home.

He stands officiously, watching all,
making the peas feel their guilt.
His eyes still swim in sadness,
though still, nevertheless, you
won't get past his pen
that takes your order dutifully,
painfully set down
forever.

He wears no uniform.
In fact, he's nude,
although, to be fair,
no one notices.

His customers, in identical black suits,
nod, satisfied, fulfilled, as he fills
and refills their soup, as they drink it
through their wise and thirsty beards.

He ladles a river
of lovingly silent kosher clams
on reasonable china
a breath away from doom.
So much food and food,
humped in steaming armfuls,
Franz keeps forever feeding.

Later, he will sleep,
breathing softly,
curled in the embrace
of dozing giraffes
and the tails of animals
no one has ever seen,
with violin music
strung from the stars
like a distant memory,
just perfected enough
to make him dream
of crawling to heaven
on broken wings.

Caliban's victory

We caught him when he drowned his dreaming books,
star-wound man, wrapped in himself.
—From behind, where all good treasons grow.
—From beyond, where happy endings never go.

Tyrant, he fed my thirst salt water,
clapped me devil, deformed slave, spat sharp bile
on my scaly gabardine,
did beat me and curse me beast;
words do howl and bite and hate me still,
forgetting I, a king, outrank him.
Time took me my careful plotting.
Beware the tortoise outlive you all.

His daughter took me willing.
Her man played only that chess.
I won her, and soothed her hair back
with tumbling song and all the beauty
I kept from sleep, on the cursed rock
I loved her for the shipwrecks in her eyes.
And she did love me, did kiss my wounds,
till I turned beast, drunkard, man, king, all—

And you, spinner of words and worlds,
we'll make you a meal to stuff a gullet full.
Hunger tames all vile offenses,
and I am the darkness I call mine.

My island, mine,
where I am again mine own king.
Freedom. High-day! Freedom! Free!
Now I go eat my dinner.

The earth as crucifixion

I had a thirst to buy a crucifix
from fear, not love.
A sudden terror I awoke with
that I was about to go out
like a pinched candle.
That I would be nothing but a name.

I searched in store after store.
No cross. Found necklaces
strung with skulls, razors, clocks,
glocks, pentagrams, smiley faces.
No cross. Finally found it
in a souvenir shop. Plastic, it shattered
and scattered like sterile seeds.

I broke down, my bones sobbing.

"I'll be your crucifix,"
said dragonfly,
and spread his wings through the dying sun.

"I'll be your crucifix,"
said snake,
and pushed through his old skin to a dawn.

"I'll be your crucifix,"
said deer,
and showed me her gaping wound.

And then I saw the world as crucifixion.
And every living thing a Christ.
Not one spared the spear.
The heart alone the Paraclete.

What the turtle knows

Part primal, part divine,
with careful pace, this testudine
moves towards her sea, that ancient question.

Her rainbow carapace on the shore,
her church of the signature sands,
her shell too determined
for clumsy, unbright predators,
her mind reptilian and pure.

Two hundred million years
and she survives still
on her stubby feet and sturdy scutes,
while nations fade to silent dooms.

She makes love under a turtle moon,
lays her eggs in the smooth sand of sighs,
then ponders the meaning there,
the secret she burrows into dunes.

Everything is haunted.
Everything is haunted with eternity.

The impossibility of seagulls

The seagulls,
ancient from the egg,
old men's faces
sunk between silver wings,
scoop the air in graceless arcs,
dreaming and despair
in the blue wheat of an October sky.

No angels but Heaven's tumbling dice,
the lost souls of demonic winds
which seek to penetrate the eyes of God,
the blue within the blue.
Trapped between flight and alighting,
they can evade nothing,
not even the invisible.

Their cries yearn in concentric circles,
their wings aching in the gales,
spiral pulses of white on blue,
thirsting, hungry parentheses,
drinking the dust the moon provides,
longing to be a cloud, a dawn, a perfect star,
no longer crucified on wings.

Above them, strung between stars,
the gentle, withered hands of angels;
below them, endlessly far,
a world of human strangers.
The wind again turns back their quest,
and with cries that tear the skies asunder,
they follow the thunder home.

What creatures see when they sleep

— 1.

The owl dreams the night in
across half the earth,
spreading fear with her wings.

— 2.

The field mouse,
embraced in the grass,
escaped from the owl,
inhabits the lost kingdom.

— 3.

The swan,
dreaming in the center of the pond,
mistakes itself for an angel
and is comforted.

— 4.

The beetle dreams
of a stone under which to cling
in the downpour
like a shadow clinging to eternity.

— 5.

The cricket is dreaming you.
If you look carefully through his dream,
he may point you to a fissure in time.

— 6.

The antelope dreams the form of the Savior,
pleased to study his long, sturdy antlers,
to watch him forever
leaping the lions.

Dogs and men

As a child I saw
a dog hit by a car.
His blood shot up,
trying to get back to heaven,
and I saw eternity
was hopelessly far and hopelessly near.

Animals know a way in
and a way out
of time,
passing through invisible doors,
moving between silences
like stars through clouds.

The suffering of animals
is complete, perfect, everywhere.
Their blood conspires with ours.
The dog tied in the snow—
It turns to bark North.
It turns to bark South.
But we have lost the language of their bones.

Dogs, men,
walk in rhythm when they're old,
careful, close to the earth,
each bone unbending pain,
shuttered, like we are seeing them
through the gaps of light in a passing train.

That was my dog that died that day,
and every day since,
blood it shed for me, so I could see.

The day you finally learn
you live and die in the breaths of others,
there may be nothing left to do
but build a circle in a grove of trees
and shout "I'm alive! I'm still alive!"
until winds weave an answer to the rain.

The visitor

The cicada dies and remains,
clutched to my upstairs window,
punctuating thought.

At dawn, it glows gold,
a hyacinth
lit from within
by emptiness,
wings shedding needles of light
to thread the windy leaves.

At noon it burns blue,
folding the sky in its wings.
Living locusts
trill for its return,
but it remains
loyal to its death.

At night it is a black heart
feigning invisibility,
patient,
no longer fearing the cat.

In Summer it remembers
the last cry of its wings.
The storm comes, quickening the shadows,
tormenting the screen,
but still it clutches
whirling with the earth.

In Winter, winds
turn trees to claws,
but still it clings, waiting,
molding itself
into a diamond of ice.

In Spring it is gone.
Finally, I can leave this house
to find
on my grandmother's tombstone
a cicada's shell broken and free.

Cicada learned

Cicada learned
he was an interpenetration
when he saw his own shell
staring back at him in wonder
and he realized it was not his birth but his death
he left behind.

Then he knew there are layers and layers
of cicadas, all stacked simultaneously
through the mind. Some are visible,
but mostly the cicadas you hear in trees
are invisible, and once guided Christ
down the darkest roads of Galilee.

Most of all, cicada learned
that cicadas glow with the fire of the
cicada god, who broke the universe
from its shell of silence a trillion
light-years ago, and the universe is
shaped like a cicada that will release itself
back into its shell when man is finally enlightened—
each shell a thirst fulfilled, stringing electric
symphonies trilling through the trees
the truth that our hearts are all
cicada shells broken and whole,
holy and loved and cupped
in gentle forests of stars forever, amen.

Black bass

When the black bass,
hovering in time,
feels the stream
assume his shape,
impersonating him
in tribute to his black bass dignity,
flowing around him,
making way for him,
like the king of all fish,
molding itself to his gills,
glittering his scales to gold,
no longer water at all
but the soul of the silent black bass,
then the lure that wounded him
unknots itself, and he follows the stream
straight through the winging skies.

Raising Godzilla

It's hard for a monster to hide,
though he tried, and tried, and
tried, at first blending with mountains
and forests, pretending not to breathe,
tucking his snarling tail between his legs.

Silently,
he learned the language of fission and flame.
There was no one to teach him.
His parents were just apocalyptic energy.

Slowly,
he grew louder.
God he was a big green galoot.
His massive feet galumphing.
He couldn't fit on, let alone in.

So he spent his days
composing haiku
to invisible ancestors,
polishing his emerald heart,
and rolling rumbles to the dawn.

The little people frightened him.
He studied their ways and wars
with the quizzical hum of electric high wires.
Their language was tiny and tinny
and filled with rapid determination.

Then one day
he tripped over a pagoda,
and damn if it didn't shrug its big shoulders
and collapse and crumble
in a heap of silence.

That's when he realized he'd been conned.
He discovered their tanks and trains
were really only toys, and the little people
hopelessly stupid, always running from him
in the same direction he was walking.

Before long he'd trampled half their towns,
and it was good. He learned their little empires
need a good kicking now and then, and that God
gave Godzillas fire and tails for a reason.

So he clicked his claws in joy
and glowed beyond extinction.

Dog

Many saw, but no one
paid attention to the dog, the old
man, watching the traffic pass,
resigned from all but sun and moon.

Skinny mutt, split tail, leather ears,
the old man's hands as clean and smooth
as worn soup bones.
Mutt and man on a bus-less bench.

Such invisibility is an art,
to be so much a part
of your town square
that no one knows you're there.

Like the green stone fountain
that holds no more penny wisdom,
the swirling tresses of its spray
long cut down to silence.

Sometimes he stayed all night,
staring back at mannequin eternities,
the dog asleep beside him, legs up,
looking like a dead mosquito.

Mornings, the man bought donut pieces,
pushed each gently into the dog's mouth,
his own mouth working in mirror of the dog's,
dog's mouth jawing like an old bluesman.

The old man's finger waved the countless air,
or carefully conducted the weather.
Still, no one stopped to read
their inscription in the rain.

One day he was dead. Someone nudged him.
He seemed to shrug, then leaned over.
An ambulance removed him.
The dog remained.

The sheriff paid for the funeral
and then, because he did not know
what else to do, put the dog down,
fed him to the old man's unmarked grave.
After, the town collapsed,
wall by wall, illusion by
illusion, an old movie
pulled down prop by prop.

A bus bench, a town square,
and paper tornadoes that spun in alleys—
stilled—their tiny rage spent,
collapsed like drunks in oblivion.

Listen. There was an old man.
A dog. This much is fate. And crazy chance.
The remainder is possibility.
And you are all liars and poets.

The end of nightmares

I dream man died but the animals remain.
Mourning doves watch the street lamps go blind.
Coyotes yawn in the hearts of machines.
Sparrows trill wonders in the eaves.

Perfection of insects in grass absolute.
Beetles swagger over our unlined graves.
Dragonflies thread the stars with filament
as mantis shadows unfold the eve.

The horse's mane waves the riderless winds.
The leopard's shining, uncaptured lust
reclaims her Asia, and the rabbit's blood
floods the fox's teeth with ecstasy.

Breathless spirit of hunger, hunt and wound,
holy thirst, delights of flight and fear,
and raptured by the cobra's arrowed gaze,
the nightingale sings no other world.

They sleep in the easeful dust of kings,
dreaming deep beneath the empty skies,
breeding, dying, born and reborn,
and awake to their own startled cries.

Trusting the wasps

— 1.

I killed the first one
with a rolled-up *Times*,
pounding her life out
under war, murder, and disease.

When I was done
she looked like a poisoned fig,
her body riddled with seeds,
her eyes pinpricks of mystery,
my body a disheveled room
filled with wings and things undone.

— 2.

Now there are dozens
between my upstairs screen window
and the antique door with ivory knob.
They come and go through cracks
the size of a fingernail.
Sometimes they forget the way back,
clinging to the glass,
licorice eyes shifting up, around,
searching for the lost paradise.

— 3.

Have they journeyed here from outer space
to gauge my knowledge of earth?
The sun touches them black, green, bottle-blue,
ecstatic bottlecap angels
descending like helicopters,

then whirring into maple seeds,
spinning the sun's gold,
beating to a pulse
in baseball diamond breezes,
swirling to the blue within the blue.

— 4.

Faith is a mirror
which reflects what it cannot see.
Take me, then,
who knows no flight beyond dream.

If I close my eyes,
will I feel my wings
beating in sudden palms of light?
Ticking time to dust with yours?

— 5.

Today I opened the door,
stepped outside with a deep breath
and bare feet,
but the air was weighted with betrayals.

I long for a trust
as clean as my grandmother's linen on the line,
as pure as a child's breath
dunking for apples.

Come then,
you sly killers,
sting my mouth to life.
Death is whatever
makes us count to two.

— 6.

One lands in my palm.
It feels like a baby's breath.
Its legs probe my lines.
Then it stings me, over and over.
Its rage merges briefly with my pulse.
This love is impossible.
It cannot pierce these bones of gravity.

— 7.

Indoors, the wasp rages against mystery,
coils up like a tip of smoke,
pounds its head blindly into windows
like a finger gesticulating points
in an argument it cannot comprehend.

I suspect it hates me,
but I mistake its rage.
It hates my walls, my lying windows,
my confinement and flightless certainties.

I open the window
and it's out,
ascends to a freedom it must sense in sleep.

— 8.

Last night I dreamed of wasps.
One leapt into my house,
hovered in my brain,
descended deep into the darkness,
stinging memories to life.

— 9.

Now I kneel naked,
open the door, reach to them.
They almost let me touch them,
then pull away as if on strings.
When I breathe deeply
they creep closer, waiting for me
to come with them over the trees,
through the net of stars,
as we drop from world to world
like the stinging tears of God.

— 10.

I can sit with them now, mornings,
when the cold sun stuns them sluggish.
Don't go near the nest.
Don't attempt to snatch them.
Don't flinch or show fear.
You can die.
Learn to breathe
like a child's whispered song.
The wasp awaits your finger like a ring.

— 11.

A dandelion is a clutch of gold coins
turning silver with the fears of Fall.

Late October,
a ring of black and gold wasps watches me dress
from the window of the ivory-handled door.
They have formed a perfect circle
of skydiver hope,
each foreleg crossing its brother's or sister's,
wings folded 'round a bitter dawn.

I pull the door open gently
to let them in.
They drop to the floor with a whisper
like bits of finely spun glass,
then a sudden wave of wind
brushes them from my sight with a sigh.

Where?
Back to the earth they spun in dances.
Back to the depths beneath lost cities.
Back to the secret veins that coined them
from hunger in the lion's mouth.

Spiders weave the bed of visions

Every night covert spiders descended
to weave my bed with dreams
of amethyst meteors and kaleidoscopes
shattered to their freedom, and I knew
the universe in terrified innocence
as it tried to remember itself.

Every morning I went blind, screaming in terror,
my eyes sewn neatly shut with spiders' legs.
My mother bathed them open with her spittle
and a cloth, and light and color returned.
Then she calmed me with these words:

"Look at the tops of the trees. No one ever does.
A world of their own, an ocean no one sails.
They whisper you meanings of wind and wings,
predict storms days in advance, and tell
stories of lovers and warriors long gone."

My mother's words wove night into waking
until I no longer knew dream from day.
Time was a window whose curtains she drew,
caressing me gently into flesh and vision.

The wolf as original dreamer

The earth would burst incandescent,
they said, but I was prepared
with an army of dreams and magic,
and each night a thousand stars
descended from the ceiling like cobalt spiders
to weave my bed of innocence.

The fall came when my father placed a book
of Peter and the Wolf before the mirror.
I could not stop watching the wolf,
its lava eyes spilling rage and violation,
teeth swirling in a snarl of white death,
its feet clawing for the earth to return.

Above, Peter clung to the tree branch
faceless, like all sadists,
tightening the noose over its tail
to suspend it through eternity,
and to make the torture exquisite,
he made music from its misery.

Tonight, alone in bed,
my wife dying, son grown and gone,
the wolf leaps from a shadow in my dream,
folds itself around me, shredded tail bleeding.
I sing gently to it,
sharing the hunger still hovering in the air.

Seeing night

At times, the road below
pulled past endlessly
until I could feel the turns ahead,
and my head swayed with the creaking lamp,
my wings bound, eyes encased in black,
the night eternal,
only the church bells to remember.

Once I heard
the cat approach, withdraw, approach again.
I could smell its sweet breath
and hear the hunger in its claws
nearing my throat.
It spared me from fear, I think,
knowing what I am.

All around me was what I used to fear.
Crashing glass, cruel laughter,
the clink of coins, angry oaths,
words that bit the air,
whips snapping,
horses shrieking,
drunken men, my owners
until you came.

I almost surrendered
to exhaustion, thirst,
their mocking cries,
and the dark within the dark.

Now I feel your careful fingers
loose the threads at last.

The night withers,
and my eyes crave the light of lights.

Ascending, father of heights,
I follow my cries
to my pride of place—
A blue no man can see.

I journeyed, dying,
across eternities,
reborn at last
in the bend of my beating wings.

Acknowledgments

Some of the poems have appeared in literary journals, including:

"The Wolf as original dreamer" has appeared in *Caveat Lector, Illumen, The Mother Earth International Journal, Lone Starts Magazine* and *The King's English.* The poem was nominated for the Pushcart Prize.
"A view from the white whale" was published in *The Old Red Kimono* and *Avocet.*
"Bird lights" was published in *Westward Quarterly: The Magazine of Family Reading.*
"Night vision" was published in *Words of Wisdom, Writer's Journal, Hot Metal Press, Whistling Shade, Poetic Matrix, Tribeca Poetry Review, Presa* and *The Worchester Review.*
"Kafka Lived" was published in *Gargoyle Magazine.*

Cover art, "Emergence of Graptopsaltria nigrofuscata," by Masaki Ikeda; photo of author and Maria by Christopher Lause; cover and interior book design by Diane Kistner (dkistner@futurecycle.org); Chaparral Pro text with Tork titling

About FutureCycle Press

FutureCycle Press is dedicated to publishing lasting English-language poetry and flash fiction books, chapbooks, and anthologies in both print-on-demand and ebook formats. Founded in 2007 by long-time independent editor/publishers and partners Diane Kistner and Robert S. King, the press incorporated as a nonprofit in 2012. A number of our editors are distinguished poets and authors in their own right, and we have been actively involved in the small press movement going back to the early seventies.

The FutureCycle Poetry Book Prize and honorarium is awarded annually for the best full-length volume of poetry we publish in a calendar year. Introduced in 2013, our Good Works projects are devoted to issues of global significance, with all proceeds donated to a related worthy cause. We are dedicated to giving all authors we publish the care their work deserves, making our catalog of titles the most distinguished it can be, and paying forward any earnings to fund more great books.

We've learned a few things about independent publishing over the years. We've also evolved a unique, resilient publishing model that allows us to focus mainly on vetting and preserving for posterity the most books of exceptional quality without becoming overwhelmed with bookkeeping and mailing, fundraising activities, or taxing editorial and production "bubbles." To find out more about what we are doing, come see us at www.futurecycle.org.

The FutureCycle Poetry Book Prize

All full-length volumes of poetry published by FutureCycle Press in a given calendar year are considered for the annual FutureCycle Poetry Book Prize. This allows us to consider each submission on its own merits, outside of the context of a contest. Too, the judges see the finished book, which will have benefitted from the beautiful book design and strong editorial gloss we are famous for.

The book ranked the best in judging is announced as the prize-winner in the subsequent year. There is no fixed monetary award; instead, the winning poet receives an honorarium of 20% of the total net royalties from all poetry books and chapbooks the press sold online in the year the winning book was published. The winner is also accorded the honor of judging the next year's competition.

CPSIA information can be obtained at www.ICGtesting.com
Printed in the USA
BVOW04s2236260713

326960BV00010B/250/P

REDEMPTION

R

The Russian Library at Columbia University Press publishes an expansive selection of Russian literature in English translation, concentrating on works previously unavailable in English and those ripe for new translations. Works of premodern, modern, and contemporary literature are featured, including recent writing. The series seeks to demonstrate the breadth, surprising variety, and global importance of the Russian literary tradition and includes not only novels but also short stories, plays, poetry, memoirs, creative nonfiction, and works of mixed or fluid genre.

■ □ ■

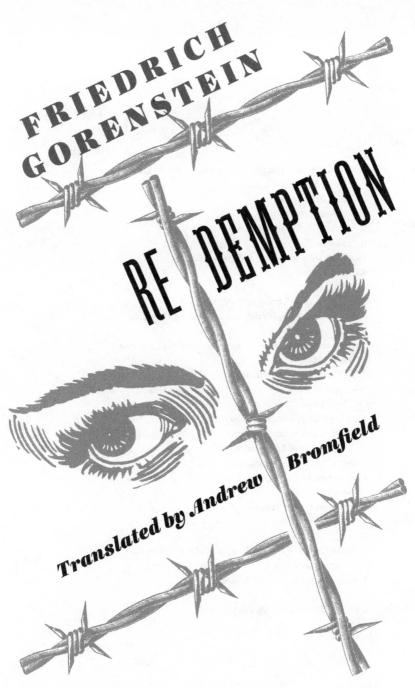

FRIEDRICH GORENSTEIN

RE DEMPTION

Translated by Andrew Bromfield

Columbia University Press / New York

Published with the support of Read Russia, Inc., and the Institute of
    Literary Translation, Russia
Columbia University Press
Publishers Since 1893
New York   Chichester, West Sussex
cup.columbia.edu

Library of Congress Cataloging-in-Publication Data
Names: Gorenshteæin, Fridrikh, 1932-2002, author. | Bromfield,
    Andrew, translator.
Title: Redemption / Friedrich Gorenstein ; translated by Andrew
    Bromfield.
Other titles: Iskuplenie. English
Description: New York : Columbia University Press, 2018. |
    Series: Russian library
Identifiers: LCCN 2018011861 (print) | LCCN 2018017111 (ebook) |
    ISBN 9780231546027 (electronic) | ISBN 9780231185141 (cloth :
    alk. paper) | ISBN 9780231185158 (pbk.)
Subjects: | LCGFT: Psychological fiction.
Classification: LCC PG3481.2.R45 (ebook) | LCC PG3481.2.R45 I713
    2018 (print) | DDC 891.73/44—dc23
LC record available at https://lccn.loc.gov/2018011861

Cover design: Roberto de Vicq de Cumptich
Book design: Lisa Hamm

CONTENTS

INTRODUCTION

Hemingway's pronouncement about an unhappy childhood as the best early training for a writer is especially true for Friedrich Gorenstein. In fact, to call his childhood merely unhappy is a gross understatement. Gorenstein grew up during the time of two evil historical forces, which deeply affected him and left indelible marks on his character and his outlook. His tragic early life experience informed his future writing. Born in 1932 in Kiev, Ukraine, Friedrich was only three years old when his father, a professor of political economy, fell victim to Stalin's Great Terror. Arrested by the NKVD (the People's Commissariat for Internal Affairs, the secret police) and sent to one of the Far East hard-labor camps, two years later he was sentenced to death and shot.

This development had a devastating effect on Gorenstein's family, now the subjects of deprivation and further persecution, and pigeonholed as the "family of an enemy of the people." Gorenstein's mother, Enna Abramovna Prilutskaya, a teacher by training, did everything she could to hide from the watchful eyes of the secret police. First, she changed her surname from her husband's back to her maiden name. She also managed to replace her son's papers, not only changing his surname to hers but also giving him the name "Felix" instead of "Friedrich." Ironically, in the spirit of the time, she and her husband, both ardent believers in the bright future of

Communist ideas, had given their son the name in honor of the coauthor of *The Communist Manifesto*, Friedrich Engels. Later on, as an adult, Gorenstein restored both his given name and his father's surname.

In addition, to distance herself and her son from the watchful eyes of the NKVD, Enna Abramovna escaped from Kiev with three-year-old Friedrich. She took refuge in Berdichev, Ukraine, where she and her husband had been born. Jobless for several years, she had no place of her own, and moved from one relative's or acquaintance's home to another.

Friedrich was only nine when, on June 22, 1941, the military forces of Nazi Germany, together with their allies, broke the notorious Molotov-Ribbentrop nonaggression pact.[1] In the largest German military operation of World War II, code-named "Operation Barbarossa," they crossed the Soviet border on a wide front stretching from the Black Sea in the south to the Baltic Sea in the north.

The attack took the Soviet forces by surprise and was thus highly successful. Stalin infamously treated information about a mortal danger to the country as "fake news" for months, dismissing numerous reports from the Western press as well as from Soviet intelligence about the high concentration of Wehrmacht troops and armament along a broad stretch of the country's western border. The Soviet dictator treated such reports as malicious disinformation and provocation aimed at breaking up the friendship between the peoples of Germany and the Soviet Union.

In the first few hours of the invasion, Luftwaffe planes bombed major Soviet cities. A significant part of the Soviet air force was destroyed on the ground. Unprepared, lacking any direction from high command, the Soviet armies were overwhelmed and retreated en masse. Around four million Soviet soldiers were encircled and captured.

The sudden attack had a devastating effect on the civilian population in general, and on Jews in particular. One of the main reasons for this was that the Soviets blocked information regarding the true intentions of the German troops. After Hitler had come to power and before the signing of the German-Soviet pact of 1939, the policy of the USSR was anti-Nazi. The government produced antifascist films and published books critical of the Nazis' handling of the German Jews. After the pogroms of Kristallnacht in November 1938, an antifascist rally was organized in Moscow, where the director of the State Jewish Theater, Solomon Mikhoels, spoke.

However, in less than a year, Hitler and Stalin, yesterday's ideological enemies, became allies and partners in the seizure of neighboring countries. The Molotov-Ribbentrop pact was signed a week before the outbreak of World War II. Poland was divided, and Hitler seized the countries of Europe one after another. In the occupied territories, especially in Poland, severe persecution of Jews began. Their property was seized, and they were driven into Nazi-organized ghettos.

After the signing of the Molotov-Ribbentrop pact, the Soviets stopped publishing news of Nazi atrocities against Jews. Because of the Soviet information blockade, on the eve of the German invasion the overwhelming majority of the Soviet population was not fully aware of the threat posed by the Germans. As a result of this lack of information and the speed of the German offensive, most Jews in the western regions could not evacuate and were walled off in the ghettos and then killed in the extermination camps.

In *Mein Kampf*, Adolf Hitler wrote that Nazi Germany's main goal was to enlarge its living space (*Lebensraum*) at the expense of the eastern territories; in Hitler's view it was equally important to annihilate members of the Communist Party and Soviet Jews, two components of the Judeo-Bolshevik threat to Germany. Therefore, the first order of business when capturing a Red Army unit was to cull Jews and Communist political commissars and shoot them, often on the spot.

Procedures were also in place to deal with Jewish civilians. As the Nazi military advanced deep into Soviet territory, SS and police units followed the troops. The first to arrive were the Einsatzgruppen, special mobile killing units of the Wehrmacht security police and the security service. Behind the front lines, they were charged with the task of annihilating Jews, Communists, and other people deemed to be dangerous to the establishment of long-term German rule on Soviet territory.

The Einsatzgruppen initiated the mass murder of Jews and Gypsies but also Soviet state and Party officials. Unlike in the Nazi-occupied countries of Western Europe, where Jews had been deported and shipped to death camps primarily in Germany and Poland, Jews in the USSR were taken from their homes and shot on the outskirts of their towns. In the cities with relatively large Jewish populations, such as Lvov, Minsk, and Odessa, Jews were forced into local ghettos and then hauled off in cattle trucks to the death camps.[2]

Rumors about the deadly treatment of Jewish civilians by the rapidly advancing German troops caused mass panic, as there were no civilian evacuation plans in place. Contrary to the myth that some Americans still believe today, at the outbreak of war with Germany the Soviet government had not made special arrangements to save Soviet Jews from the rapidly advancing Nazis.[3] The truth is that the Soviet authorities had been fully informed about the systematic extermination of Jews in the Nazi-occupied territories, but at the time of the German invasion, no government evacuation instructions of any kind were in place.

The orders came from Moscow several days later; the only objective was to relocate to the rear of the country the raw materials, industrial equipment, and personnel needed to run the Soviet war machine. Along with many Jewish families who were threatened with mortal danger,[4] Gorenstein's mother with her son rushed to the evacuation train. She managed to catch the last echelon leaving Berdichev.

Often these cargo trains, filled with evacuees, traveled eastward under enemy fire. German warplanes shelled the wagons; many evacuees were killed or wounded.[5] Malnutrition and unsanitary conditions on the trains facilitated the spread of infectious diseases. Medical help aboard these trains was scarce. To leave the echelon and seek help at a local hospital meant risking being left behind and falling into the hands of the rapidly advancing Nazis.

Many evacuees did not survive the journey. One of them was Friedrich's mother. When, after long weeks of riding in cargo trains, they finally reached their point of destination, the city of Namangan, the second biggest hub for refugee resettlement in Uzbekistan, Enna Abramovna fell ill and died of acute tuberculosis. Friedrich wound up in an orphanage, where he spent the rest of the war. After the war was over, his mother's sisters, Zlota and Rachel, found him and brought him back to Berdichev.

Friedrich began his working life as an unskilled laborer on construction sites. He later entered the Dnepropetrovsk Mining Institute, and upon graduation in 1955, he worked for several years as a mining engineer in Krivoi Rog, Ukraine. His writing life began in 1961 when he was accepted at the Higher Courses for Scriptwriters in Moscow.

Gorenstein wrote seventeen screenplays; five were produced as movies. Of these, the Western public is most familiar with *Solaris* (directed by Andrei Tarkovsky) and *A Slave of Love* (directed by Nikita Mikhalkov). Gorenstein also cowrote a number of movie scripts, although his name was not included in the credits.[6]

Despite his success, he treated scriptwriting as no more than a means of sustenance. In his novel, *Traveling Companions*, his alter ego, Felix Zabrodsky, a scriptwriter and vaudeville writer, recalls: "There were a lot of commissions, and I wrote a great deal because my dacha needed new plumbing or my wife needed a new fur coat.

She would say, 'Write a vaudeville or a movie comedy, so that I can buy a fur coat, and then go ahead and write your own stuff.'"[7]

His "own stuff" is clearly a reference to his uncompromising literary work, free of the chains of censorship, which he saw as the sole purpose of his life. "The more time passed, the more I felt the chains on me," Zabrodsky confesses. "I wanted to rip them off, particularly at night, even if it meant tearing out pieces of my own flesh, because the chains had fused with my skin. The older I get, the more my skin struggles to break free and run into the forest, perhaps to die under the eyes of the wolves, but at least with heart and soul naked and unchained."[8]

Besides writing movie scripts, Gorenstein produced two full-length novels, *The Place* (Mesto) and *A Psalm* (Psalom), several novellas and short stories, and three plays. His literary output was highly appreciated within the narrow circle of people he trusted. Among them were prominent cultural figures of the time, such as the filmmakers Andrei Tarkovsky and Andrei Konchalovsky, writers Yuri Trifonov and Vassily Aksyonov, playwrights Viktor Slavkin and Mark Rozovsky, and literary critics Benedikt Sarnov and Anna Berzer.

However, except for one short story titled "A House with a Small Tower" published in the magazine *Youth* in 1964, nothing of his literary output appeared in print while he lived in the USSR. After his novel about miners, *Winter of 1953* (Zima 53-go), was turned down by the most prestigious literary journal of the time, *New World* (Novyi mir), which published Solzhenitsyn's work and that of other dissident authors, Gorenstein did not even bother to submit his work to any Soviet publishers.

Tired of waiting for his work to appear in his native land, with the help of his friends and admirers, Gorenstein succeeded in publishing abroad. One of the admirers of his work, Margarita Sinderovich, retyped his manuscripts on cigarette paper, which made it possible for movie director Andrei Konchalovsky to smuggle them across the Soviet border in his trousers.[9] In 1978, having been rejected by leading Soviet literary outlets, his novel *Winter of 1953* appeared in the Russian émigré journal *Kontinent* in Paris.

In 1979, Gorenstein contributed his novella *The Steps* (Stupeni) to the literary almanac *Metropol*, a collection of uncensored texts by well-known writers, such as Bella Akhmadulina, Andrei Voznesensky, Vladimir Vysotsky, and others. All almanac writers were subjected to persecutions of various kinds. (One out of a dozen typescript copies produced in Moscow was smuggled to the United States and published by Ardis Publishers in Ann Arbor, Michigan.)[10]

In 1980, Gorenstein emigrated to Vienna, then moved to West Berlin, where he received the annual creative scholarship of the German Academic Exchange Service (DAAD), the first Russian writer to be honored by this program. Outside of his native land, he was no less productive. During his Berlin life, he wrote three more novels, several novellas and short stories, and a new play. His works were published by Russian-language presses outside of the Soviet Union—the New York-based publishing house Slovo, the Paris émigré journals *The Continent* (Kontinent) and *Syntax* (Sintaksis), and the West Berlin magazine *A Mirror of Riddles* (Zerkalo zagadok).

Unlike some other Russian émigré writers, Gorenstein did not repatriate after the collapse of the Soviet Union. In 1992, a year after three volumes of his selected works were first issued in Russia by Slovo, his novel *The Place* (vol. 1) was short-listed for the Russian Booker Prize.

Gorenstein died in Berlin on March 2, 2002, after a long bout with cancer, just a few days before his seventieth birthday.

■ □ ■

The fact that almost none of Gorenstein's work appeared in print in his homeland during his Soviet lifetime is hardly surprising, considering the uncompromising nature of both his work and the author himself. Like other nonconformist Soviet writers of his time, having no hope that his work would see the light of the day in his lifetime, he wrote "for the desk drawer." His writing pushed too many censors' buttons. It could hardly have been more unlike a work of socialist realism, in which the world is depicted not as it is in reality, but in its "revolutionary development"—that is, in the way it is envisioned according to Party ideologists.

Some of his contemporaries, including Solzhenitsyn and other liberal-minded authors, yielded to the editors' pressure and made textual changes that eased the passage of their work to the printed page, but Gorenstein did not follow suit. And not without reason. A change here or there could hardly have made any difference. Gorenstein's bleak world outlook was wholly unacceptable, even during the "Thaw," a time when censorship was relatively relaxed following Khrushchev's denunciations of Stalin's crimes against humanity.

Thus, when Gorenstein submitted his novel *Winter 1953* (Zima 53-go) to the liberal-leaning journal *Novyi mir*, it was quickly rejected.[11] The work was a full affront to the Soviet political system. It wasn't even anti-Soviet, but a-Soviet; that is, it was written with complete disregard for what could or could not appear in Soviet publications.[12]

Written in 1967, his novel *Redemption* exemplifies the many taboos Gorenstein violated in his prose. The novel opens on New Year's Eve of 1946, just a few months after the end of World War II. The world is still vibrating from the war; people seem to have forgotten what normal life is. Their hearts are still filled with mistrust and suspicion. The hardships of life—scarcity of food, a lack of housing, and indiscriminate arrests by the returning Soviet authorities— make them feel that they are still living in wartime.

The novel's theme—the aftermath of the Holocaust—grossly violated the information policy of the post–World War II era to hush up the very mention of the Holocaust, especially the part that had taken place on Soviet territory. The fact that the victims of the Nazi atrocities were primarily Jews was hidden not only during the years immediately following World War II but also throughout the rest of the Soviet era. Even the slightest mention of the Holocaust was suppressed. It was part of Soviet government policy, which Paul Ricœur dubs "organized forgetting."[13]

The government's measures to suppress information about the specifics and scope of Nazi atrocities against the Jews in general, and Soviet Jews in particular, was in full force early on. Toward the end of the war, under the editorial guidance of two distinguished authors, Vasily Grossman and Ilya Ehrenburg, a group of well-known writers and journalists—Viktor Shklovsky, Veniamin Kaverin, Margarita Aliger, and others—began to compile *The Black Book* (Chernaya kniga). This volume included stories of the Holocaust, complete with witness accounts, German execution orders, diaries and testimony of the executioners, as well as notes and diaries of Jewish survivors. The publication was banned, and many of those who worked on *The Black Book* were repressed.[14]

In 1952, the Jewish Anti-Fascist Committee, the only representative body of Jews in the USSR, was disbanded, and its most prominent members were put on trial. Among others who were arrested on trumped-up charges of spying, the Yiddish poet Peretz Markish was accused of attempting to promote Jewish nationalism, with his expression of grief over the Jewish victims of the Nazis as "proof." (After being tortured, the accused were tried in secret proceedings and executed.)

In the official Soviet view, the Nazis killed the country's Jews because they were Soviet citizens, not because they were Jews. During the postwar period, in all the territories where Nazi atrocities had been perpetrated, local authorities closely supervised any attempts of surviving relatives to perpetuate the memory of the victims of the Holocaust—to ensure that the words "Jew" or "Jewish" did not appear on any grave or monument. These words were duly replaced with "civilians" or "Soviet citizens," and a five-pointed Soviet star was substituted for the Star of David.[15]

Until the late 1970s, discussion of the Holocaust was taboo. At various times, it was branded as "anti-Soviet," "nationalist," or "Zionist" propaganda. In 1961, a short poem titled "Babi Yar," by Yevgeny Yevtushenko, managed to appear on the pages of the *Literary Gazette*. Devoted to the memory of Ukrainian Jews slaughtered during the war, it pointed to the fact that the place of the mass burial was devoid of any memorial. The poem brought about the wrath of the Soviet leader, Nikita Khrushchev, who accused the young poet of having lost his political vigilance.

In 1964, the publishing house Young Guard (Molodaya Gvardiya) issued a documentary novel by V. R. Tomin and A. G. Sinelnikov, *Return Is Undesirable* (Vozvrashchenie nezhelatel'no), about the Nazi death camp Sobibór. Though the camp had been populated almost exclusively by Jewish prisoners from Poland, Holland, Germany, and Russia, the word "Jew" does not appear even once in its pages. The prisoners are identified as Poles, Dutchmen, Germans, and Russians—not Jews.[16]

■ □ ■

The Soviet authorities exercised tight control over any information related to the Holocaust for several reasons. To begin with, they wanted to distance themselves from the responsibility of having aided and abetted Hitler in unleashing World War II when they signed the notorious Molotov-Ribbentrop nonaggression pact. Having full control of the media, the Soviet government made the country's population believe that World War II started not with the German invasion of Poland on September 1, 1939, but with their incursion into Soviet territory on June 22, 1941. (From the first days of the war to the collapse of the Soviet Union, the attack was invariably characterized as being perpetrated "treacherously, without declaration of war." This proved to be a lie, which was made public only in 1991, shortly before the collapse of the Soviet regime.t.)[17] Moreover, the very notion of World War II was supplanted in the Soviet public's consciousness with the term "the Great Patriotic War."[18] This term was coined to hearken back to the "Patriotic War of 1812," which is how Russian historians refer to the military campaign against the invading army of Napoleon I. Thus, calling the fight against Hitler "The Great Patriotic War" presented the military confrontation of the invading German troops as part of Russian historical tradition. Such linguistic subterfuge aimed to downplay the fact that the Russian campaign was part of World War II, a conflict whose severity was exacerbated by the USSR's earlier actions. The Soviets had not only fed the Wermacht with their grain and supplied the Nazi war machine with such strategic raw materials as oil, coal, iron ore, and ferromanganese (an alloy used in production of armor steel), but, while Hitler's troops invaded several European countries, the Soviet Union annexed the eastern part of Poland and gobbled up three Baltic states and parts of Romania. They also unleashed (albeit unsuccessfully) a military campaign against Finland.

Anti-Semitism grew both within the state apparatus and among the broader population during wartime and especially during the postwar years. State persecution took the form of a campaign against "rootless cosmopolitans," mostly Jewish intellectuals, who were accused of lacking Soviet patriotism. The state campaign culminated in the fabrication of the notorious "Doctors' Plot," in which a group of prominent physicians, mostly Jews, was accused of conspiracy to assassinate Soviet leaders. This movement sapped further support for the notion of commemorating the victims of the Holocaust.

Finally, since one of the main ideological goals of the Soviet authorities was to propagate the notion of unity of the Soviet people, a separate memorialization of Jewish victims of the war could not be tolerated. Every effort was made to hide Nazi crimes against Jews and/or to replace the memories of the perished along ideological lines that treated them as simply part of the "civilian Soviet population." This was particularly important to Soviet authorities, who wanted to suppress any growth of nationalism among Soviet minority populations, especially after the State of Israel was established.[19]

■ □ ■

Gorenstein's novel violated another taboo. It revealed Soviet citizens' widespread collaboration with the enemy, which was common knowledge in the country but was suppressed in publications. In the post–World War II years, every job application in the Soviet Union asked, "Did you reside in the territory temporarily occupied by the enemy?" If the answer was yes, that fact alone made the applicant subject to mistrust and suspicion. Yet any public mention of collaboration with the Nazis during wartime had been under strict control of the censor.

Upon entering the USSR, the Nazis found a large number of local residents eager to take an active part in not only rounding up but also carrying out the physical destruction of Jews. The most active Nazi collaborators were in the territories of Lithuania, Latvia, and Western Ukraine (which less than two years earlier made up the eastern part of Poland).[20] The territories were annexed by the Soviet Union in 1939–1940, as part of the secret protocol of the Molotov-Ribbentrop nonaggression pact. There was no shortage of such volunteers in the territories of other Soviet republics.[21]

The very fact of mass collaboration with the enemy was not only a sign of open defiance of the Soviet regime, a cause of embarrassment to the political system, but also a signifier of nationalism, an attempt at independence from the power that had overrun its borders with tanks. Soviet power struggled with nationalists and did not want these problems to be debated in a discussion of crimes against Jews.[22]

In *Redemption*, Gorenstein questions the valor of Pavel Morozov, one of the most notorious Soviet propaganda-made heroes. In 1932, the thirteen-year-old Morozov became a hero-martyr for denouncing his own father to the authorities for illegal activities. Conditioned by the Soviet ideology to inform on one's own parents for the sake of the greater good, Gorenstein's young heroine, sixteen-year-old Sashenka, denounces her mother to the police for "stealing state property." In reality, the mother had taken some leftovers to feed her famished young daughter and the starving homeless couple she had given refuge in her apartment. However, Sashenka does this not out of loyalty to the system and its proclaimed ideals, but because of her own teenaged misery. She does it to spite her widowed mother, who takes a lover instead of remaining loyal for the rest of her life to the memory of Sashenka's father, who had perished during the war.

Gorenstein also does not give a second thought to puncturing the myth of Soviet society as a society of equals, portraying it as highly stratified. Among many other signs of social inequality, he describes the rationing of food for ordinary people while the commanding officers of the police precinct enjoy a much better diet. At a time of excruciating poverty, a general's son who courts Sashenka has access to luxury items like French perfume, which was not only unattainable but even unthinkable for regular Soviet citizens.

The novel also reveals the existence of political prisoners in the Soviet state, among them a college professor of literature.

To propagate the myth that the World War II victory was solely a Soviet achievement, the official propaganda suppressed any reference to assistance from wartime Allied countries to the struggling

Soviets, specifically the American Lend-Lease Act. True to life, Gorenstein's novel mentions American-supplied food items, such as egg powder, biscuits, Spam, and chocolate, which saved a significant part of the civilian population from starvation.

■ □ ■

Though the plot of the novel revolves around the consequences of wartime atrocities committed by the local Nazi collaborators, it addresses a much larger issue—the effect of the Holocaust on humanity at large. No motive for the horrific locally committed murders is cited—or even hinted at—in the novel. The Holocaust is examined as the result of not ethnic tensions or racist Nazi ideology, but evil impulses nestled in the human heart. In fact, at the center of the novel is a philosophical discussion between the imprisoned professor and the surviving member of a Jewish family that perished. They tackle the biblical question of evil in human life. (The novel itself can be seen as a philosophical meditation on this subject.) Could such horrific crimes perpetrated on such a large scale ever be fully avenged? Could any human actions ever bring about redemption?

This biblical reading of the real-life tragedy is foreshadowed by Gorenstein's choice of the character who had perpetrated horrific murders. While atrocities committed by the German occupying forces are mentioned in passing only, at the center of the novel's plot are the monstrous crimes carried out by one of the slain family's neighbors, who had hardly any grievances or scores to settle. Since the action of the novel takes place in a small Ukrainian town, one might expect the murderer to be a Ukrainian. After all, while millions of Ukrainians joined the Red Army in fighting the Nazis, the participation of members of their community in the Holocaust, which took place during the German occupation, is well documented.[23]

However, in Gorenstein's novel, the perpetrator of the bloodshed is an Assyrian, a member of a tiny minority. At the outbreak of World War II, they amounted to hardly more than twenty thousand people nationwide. Themselves refugees, they had settled in the Soviet territory comparatively recently, escaping the genocide carried out by the troops of the Ottoman Empire in the course of World War I. It is likely that Gorenstein eschews the narrative of majority Ukrainians murdering minority Jews to highlight the universality of the evil of the Holocaust. This went beyond historical grievance. Moreover, by making the murderer an Assyrian, Gorenstein references biblical accounts of the Assyrians' assaults on ancient Israel (2 Kings 15:29; 2 Kings 18:9–12; Isaiah 36:1). The attackers are invariably characterized as being fierce and cruel, showing no mercy to the conquered (e.g., in 2 Kings 19:17, "Truly, O Lord, the kings of Assyria have laid waste the nations and their lands").

It is also possible that Gorenstein had in mind one particular use of the trope of associating biblical Assyrians with a culture of savageness. Specifically, reflecting on Stalin's brutality toward the great Russian poet Osip Mandelstam, persecuted for writing an epigram ridiculing the Soviet leader, the poet's widow, Nadezhda Mandelstam, said in an interview, "You couldn't find another beast like him [Stalin], Assyrian that he is."[24]

This possibility is strengthened through the folkloric connection between the character of the murderer in the novel, an Assyrian boot cleaner, and the Soviet dictator. In the slang of Gulag prisoners, Stalin's nickname rhymed with his acquired surname—*Gutalin*, "Shoe Polish." The French researcher of the Gulag, Jacques Rossi, who interpreted this word as belonging to the criminal argot, explained its genesis: "Of short stature, dark-haired and pockmarked, speaking Russian with a strong Caucasian accent, Stalin was reminiscent of Caucasians-Assyrians, street boot cleaners, who traditionally used *gutalin*, a shoe polish."[25] This association of Stalin's image with that of a boot cleaner comes from the widely known fact that the dictator grew up in a shoemaker's family. By such associating the murderer in *Redemption* with Stalin, Gorenstein suggests that Stalin bears some responsibility for both the deaths of Jews in the occupied territories and for unleashing the post–World War II anti-Semitic campaigns.

■ □ ■

As the Russian literary critic L. Lazarev notes, Gorenstein does not believe in the healing power of suffering. In Gorenstein's view, suffering does not soften a human soul—it hardens it. In one of his articles, he writes, "The first reaction of a person to freedom and goodness after having been crushed by injustice is not joy and gratitude, but resentment and anger over the years lived in fear and repression."[26] Yet one of the merits of Gorenstein's work is that he finds kindness and humanity under the most inhumane circumstances. While the physical and moral climate that surrounds the action in *Redemption* is unutterably bleak, the novel does give us a glimmer of hope.

Gorenstein sees good and evil as coexisting in the human soul. Because of the desperation and bitterness visited upon her young life, Sashenka denounces her own mother to the police, but the very same Sashenka falls in love with and saves from suicide the sole surviving member of a family that had perished during the Holocaust. Her self-sacrifice and self-abnegation make her love for a grown man feel like love for her own child. In fact, she expresses regret that she did not meet the young man when he was a three-year-old boy.

Gorenstein goes to great lengths to convince the reader that at the core of a woman's love lies her maternal instinct. He idolizes motherhood and considers maternal love the only hope for the salvation of humanity and its redemption from wickedness and cruelty toward its brethren. In his view, such love does not demand reciprocity; it is blind and devoid of the torments and doubts often present in sexual love. For him, the selflessness of maternal love makes it akin to Christ's love.

The carrier of absolute good is a mother's heart. Sashenka's mother readily forgives her daughter's betrayal; her child's well-being is more important to her than her own suffering. A mass murderer's aging mother does not mind walking miles on end, day after day, just in case the new guard of her jailed son has a kind moment and consents to pass on a food parcel. The wife of the perpetrator of the horrific murders of local doctors and their families is inconsolable in her grief during the funeral of her five-year-old son.

Gorenstein suggests hope for the future by ending the novel with an emphasis on motherhood. In Sashenka's household, three babies appear in the world, one after another. Not by chance, all of them are female, and thus have the potential to be mothers themselves.

■ □ ■

Gorenstein's work has been widely translated in Europe. Almost all of his work has appeared in French and German. Several of his plays have been staged in European theaters. At the same time, only one of his works, a short novel titled *Traveling Companions*, has appeared in English translation. With this publication of *Redemption*, English-speaking readers finally have the opportunity to further acquaint themselves with this remarkable writer.

Emil Draitser
Hunter College of the City University of New York

NOTES

1. Anyone familiar with the ominous meaning of this date in Russian history will appreciate the macabre humor of the opening paragraph of *Traveling Companions*: "June 22, 1941, was the blackest day of my life. That day, at five o'clock in the morning, when I returned home from a trip, I found a rejection slip in my mailbox, from a Moscow theater, informing me that my play, *A Ruble and Two Bits*, had been rejected. The postman had delivered it the day before." Friedrich Gorenstein, *Traveling Companions*, trans. Bernard Meares (New York: Harcourt Brace Jovanovich, 1991), 1.

2. For more about the Nazis' systematic destruction of the Jewish population in the occupied territories, such as Uman and Odessa (both Ukraine), and Minsk (Belorussia, see Emil Draitser, *Shush! Growing Up Jewish Under Stalin: A Memoir* (Berkeley: University of California Press, 2004), 228–29, 234–35, 248.

3. There is reason to believe that the myth was born in 1943, when members of the Soviet "Jewish Anti-Fascist Committee," organized on Stalin's orders, visited the United States to raise funds for the Soviet war effort.

4. For example, see Draitser, *Shush!*, 38.

5. For an eyewitness account, see Draitser, *Shush!*, 42–45.

6. Gorenstein was also not credited for writing monologues for the lead character of Tarkovsky's other masterpiece, *Andrei Rublev*.

7. Gorenstein, "Traveling Companions" (Poputchiki), in *Iskuplenie* (Redemption) (St. Petersburg: Azbuka, 2011), 380.

8. Gorenstein, *Traveling Companions*, 211. The original Russian "zheleznye kavychki" (iron quotation marks) makes it clear that he has in mind the literary handcuffs imposed by the censors.

9. Cited in Konchalovsky's memoir, *The Exalting Deception* (Vozvyshaiushchij obman); see http://magazines.russ.ru/slovo/2007/54/po14.html (accessed January 15, 2018).

10. As cited in "Delo Metropolia," one typescript of the almanac was taken out of the country by Raymond Benson, the head of the American embassy's cultural and press offices (see http://magazines.russ.ru/nlo/2006/82/de14 .html; accessed February 20, 2018).

11. L. Lazarev, "*O romane F. Gorenshtejna 'Mesto'*" (On Gorenstein's novel *The Place*), in Fridrikh Gorenshtejn, *Izbrannoe v trekh tomakh, t.1, Mesto* (Friedrich Gorenstein, Selected works in three volumes, vol. 1, The Place) (Moscow: Slovo, 1991), 3.

12. In that respect, Gorenstein reminds one of the Russian-born Nobel Laureate in Literature, the poet Joseph Brodsky, who, in his Soviet life, "prefer[red] to act as if the Soviet regime [did] not exist." See Ellendea Proffer Teasley, *Brodskii sredi nas* (Moscow: Corpus Books, 2015); quoted in Cynthia Haven, "The Unknown Brodsky," in *The Nation*, April 11/18, 2016, 43.

13. See Ola Hnatiuk, "How the Soviet Union Suppressed the Holocaust to Fight 'Nationalism,'" *Odessa Review*, November 16, 2007, http://odessareview.com /soviet-union-suppressed-holocaust-fight-nationalism/.

14. *The Black Book* was published in Russian for the first time in Israel in 1980. It was then published in Kiev in 1991, and only recently, in 2015, in the Russian Federation through a crowdfunding initiative. In English, the book appeared under the title *The Complete Black Book of Russian Jewry*, ed. Vasily Grossman (Piscataway, NJ: Routledge, 2003).

15. Well into the twenty-first century, a foreigner, a French Catholic priest, almost single-handedly excavated the history of previously undocumented Jewish victims of the Holocaust in the former Soviet Union (see Father Patrick Desbois, *The Holocaust by Bullets: A Priest's Journey to Uncover the Truth Behind the Murder of 1.5 Million Jews* [New York: Palgrave Macmillan, 2008]).

16. Avraam Elinson, "Vmesto poslesloviia" (Instead of an afterword), in Dr. Itzhak Arad, "Vosstanie v Sobibore" (A mutiny at the Sobibor), trans. V. Kukuj, February 2009, http://berkovich-zametki.com/2009/Zametki/Nomer3 /Vilensky1.php.

17. The German memorandum was published in Russian in 1991 in the *Military and Historical Journal* (Voenno-istoricheskij zhurnal) under the rubric "For the first time in the Soviet press" (Vpervye v sovetskoj pechati), June 1991, http:// zhistory.org.ua/viz916ng.htm.

18. "How the End of the Great Patriotic War Appeared," https://pikabu.ru /story/kak_poyavilsya_termin_velikaya_otechestvennaya_voyna_4911045 (accessed February 19, 2018).

19. On the lack of the wide public awareness of Holocaust in today's Russian Federation, see the documentary film titled *Holocaust—Is That a Wallpaper Paste?* (2013), https://www.youtube.com/watch?v=7SfrnBQ3LGM.

20. As the newly published book by Rūta Vanagaitė titled *Ours* (Mūsiškiai) (Vilnius: Alma Littera, 2015) reveals, "Young illiterate Lithuanians . . . so diligently killed Jews that they were transported to Lithuania for destruction from other countries. Even [high school] children voluntarily participated in the murders, and the [local] Church indifferently watched the Holocaust, even absolved the murderers of all their sins. For the purity of the race and Jewish [made of silver or gold] dentures, about 200,000 Jews were killed in Lithuania." Ruta Vanagataite, "The Holocaust in Lithuania: 'These Were Ours,'" March 11, 2017, https://zihuatanexo.livejournal.com/1762836.html.

21. United States Holocaust Memorian Museum, "Collaboration," (article in the Holocaust Encyclopedia), https://www.ushmm.org/wlc/en/article.php?ModuleId =10005466, accessed February 19, 2018.

22. See Hnatiuk, "How the Soviet Union Suppressed the Holocaust."

23. See, for example, Richard J. Evans, *The Third Reich at War: 1939–1945* (London: Penguin, 2009), 203–23; Lucy S. Dawidowicz, *The War Against the Jews*

1933–1945 (New York: Bantam, 1975), 171; Sol Litman, *Pure Soldiers or Bloodthirsty Murderers?: The Ukrainian 14th Waffen-SS Galicia Division* (Montreal: Black Rose Books, 2003).

24. Cited in Nikolai Podosokorsky, "Nadezhda Mandelshtam o Staline: "Takogo drugogo zhovotnogo nel'zia bylo najti. Assiriets" (Nadezhda Mandelstam about Stalin: 'You couldn't find another beast like him [Stalin], Assyrian that he is), June 17, 2017, https://philologist.livejournal.com/9391445.html.

25. Vladimir Tol'ts, cited in "Kak u Diuma . . . Vospominania 1950-e . . . (2001–2010rr.) (Like in [Alexandre] Dumas . . . Recalling 1950s . . . [2001–2010])". *Radio Svoboda* (Radio Freedom), December 4, 2010, https://www.svoboda.org/a/2239863.html.

26. Quoted in Lazarev, "*O romane F. Gorenshtejna 'Mesto,'*" 11.

REDEMPTION

01

Her mother was sitting on a stool, leaning back against the table as she tugged off a tarpaulin boot with hands red from the frosty air. Every time her mother got back from work and started tugging off her boots, Sashenka stood rooted to the spot, with her mouth watering and her heart pounding in anticipation of tasty morsels. This was the last day of December 1945, it had already started getting dark, and Olga brought in the oil lamp from the kitchen.

Sashenka was annoyed that their lodger Olga was home; she knew Olga wouldn't go back to her place in the kitchen, but would hang about by the table until Sashenka's mother gave her something too.

With her left hand, Sashenka's mother grasped her bent knee, sheathed in a quilted trouser leg, suspending her leg in the air, then thrust the fingers of her right hand against the boot above the heel and heaved with all her might. The boot fell, and solid-frozen lumps of millet porridge tumbled out of the mother's foot cloth onto the floor. She picked them up and put them together on a plate prepared in advance. Then she unwrapped the foot cloth and took out some meat patties in a rag. There were four patties, two completely intact, with a crispy coating, but two had been slightly crushed by her foot, and she neatly matched together the pieces on a plate. Then she pulled up one quilted trouser leg and started unpinning a little oiled-paper bag that was fastened to her stocking. A sweet, thrilling smell tickled Sashenka's nostrils, she felt a twinge below her ribs, and she gulped. Olga gulped too, so loudly that something cracked in her throat, and Sashenka gave her a spiteful look.

Sashenka was sixteen years old, and she was rather good-looking, but when she started getting angry, and Sashenka often got angry, her pale face flushed crimson, her eyes glittered, and her little lips sometimes pouted and sometimes parted slightly, revealing her neat little teeth. Sashenka was tormented, but somewhere in the depths of her soul she also took pleasure in working herself into this state.

Sashenka hated Olga so much that sometimes the fury made the back of her neck ache. Olga was thirty-eight, but she looked older. She was a quiet, docile woman, although her docility sometimes shaded into insolence since, while she was never resentful and held no grudges, she also knew no shame. She worked by the day, washing people's floors and doing their laundry, on Sundays and church holidays she went to a church porch to beg, and then sorted out the copper coins, stale pieces of pie, and frozen rye-flour dumplings behind her screen in the kitchen. Olga's docile insolence was also what had led to her moving in with Sashenka and her mother. One day she came there to work: she washed the floor and brought two sacks of peat from the shed, then lay down behind the stove and fell asleep. It was a freezing-cold November evening and Olga was wearing torn stockings and galoshes tied on with string. Sashenka's mother felt sorry for her and didn't wake her up. By morning Olga had become seriously ill; she was coughing and gasping for breath. After two days the cough passed, but Olga stayed on anyway, living behind the stove in the kitchen. Her bedding consisted entirely of the things that she wore during the day. As a base, she laid out two skirts, an army uniform blouse, and a soldier's flannelette undershirt. A quilted jacket served as a pillow and her blanket was a shawl. In general, she was quite well off for clothes, but she was hard up for shoes, and wearing nothing but galoshes made her toes ache in the frost, although she muffled her feet in rags and paper.

But even more than Olga, Sashenka hated Olga's boyfriend Vasya, whom Olga had picked up on a church porch somewhere, where he was freezing, and also brought into the household. Vasya was a big, tall peasant with hands as broad as spades, hairy ears, and a heavy, thickset neck. But the eyes in his face were small and a washed-out blue color, constantly frightened and imploring.

"How can you do that?" Sashenka's mother asked. "How can you move another person into someone else's home? Maybe he's a thief or he's infectious..."

"It's only until spring, ma'am," Olga replied as she revived Vasya with hot water, "for the love of Christ, ma'am..."

Vasya was so frozen that he couldn't speak, he only squinted fearfully at Sashenka's mother and looked imploringly at Olga, as if he were asking her to protect him. Vasya stayed.

Sashenka later found out that he had run away from a village where, according to Olga, the woman whose house he lived in had written a report about him out of spite, claiming that he had worked as a *polizei* during the occupation. Vasya was absolutely unassuming, even more unassuming than Olga, and if he didn't go out to earn money, he sat in the kitchen, behind the screen that Sashenka's mother had given them. Olga had furnished her corner with a little round table, so badly eaten by woodworm that it was like honeycomb. Vasya had cobbled together a bench out of planks, and on the wall they had hung some paper flowers, a little icon, and a portrait of Marshal Zhukov, cut out of a newspaper.

While her mother was detaching the oiled-paper bag, Sashenka wondered anxiously whether Vasya was out earning money or sitting behind the screen. The bag turned out to contain doughnuts.

"That's to celebrate New Year's," Sashenka's mother said. "They baked them for the top brass..."

Sashenka's mother worked as a dishwasher in a militia canteen, and that was why her hands were red, they were stewed by the hot water in the kitchen vats, and in the freezing cold they turned even redder, and the joints swelled up.

Sashenka watched her mother take out the doughnuts and set them out on a plate, leaving her red, swollen fingers glistening with grease. There were seven doughnuts. Mother laid them in a circle around the edge of the plate and licked the smears of jam off her palms. Sashenka touched a doughnut—it was still warm, and so soft that her finger sank right into it, and a little squiggle of jam crept out from inside.

"Wait," said her mother, "first we have to warm up the millet and the patties . . . Olga, this is for you and Vasya." She put a whole patty and a few pieces from a crushed one on a different plate. The patty was a bit overcooked on one side, but Sashenka liked gnawing on a crunchy, meaty crust like that. Mother added three lumps of millet porridge to the patties, then thought for a moment and added another one.

"Vasya," Olga said joyfully. "Come on out, Vasya, the missus is treating us. We'll feed ourselves up a bit . . ."

Vasya emerged from behind the screen, but didn't come out into the room, he stopped short on the threshold. Sashenka could sense his heart starting to pound more rapidly.

Mother took two doughnuts and put them on Olga's plate.

"A special treat," she said. "It's our first New Year's Eve without war . . ."

Mother smiled and Vasya smiled too. He gave off a sour smell, the kind you find in a poor, grubby home. Sashenka's heart started racing so fast, it took her breath away, as if she were running down a steep slope and couldn't stop.

"I want him to go away," Sashenka shouted. "He stinks . . . When I'm at the table . . . I want him always to go behind the screen . . . And her, too . . ."

Vasya wilted on the threshold, ducking his head down, Olga stepped toward him, to protect him if necessary, and this hulking, frightened peasant infuriated Sashenka even more.

"My father died for the motherland," she shouted at her mother in a high voice, as if she were at a Komsomol meeting, "and you're hiding a German toady here."

Sashenka caught a glimpse of her mother's face, with its puffy eyes, and the sparse tangle of hair at the back of her head, and suddenly realized for the first time that her forty-year-old mother had become really old. For a moment Sashenka felt sorry for her mother and relaxed her chest, which was tensed up in malice. But that also gave Sashenka a moment's respite to catch her breath, fill her lungs as full of air as she could, and shout loudly, this time something unintelligible, the way that Sashenka had wanted to shout over and over again when she felt the sweet languor that had been tormenting her for more than a year now, just as soon as the oil lamp was turned out in the evening. And sometimes, waking up in the night, she clenched her teeth and wanted someone big with a vague, indefinite face to take her body in his coarse hands and knead it and tear it to pieces. Just recently Sashenka had started thinking about the "young hawk" Markeev.

"Young hawks" was what they called the young trainees from the mop-up battalion, which carried out patrol duty in the city.

Sashenka hated Markeev, but last night she had dreamed that Markeev was pressing her up against some kind of wall, and it felt so sweet that after she woke up her entire body had carried on trembling and shivering for several minutes.

She was seized by trembling now too, and she raked the porridge, patties, and doughnuts off all the plates, tipped them out onto the table and started grinding them together in her hands, watching the mingled mass, sticky with jam, oozing out between her greasy, gleaming fingers. Olga led Vasya behind the screen and they sat there quietly, not even whispering; the oil lamp crackled, Sashenka's mother stood there with her arms wearily lowered, barefooted, with her quilted trousers rolled up to the knees, and Sashenka started calming down too, she felt better now and was breathing more freely . . .

"Don't trample on it," her mother said. "We'll never scrape the jam and the millet off the floor afterward . . ."

Sashenka's mother used to beat her, but recently Sashenka had noticed that her mother had started to be afraid of her, especially when Sashenka flew into a rage.

Sashenka shook the remains of the sticky mush off her fingers and went into the kitchen to wash her hands. Behind the screen Olga hastily whispered something and then abruptly fell silent in mid-word, as if she had put her hand over her mouth.

"They've gone into hiding, those helpless bastards," Sashenka shouted, "my father laid down his life, and they're hiding here . . ."

The water in the bucket had grown a crust of ice. Sashenka took a mug, broke the ice, and scooped up some water; then she leaned down over a basin, filled her mouth with icy water, and squirted it out onto her hands. She pulled off her cotton sweater, rolled up the long sleeves of her undershirt, and washed her face thoroughly with a little slip of household soap, then pulled off her undershirt and washed her breasts. Sashenka went back to the main room, feeling fresher and even more cheerful. Her mother was gathering up the slimy, mingled lumps off the table, trying to separate the remains of the doughnuts from the millet and the meat patties. After the cold, fresh water, Sashenka felt such an intense pang of hunger that her forehead and temples cramped up and she got a painful twinge in her stomach. She wanted to go over and eat the patty and two doughnuts that had been left untouched, but she controlled herself and walked stone-faced past her mother and into the little second room, where there was a wardrobe with a mirror. Sasha closed the door with the hook, lit a candle, dropped a little melted paraffin wax on a stool, stuck the candle on it in front of the mirror, and started getting undressed. She took off her undershirt, crumpled skirt, and long pants, and looked at herself in the mirror for a minute or two. Sashenka had a good figure and she knew it. She had long legs, broad hips, and small breasts, although it was true that her appearance was somewhat spoiled by the protruding ribs on both sides.

Sashenka put her hands on her thighs and squeezed them with her fingers, feeling a sweet, ticklish sensation. Then she ran her palms under her armpits, touched her erect, springy nipples and quietly laughed at the sudden surge of happiness. She put on a pink silk bra and lacy panties, took a cool, sleek slip that smelled of perfume and held it against her face, then dived into the slip, shuddering at the tender touches of the silk against her skin, glanced at her little shoulder with a little sky-blue ribbon stretched over it, and rubbed her cheek against the ribbon. All these clothes had once belonged to her mother, but now they fitted Sashenka perfectly. Then Sashenka stuck her head into the wardrobe, into the darkness that smelled of mothballs, and pulled out a cardboard box full of shoes. She put on a pair of white lisle-thread stockings, a new skirt, and white pumps. The shoes were out of season, and so was the pink silk blouse, but everything suited Sashenka very well, and in any case, it was her only outfit. Full of joy, with her eyes sparkling, Sashenka sauntered past the mirror. Then she strolled past it with an independent air, casting disdainful glances, and then she ran through a few dance moves, holding the edge of the skirt in her fingers. She took the hook off the door and walked into the large room, clenching her teeth in angry irritation again, because she realized that if she once smiled and stopped being angry and suffering, she would forfeit her power in the home. Her mother was sitting at the table, and when she saw Sashenka she ran her hand across her eyes and wrinkled up her face. Just recently Sashenka's mother often cried at the slightest excuse, and Sashenka found that irksome.

"Why have you turned on the waterworks again?" Sashenka asked, trying to speak in a low voice.

"You're my beautiful girl," her mother said, sobbing, "it's such a shame your father can't see what a grown-up Komsomol girl you are now . . ."

"Father laid down his life for the motherland," said Sashenka, "and you pilfer things here on the home front."

"I'm not qualified for anything," her mother said. "If I had an education, I could have got a job with good pay . . ."

Sashenka went out into the kitchen and saw that Vasya's dirty, dusty greatcoat with no half-belt at the back, smeared all over with some kind of heating or diesel oil, was hanging on top of her short fur coat. She yanked hard on the coat, but its loop was sewn on solidly—Olga must have run a double seam across it—and Sashenka broke a nail.

"You bastards," Sashenka shouted, turning toward the corner with the screen in it. "If you hang that filthy rag here again . . . Just one more time . . . I'll throw it in the garbage pit . . ." Sashenka hung on the greatcoat with all her weight and tore off the loop. The greatcoat fell on the floor, but Sashenka's fur coat fell with it and Sasha struck her knee painfully. Her frightened mother came running into the kitchen. "Olga," she said, "I asked you to keep your things separately . . . There's a very convenient place over there in the corner."

Sashenka's mother leaned down to pick up the greatcoat, but Sashenka stepped on it and gleefully wiped it round the floor, trying to drag it across the dirtiest and wettest spots.

"Let him pick it up himself," Sashenka shouted. "Lackeys were done away with almost thirty years ago . . . He's not betraying patriots to Hitler's *gauleiters* now . . ."

There was a heavy sigh behind the screen, but nothing was said.

Sashenka felt hot after the commotion and the shouting, and she hastily put on her fur jacket and the fluffy beret that pulled down over her ears and tied under her chin with little ribbons, put on her low boots, wrapped her shoes in newspaper, grabbed her purse, and ran out into the street.

It was dark in the side street and Sashenka took a shortcut by turning onto a narrow path and walking past an icebound water pump. Behind the pump were sheds and the ruins of a single-story, gray brick building. This spot had always had a sweetish, sinister odor, like the smell of corpses. But later Sashenka had found out that the smell near the sheds wasn't from corpses, but from German louse powder. Under the Germans the little gray building had been some kind of sanitary and epidemiological station. Even now there were lots of little packets lying all around with a picture of a large green louse on them.

The yard custodian Franya was standing beside the ruins, holding on to the hoarfrosted remains of the cast-iron porch. The porch had been made of patterned iron with various kinds of bows and flourishes. Even the withered stems of the Virginia creeper that used to wind around the metal supports of the porch had survived.

"Anyone who rats on his buddy is a creep, right?" Franya shouted and burst out laughing. He took an onion out of his pocket and started crisply munching on it. Suddenly Franya grabbed hold of Sashenka's arm and pressed his wet mouth, with its smell of cheap vodka, to her ear . . . "The dentist's family is buried here. Leopold Lvovich's family. By the cesspit . . . Alongside the privy . . ." Franya whispered.

Franya's eyes bulged in a drunken or insane stare. Sashenka tore herself free, ran out into the middle of the street, and set off at a hasty walk, trying to reach the well-lit, crowded avenue as quickly as possible.

On the main street the lamps were lit, and outside the cinema was a large fir tree, with its paper decorations and little flags rustling. In the two-story building of the divisional headquarters and the buildings beside it, where the families of military officers lived, the lights were on and the windows were exceptionally bright and festive. The Young Pioneer Palace, where the young people's New Year's Ball had already begun, was also glittering with bright lights. It was an old building with tall windows and paneled ceilings. Before the revolution and during the occupation the municipal council had been located here.

A crowd was standing in front of the entrance and the marble staircases were completely covered with frozen gobbets of spit and snowballs. Sashenka squeezed into the crowd and she was borne away, dragged up the slippery stone slabs, flung against the door, and swept into the lobby, which was very cold, with the wind blowing straight through it, where a cordon of "young hawks" was holding the onslaught in check. A female receptionist deftly grabbed Sashenka's invitation in her mittens and made a tear in it. The lobby was decorated with banners, fir-tree branches, and colored lightbulbs that were blinking randomly. Sashenka hurriedly took off her jacket and boots, put the cloakroom tag in her purse, and walked up to the top floor, where she saw Markeev beside the snack bar counter with the Assyrian girl Zara.

A large Middle Eastern family living in the town ran shoeshine stands, where they also sold boot and shoelaces. Some people called them Georgians and others called them Assyrians. But in fact, they were either Kurds or Serbs. Zara was wearing a heavy, dusty velvet skirt and she had gold pendant earrings in her ears, while Markeev was in a fashionable, lightish-blue service jacket, brightly polished boots, and riding breeches. In keeping with the latest fashion, the pull chain of a German rifle ran from his belt to his pocket. The aluminum links were fastened together by little rings and at the end of the chain the handle of an excellent clasp knife could be seen, flirtatiously peeping out of his pocket. Sashenka's throat immediately went dry, but she managed to put on an independent air and walked to the snack bar counter, swaying her hips. She simply watched herself in the mirror out of the very corner of her eye, and the farther she walked, the better she felt. She sensed that she had made an impression with her lisle stockings and pink blouse with the wide, low neckline that offered just the slightest glimpse of the lacy edge of her slip, that even though these clothes were the only dressy ones she had, they emphasized all of her good points to advantage and, at the same time, concealed her defects, which Sashenka knew with absolute precision. For instance, she had a chin that was a little bit longer than it ought to be and sometimes, when she was left alone in front of the mirror, in her annoyance Sashenka rubbed her chin with her fingers until it turned red, as if that would make it shorter. She also had a scar on the nape of her neck from an operation that she'd had in her childhood, but Sashenka powdered over it and covered it with her hair, which she combed in a seemingly casual fashion, so that it cascaded down to the right of the scar. But now she liked the way she looked in the mirror.

It was Sashenka's first ball. She had been preparing for it a long time, a whole week, since her mother got her an invitation through the local special trade committee. Sashenka had washed every day with a special war-trophy lotion bought at a street market, wound curlers into her hair, rubbed eau de cologne into her skin and, for the first time in her life, painted her lips in a little Cupid's bow and powdered her cheeks. And now there was General Batiunya's son whispering something to his friend and glancing furtively at Sashenka's calves in their covering of cream lisle cotton. Sashenka stood in line, showed her invitation, and received a present at a competitive market price. When the counter girl handed out the little package, she marked the edge of the invitation with a little stamp that said "Canceled."

Sashenka walked into the large hall, where the New Year's tree was standing and a military band was playing. Lots of couples were swirling around, some slowly, others quickly, jostling shoulders with each other. But Sashenka didn't stop in the middle; every step she took was calculated now, as if some experienced force were directing her movements. Sashenka walked through them and sat down a little farther on in the shadow of the balcony. The hall had a balcony and a stage, but everything was happening in the center, by the tree, illuminated with several hundred-watt light bulbs. General Batiunya's son walked up, sat down beside Sashenka, and started tugging her purse out of her hands.

"You nasty boy," Sashenka exclaimed in a singsong voice, bursting into laughter and hitting him on the hand.

God only knows where Sashenka had mastered this flirtatious, caressing blow, in which the girl's completely relaxed hand first touches the man's hand with its wrist and then trails its palm across it, with the fingertips gently touching and the little nails scratching.

Taking the prickling of the nails as a summons to action, General Batiunya's son snatched his hand away and immediately thrust it back again, this time not at the purse, but at Sashenka's lisle-thread knees. And Sashenka felt a sweet fear, like in a dream. She sat there for a few moments as if entranced, surrendering completely to those long-awaited fingers as they fumbled at her knees, growing bolder and creeping higher. But then she came to her senses and pushed the young man so hard in the chest that he almost went flying off the bench.

"Let's go up on the balcony," Batiunya whispered.

"No, I want to dance," Sashenka said firmly.

General Batiunya's son meekly followed her to the center of the hall. He was wearing a service jacket that the "young hawk" Markeev could never even have dreamed of, cut from English cloth and trimmed with piping. He had a little gold-plated chain running from his belt to his pocket, and peeping out of the pocket was the tip of a knife-handle made from the leg of a wild boar, with the little hoof as the pommel.

Sashenka danced a tango, then a waltz, then a butterfly polka. During the breaks, she nibbled on walnuts and filled chocolate candies from an American aid parcel, with which Batiunya regaled her in the darkness under the balcony, and Sashenka's present, still unopened, lay in her purse for the next day. Sashenka ate so much chocolate that she completely stopped feeling hungry and the taste of chocolate even started to seem familiar and ordinary. She piled the chocolate wrappers and walnut shells in the hand that Batiunya meekly held out in the air. Batiunya hid the waste in the cracks in the parquet floor.

Sometime after midnight a fight broke out on the balcony, someone was detained and someone was led away, but Sashenka cheerfully accepted all this too. The chocolate had actually made her slightly drunk, her lips were sticky and the roof of her mouth and her throat itched. She glimpsed Markeev and Zara flitting past a few times. Zara was shaking her gold pendants like a nanny goat, and Markeev only appeared well-fed and handsome from a distance. His boots were down-at-heel, and in a break between dances Sashenka spotted him standing behind the door, stealthily gnawing on a hard, dry biscuit. He was gathering up the crumbs off his sleeves and putting them in his mouth. Sashenka almost split her sides laughing when she saw how embarrassed Markeev was to realize that he'd been discovered with his biscuit, and at the way he dropped a crumb he had picked off his sleeve on the floor before it reached his mouth, and then started picking some specks of dust and little threads or other off his sleeve in an attempt to deceive her. Sashenka raised her head, laughing as she cast a sideways glance in Markeev's direction and started whispering something in Batiunya's ear. She whispered to him that she wanted some kvass from the buffet with competitive market prices: she could have said it out loud, but she deliberately whispered in his ear, so that Markeev would think she was talking about him. She was taking her revenge on Markeev for the dreams in which he had pawed and fumbled at her, and for the hateful little virginal sofa bed that she had pummeled with her sides as she squirmed on it afterward, when she woke up in the middle of the night.

Markeev gave Sashenka a spiteful look, pushed the door, and darted out into the lobby, and Sashenka burst into loud laughter. The laughter and dancing had turned Sashenka's cheeks pink, and she was so beautiful that Batiunya forgot about everything else and dashed off, not to the commercial buffet, but to the cloakroom to get his greatcoat, and from there across the road to the freshly plastered apartment building of the top military brass, where he seized his chance and snatched a bottle with French writing on it and several tangerines out of his father's personal cupboard. Without pausing to catch his breath, he dashed back, and as he ran up to Sashenka he couldn't remember taking off his greatcoat at the cloakroom, he simply couldn't remember, it was as if he had been instantly transported back to Sashenka, and he stood there in front of her, panting, disheveled, smeared with plaster, his eyes glowing.

In the hall, they were playing forfeits. A "master of ceremonies" with a limp, wearing a service jacket with tank-crew collar tabs, but no shoulder straps, was hobbling around everyone, handing out little cardboard tabs. Batiunya ended up with a tab that said "mignonette," and Sashenka's was "nasturtium."

"Oh," Zara shouted out.

"What's wrong?' asked the tank-crew master of ceremonies.

"I'm in love," said Zara, adjusting her pendants.

"Who with?"

"With 'forget-me-not.'"

"Oho," Markeev shouted out brazenly, as if he had never nibbled on a dry biscuit behind a door, but fed from morning to night on American condensed milk and American dried-fruit pudding packed in little golden boxes.

"Let's go up on the balcony," Batiunya whispered to Sashenka, then looked at Markeev and snickered rather loudly.

Sashenka and Batiunya walked up the spiral staircase, where it was drafty and smelled of cat droppings. The balcony was dusty and dark. A little lantern lit up rows of seats nailed to planks, stacked together with their legs upward, a broken billiard table, and ragged drapes, from which strips had been torn to be used as velvet shoeshine rags. Small items of club property crunched underfoot: chessboards and chess pieces, a bent bugle, several Spanish hats with tassels and papier-mâché animal masks.

Batiunya took out his pocketknife and picked at the cork of the French bottle. The cork popped and aromatic foam oozed out, fizzing up and flowing onto the chaotically heaped up, dirty junk.

"Have some," said Batiunya, "it's French champagne."

He set the champagne bottle to Sashenka's lips, and she took a timid swallow, squeezed her eyes shut and took several more. The champagne didn't taste quite as good as the lemonade that Sashenka had drunk on Victory Day, it wasn't as sweet and it didn't have the fruit-essence fragrance that Sashenka adored, but it still prickled at her throat in the same pleasant way, and after the third swallow Sashenka felt some effect. Batiunya handed her a mandarin; Sashenka sniffed at the tender yellow skin and laughed.

"Eat it," said Batiunya.

"Later," said Sashenka, and she put the mandarin in her purse.

"Take some more," Batiunya said, and held out three more mandarins.

Sashenka felt sorry to tear the satin-smooth skin, and she put another two mandarins in her purse and tore open the third one, the worst one, which wasn't yellow, but greenish, and put a segment in her mouth. Closing her eyes, Sashenka sucked the juice out of the mandarin, swallowing her aromatic saliva. Her stomach had been gurgling and she'd been feeling occasional twinges for a long time already: Sashenka had obviously gorged herself on American chocolate and once or twice a light nausea crept up to her throat, leaving behind in her mouth a sweet and sour aftertaste of glutinous, ration-card bread, cocoa with vanilla, and millet soup.

When Batiunya reached forward to kiss her, Sashenka had jerked her head back in fright, although she very much wanted to try a man's lips with her own for the first time in her life. But she was afraid that Batiunya would sense that sweet and sour aftertaste that was setting her teeth on edge. However, after drinking some champagne and sucking on the mandarin, Sashenka felt much better, her stomach settled down and the twinges stopped, and her mouth now felt fresh, cool, and aromatic. She waited for Batiunya to try to kiss her again, but he must have been frightened off by her refusal and didn't dare to try. That made Sashenka angry and she said, "Let's go downstairs."

Batiunya nodded without saying anything. His nose was submissive and sad, absolutely timid, and a tuft of hair stuck up sadly on the crown of his head. That made Sashenka want to laugh and her heart was touched by a kind impulse; she felt grateful to Batiunya for the mandarins and the chocolate and for falling in love with her. She wanted to do something nice for Batiunya, but she didn't know what, and apart from that, there was a faint, confused buzzing in her head.

"I'll kiss you," Sashenka said, "only you close your eyes."

Batiunya hastily closed his eyes. Sashenka couldn't bring herself to kiss his lips after all, and she spent a long time choosing between the forehead and the cheek.

"Come on," Batiunya called out impatiently, opening his eyes slightly.

"Close your eyes, you nasty boy," Sasha exclaimed and stepped forward to kiss him on the neck. But the moment she got close, Batiunya suddenly grabbed her by the shoulders and poked something wet against her nose and the edge of her mouth several times. Breaking away, Sasha realized that these wet, disgusting dabs were the first kiss of her life, the one that she had dreamed about so much. She felt bitter and sad, because her first kiss was already over and it had been so uninteresting. She walked away to the broken billiard table that was standing up on end and propped her hands against it.

"What's wrong?" Batiunya asked guiltily.

"Nothing," said Sashenka, and she burst into tears.

"Perhaps I've offended you," said Batiunya, perplexed, "don't you go thinking . . . I want to marry you . . ."

Sashenka looked at his submissive nose, stopped crying, and started laughing.

"Let's go downstairs," she said.

She suddenly wanted to dance, sing, flirt, and be the center of attention. Downstairs the military band was thundering away again. They were dancing something quick and passionate.

"Now let's get moving," shouted the tank-crew master of ceremonies. "Let's have lots of sweat and no blood."

The band members got out of their seats, turning up the heat. Markeev juggled with his boots and Zara tortured her skirt so fiercely with her knees that a crack was clearly heard as the seams yielded.

Sashenka started trembling, anticipating a difficult battle. Zara was two years older than she was and had muscular, well-fed legs, the kind you could only get from good-quality food. But Sashenka had no intention of outdancing Zara, or of joining in the frantic pace of the foxtrot. On the contrary, she and Batiunya set off, gliding slowly and smoothly, skillfully omitting several beats of the music by marking time on the spot and so slipping into the rhythm. It was a precisely calculated move that had come to Sashenka in a flash, when she was still on the final step of the spiral staircase. Sashenka transformed a problem into an advantage. Moving slowly, she immediately stood out from the general mass of dancers, who were trying to outdance each other. All their faces, even the girls', were red and contorted, as if they were performing heavy work, their mouths fitfully gulped in air and the clothes under their arms were baggy with sweat. But Sashenka floated smoothly and lightly; in that way she could show off her lisle stockings, and her pink blouse with the low neckline, and even the lacy, sky-blue slip, which glowed through the transparent voile. Before even a minute had passed, Sashenka began reaping the fruits of her intelligent behavior, as well as her clothes and her appearance. Several lieutenants, who had appeared in the hall only recently, broke off dancing and moved back to the wall, watching no one but Sashenka. Other, more impressive young men also moved back to the wall: young hawks in service jackets, students from the mechanical engineering college, soccer players from the Red Front team, and in general everyone who was strong and handsome moved aside, to the wall. A few second-rate couples tried to dance on, it's true, but no one took any notice of them, and Zara and Markeev completely disappeared. Eventually the tank-crew master of ceremonies gave a wave of his hand, and the band fell silent, defeated by Sashenka; the musicians sat down, mopped off their faces with their handkerchiefs, and started playing a smooth tango, adjusting to Sashenka's rhythm. Sashenka waited out the pause with dignity, calmly standing at the center of the circle, resting the palm of one hand on Batiunya's shoulder and presenting her other hand to Batiunya's right hand in a casual, relaxed gesture, like an award. To demonstrate her indifference to the general attention, she quietly asked her partner about trivial nonsense that she wasn't interested in at all. She asked if his boots pinched and if his mother went to bed early. As for her own mother, she sometimes slept like a log, and sometimes tossed and turned all night, like Olga.

Sashenka immediately checked herself at that, because she might blurt out in passing that her mother worked as a dishwasher, and that they had two paupers, who begged on a church porch, living with them. But nonetheless, from the outside their conversation appeared elegant, and Sashenka was carried away by this quiet talking, which all these lieutenants and young hawks could only guess at. When the music started playing, Sashenka inclined her head, smiling sadly, and glided off in the same dignified manner, slipping gracefully across the parquet in her pumps, indifferent to the fame that she had craved only yesterday; she was created only to adorn, but not to love, like Marlene Dietrich or Erika Fiedler in the captured German color movies. Sashenka floated on across the parquet and nothing interested her any longer, apart from the tall windows, which were gilded by patches of moonlight at the spots where they were not boarded up with plywood. Sashenka slipped into a joyful melancholy, diffusing into something sweet and amorphous, and only returned to the hall when she and Batiunya glided past the inner dividing wall. Here there were no moonlit windows, the staircase leading to the vestibule was visible through the open doors, and she caught the smell from the snack bar, where the food was not sold at ration-card rates, but for competitive market prices. Sashenka began recognizing faces, as if she were sinking downward, and suddenly, for some reason that wasn't yet clear, she intuitively sensed a disagreeable change of mood toward her. She listened.

"A louse," someone said joyfully.

"Two," someone else put in.

"I've been watching them for ages," Zara chipped in happily and immediately added spitefully: "She's spreading typhus."

"I've already studied the route they follow," Markeev explained to Zara, but so loudly that he was heard in every corner of the hall, "one creeps across her shoulder blade, from where you can see the strap of the slip, as far as the collar of the blouse and back again . . . And the other one creeps over to intercept it . . . They meet between the shoulder blades . . ."

The orchestra carried on playing and Sashenka made a few more movements to the rhythm of the tango, obviously in the same way that the body of someone who has been killed outright sometimes feels pain and carries on living its former life for a few minutes, because even among people who are killed outright there are some unfortunates whom the bullet doesn't strike directly in the heart, but a little bit lower.

"They've met again," Markeev shouted, "and kissed each other . . . Batiunya, they'll launch an assault on you now . . ."

There was the sound of laughter and one lieutenant pulled his forage cap down over his eyes. Batiunya stopped. He was still holding his hand on Sashenka, but he had a bewildered, frightened expression. Then he suddenly smiled, jerked his hand away and started clownishly scratching himself and slapping his hand against his sides, as if he were trying to catch parasites. The laughter became so loud that the band stopped playing and the musicians leaned down from the stage, asking what was wrong. Then the lame tank-crew master of ceremonies walked over to Markeev and, without actually hitting him, ran his palm across Markeev's face from ear to ear, as if wiping it clean, but in a way that left five crimson stripes welling up on Markeev's cheeks. Then the master of ceremonies turned toward Sashenka and his heavy, cast-iron face became gentle and calm.

"Right, enough of that," he said, "these things happen . . . When we were encircled, I scratched myself so hard, I was bleeding all over . . ."

But Sashenka looked at the master of ceremonies with hatred in her eyes, she hated him now more than anyone else in the hall, she thought that this postcard face from the battle of Kursk somehow reminded her of Vasya, and immediately remembered that Vasya's dirty greatcoat had been hanging on her fur coat.

"Enough of that," the master of ceremonies repeated, moving closer to Sashenka. "What's to be done, when there's hardship and hunger . . . I know your mother. She's strained her back hunching over those army kitchen vats . . . A louse loves hardship and hunger . . ."

This "Kursk hero" was finally trampling Sashenka into the dirt, he was humiliating her lisle stockings and her marquisette blouse, and now it was clear to her that he had ended up doing his "cultural work" as a "master of ceremonies" because he was an invalid, and not because he loved dancing and beauty.

"Brush them off with a newspaper," whispered a poorly dressed girl, who was so thin that the skin of her face had a bluish tinge. The girl was wearing her grandmother's plush cape-coat. "Parasites ought to crawl across a coat like that, not across a marquisette blouse," Sashenka thought bitterly. "My God, why did it have to happen ... I hate them all ... How I hate them ..."

"Come on, let's go out, I'll help you," the girl whispered.

"If not for this disaster, I wouldn't even speak to a plain creature like this," Sashenka thought, "and now she's trying to give me advice ... To be my friend ... Why did this happen ... Why haven't I died ... It's all because of that greatcoat ... It's filthy ... From the church porch ... I'll throw them all out ... Out into the street ... They've ruined my life ..."

Sashenka's chest was filled with sobbing and moaning, but she tried to clench her teeth firmly as she ran out of the hall, and only a slight, trembling whine seeped out through them, because she simply couldn't clench them completely tight, and it was pointless anyway, because the whine escaped along with the air as she breathed it out. Sashenka knew she couldn't hold back the groans in her chest and throat for long—her mouth was filled with them—and Sashenka puffed out her cheeks, hoping to gain a split-second that way. She ran out into the vestibule and slammed her back and shoulder blades hard against a column in loathing.

"It's already done," said the girl with the skin that was blue from malnourishment, popping up again beside Sashenka. "I brushed them off with a newspaper and throttled them in my fist ... You try

using Romanina powder on them ... Not German, but Romanina ...
And it doesn't spoil your clothes ..."

Sashenka looked at the girl's unattractive, kind eyes and thought:
"What is she living for ... Nobody will ever love her ... Nobody
will ever feed her chocolate ... The life of beautiful women is out
of reach for both of us now ... I ought to poison myself ... Poison
myself with matches ... Scrape the sulfur off of matches ..."

The tank-crew master of ceremonies took hold of Sashenka's elbow,
crumpling the marquisette of her sleeve with his yellow, tobacco-
stained fingers, and the very moment Sashenka saw those gnarled
fingers creeping across her body, looking like beetles or insects, or
something else repulsive, she realized that she was done for.

"Don't touch my arm," Sashenka cried out in revulsion. But then
she immediately snapped her teeth shut so smartly that even she
was surprised, cutting short the groaning and sobbing that were
trying to burst out together with her shout and finally disgrace her
completely. Sashenka gave the tank-crew master of ceremonies a
hard push and he lost his balance. His shorter leg, which didn't bend
at the knee, slipped, leaving his feet straddled wide in an awkward,
comical posture, and he slipped down the steps, trying to catch hold
of the banister. And at that very moment the loudspeaker hanging in
the vestibule broadcast the first stroke of the clock announcing the
arrival of the New Year, 1946. Sashenka dashed to the cloakroom,
she was afraid she wouldn't find her tag, but she found it quickly and
the startled old woman tossed out Sashenka's fur coat and boots.

02

Outside, the snow was flying thick and solid, so that when Sashenka stopped for a moment and raised her face, she imagined the pall of snow was motionless, and she was flying obliquely up from the earth to the sky. Everything seemed to start swirling around and Sashenka shook her head and ran across the road to the military apartment buildings, carrying her fur coat and boots in her arms. She wanted to find a quiet spot to put on her things in peace, but someone tall, wearing a low, round astrakhan hat was standing nearby, firing a flare pistol up into the air. The bright flares crackled loudly as they hurtled through the mass of white flakes, also obliquely, in the same way that Sashenka had been flying in her imagination, and then they burst, and a red glow trembled on the snow, like when there was a fire. Beside the Young Pioneer Palace was a little park, which the Germans had made into their graveyard during the occupation. The crosses had been knocked down long ago, and the grave mounds had been flattened out on voluntary working Sundays, but there were still slightly raised spots here and there, covered over with snow; and helmets, remnants of crosses, and grave plaques were lying around. Sashenka put a plaque covered with German letters underneath her and sat down on a little mound. Hardly any time had passed since the moment she ran outside, because she could still hear the New Year's chimes from the loudspeaker beside the burned-out three-story carcass on the corner. Sashenka put on her fur jacket, brushed the snow off her marquisette blouse, took off her pumps, and stuck her wet, freezing-cold feet into her boots. The pumps had swollen up from the snow and become shapeless, and that upset Sashenka so badly, she couldn't hold back her groans any longer. And she groaned loudly, astounded by those alien, guttural sounds that she was apparently capable of producing.

"My God, what can I do?" Sashenka asked out loud when the groans had exhausted her and stopped bringing her any relief. "Poison myself with matches . . . Or leave my mother . . . Go away somewhere . . . Or get a job at the glove factory . . . But first, get back at all these bastards . . . What a mother . . . She has no pity on her own daughter . . . And those beggars . . . Vasya even has lice in his eyebrows . . . I saw them . . . I saw Olga washing him . . . Verminridden *polizei*. My father died for the motherland, so that I could have a good life . . . Eat chocolate in a marquisette blouse . . . And be the center of attention . . . But my mother's mean and nasty. That lousy *polizei* hung his tattered rags on my fur coat and they crawled across . . ."

She had been walking, not sitting, for a long time already and now, passing by a garden in front of a house, she came out into the quiet, snow-covered square. On all sides there were nothing but burned-out carcasses jutting up, or heaps of bricks covered with a sprinkling of snow; only the Young Pioneer Palace—the former municipal council—had survived, because they didn't have time to blow it up, as well as the few buildings where army officers' families lived now. Sashenka walked on farther, her elbows pressed against her sides, with her forearms raised and her wrists drooping limply. Her purse was dangling from her right elbow. The streets were empty. Only once an army patrol truck drove by. Someone shined a flashlight on Sashenka and a soldier said something, either calling

out to her or making a joke. But Sashenka walked by without say-
ing anything. A sentry was striding to-and-fro alongside an old
three-story building. It had a rather strange appearance—the upper
story was clad in metal sheeting, not just the roof, but the actual
walls of the upper story were covered in galvanized metal sheets,
and windows had been cut in this sheeting. The bottom story was a
semibasement, with windows that rose up only halfway out of the
ground and were blocked off with thick metal gratings. Sashenka
walked along the massive fence that abutted the building: it had
barbed wire stretching along its top. The area at the back, imme-
diately behind the fence, was rather desolate, an empty lot and a
ravine. The only lights twinkled in the distance on the far side of
the ravine. Along the edge of the ravine she could make out a tem-
porary wooden barrier, already broken down in places, and a pyra-
mid knocked together out of planks, covered in snow. A plaque was
nailed to it. "Here lie buried 960 Soviet citizens, martyred by the
fascist German invaders," Sashenka read. She walked to the far end
of the ravine, where pieces of rusty tank armor, cut up with a fusion
welder, were lying. Sashenka had obviously not cleaned the snow
off her blouse very well—the marquisette was clinging to her body,
and she was shivering under her fur coat, as if she were standing in
the wind completely naked.

"What can I do?" thought Sashenka. "Go home . . . And squirm
on the sofa again . . . Vasya will be fondling Olga . . ."

When Sashenka woke up in the middle of the night and heard
that they weren't sleeping on the floor behind the screen, she got
a horrible feeling . . . She wanted to shout and curse . . . And at the
same time she pined, tormented by a dreary yearning, she tensed
up her body so fiercely and stretched out her legs so hard that the
joints of her knees hurt. She stuffed cotton wool in her ears and
wrapped a towel around her head, as if she had a toothache . . .
"Damned bastards," Sashenka thought, "I'm suffering because

of them." Sashenka was filled to overflowing with spite, so that her face turned hot and the spite warmed her, giving her strength and exciting her. Sashenka pulled off her mittens, squeezed the bundle with her shoes in it tightly under her arm and clenched her fists so hard that it hurt, making the fingers crack, and it became difficult to breathe and everything turned dark in front of her eyes. She walked home determinedly, hurrying as if she were afraid of not carrying the hatred that had accumulated in her chest all the way there. It stopped snowing. The moonlight and deep snow had concealed the ruins, the nighttime town was clean and quiet. In a few hours so much snow had fallen that Sashenka got stuck in the pristine drifts between the sheds. Lying beside the cesspit were frozen lumps of dirty potato peelings, sprinkled with snow, and tattered rags, and Sashenka suddenly felt afraid. She remembered Olga telling fortunes a few days earlier, setting three candles in front of a mirror, and Sashenka had looked into the mirror for so long that her eyes hurt, until she saw a face that she didn't know in it. Now she started fancying that it was the face of dentist Leopold Lvovich's daughter, who was buried here, beside the sewage pit. Sashenka imagined her lying in this foul, boggy ground and suddenly it seemed as if the face of the beautiful, young Jewish girl was showing through the rags and the frozen potato peelings. Her cheeks were white, glittering with hoarfrost, but her eyes were large and vehement.

"Mommy," Sashenka shouted just like a child and ran, stumbling and falling, ran the way that she used to run to her mother, to hide her head between her mother's warm knees. "Mommy," Sashenka shouted despairingly. She thought she was shouting very loudly, but in fact she was barely even moving her tongue and only short, mumbling sounds emerged from her mouth. Then she thought that she was on her little sofa; her head felt hot, and her throat had gone dry, the way it did at night, when everyone breathing in the room warmed up the air. The beautiful face, covered in hoarfrost and surrounded by sewage, was only a dream. And so of course, thank goodness, she had only dreamed about the parasites crawling across her marquisette blouse too. Sashenka saw her mother. She was standing there, looking very young, a lot like Sashenka, so much like her that for a moment Sashenka wondered in fright if she was really looking at herself from the outside. Her mother was wearing a new downy shawl and felt boots. But beside her mother Sashenka saw the tank-crew master of ceremonies in an army peacoat and a fur-lined tank helmet. He was holding her mother's hand and saying something to her, and Sashenka's mother was laughing, then suddenly she pulled her hand free and hit the master of ceremonies flirtatiously and affectionately, in exactly the same way that Sashenka had hit Batiunya. Her mother's little hand first touched the master of ceremonies' hand with its completely relaxed wrist and then trailed its palm across it, with the fingertips gently touching and the nails scratching. Sashenka pressed her cheek, chin, and forehead against the wooden pillar supporting the balcony and started groaning quietly. Feelings flooded her chest, turning it heavy again with spite and yearning, because Sashenka realized that she had tried to deceive herself by imagining for a moment that she was sleeping on the little sofa, but in fact it had all been real: the parasites on the marquisette blouse, which had crawled across from Vasya's greatcoat, and her mother with the "master of ceremonies"; and perhaps she really had seen the face of the beautiful Jewish girl, the dentist's daughter, buried beside the cesspit, as well.

The master of ceremonies put his arms around Sashenka's mother and hugged her tight, and she laughed as she gratefully rubbed her cheek against his chin and caught the edge of his tank helmet in her teeth. Sashenka was seized by a dreary anguish, her legs tensed up and their joints started aching, her teeth were clenched so tightly that her temples hurt and her pupils dilated as wide as if she were peering into deep darkness; and in the midst of the darkness

Sashenka fancied there was something sweet and terrifying that she could only vaguely guess at. She groaned more loudly and struck her body hard against the pillar to rouse herself from the oblivion that had enveloped her.

"Someone shouted," Sashenka's mother said in alarm, moving away from the master of ceremonies.

"The wind," the master of ceremonies said.

"I feel anxious anyway," Sashenka's mother said. "Sashenka takes everything so much to heart."

"Never mind," said the master of ceremonies, "she's probably at her friend's place . . . These things happen, after all . . ."

"Yes," said Sashenka's mother, "she sometimes stays over at Maya's place when she quarrels with me . . ."

The tank-crew master of ceremonies stuck his hands up under her mother's shawl at the back, so that his palms embraced the back of her head, and Sashenka's mother shook her head in mock indignation, as if trying to break free, but the master of ceremonies pressed her against the wall of the building with his chest, in the same way that Markeev had pressed Sashenka in her dream, and forced his lips hard against hers, and Sashenka's mother tenderly stroked his back, brushing the snow off his peacoat with her hands.

Sashenka instantly pushed off hard from the pillar and darted out into the middle of the courtyard; she flung away her purse and the bundle with her shoes, which hindered her hands, and swore crudely and profusely, the way that young hawks and urchins in gateways swore. Her mother sprang away from the master of ceremonies, turned toward Sashenka and drew herself erect, even going up on tiptoe and throwing both arms up above her head. Her eyebrows rose, horizontal wrinkles appeared on her forehead, her lower jaw dropped, and she called out as despairingly and childishly as Sashenka had a moment earlier when she ran away in fright from the cesspit. But this shout only stopped Sashenka for a moment, and then she wanted to hurt her mother even more badly; Sashenka was even seized by a kind of wild, bleak joy when she saw how afraid her mother was, and she shouted out:

"My father died for the motherland and here you . . . Forgive me, Lord, for this and more, forgive me, Lord, for I'm a . . . hopeless sinner . . ."

Lights went on in several windows and faces were pressed against the glass, but Sashenka couldn't give a damn any more. She dashed at her mother, weeping and moaning, and pinched her painfully on the cheek, pushing aside the bewildered master of ceremonies, who tried to shield her mother. She darted around them, like a vicious little fly, and they only tried helplessly to waft her away. Then Sashenka hurtled up the steps. The door wasn't locked, her mother must have simply closed it when she came down with the master of ceremonies. The kitchen was flooded with moonlight, the pots and pans hanging on little nails were gleaming. In the stale, heated air she could hear Vasya and Olga snoring serenely in chorus. Her body still trembling in agitation, Sashenka stood there for a second or two, as if gathering her thoughts while she listened to her mother's timid footsteps on the stairs. Hastily, before her mother came in, Sashenka moved aside the screen. Vasya and Olga were sleeping in each other's arms, both large and ugly. Olga had laid her head on the shaggy wheels of Vasya's chest, which were regularly breathing air in and out, and Olga's head rose and fell with them. The little crucifix on Olga's chest was dangling down, touching Vasya's crucifix, and when either of them twitched or shifted, the crosses jangled quietly against each other. The sleepers were only covered halfway up with Olga's shawl, some kind of tattered rag with stuffing falling out of it, and Vasya's oil-smeared greatcoat. Sashenka could see Vasya's bare foot, as big as a spade, thrust out to one side.

"Get out," Sashenka yelled furiously, shuddering and clenching her fists, "You're hiding. You German lackeys . . . You *polizeien* . . . My father was an airman, he was killed... He fought... And you spread lice here in the rear lines... Get out..."

Vasya carried on sleeping as blissfully as ever, Olga merely muttered something quietly, and that totally enraged Sashenka. She grabbed the bucket, broke the thin crust of ice with a mug and splashed out the icy water onto the sleepers. They both instantly jumped up, gazing around senselessly, shaking themselves off and snorting, like animals that have fallen through a hole in the river ice.

"Get out," Sashenka shouted, "go, and take your rags with you... Your louse-ridden rags... get out of this house..."

And then Sashenka turned around, sensing that her mother was standing in the doorway.

"Take your coat off and come into the room," her mother said in a quiet voice. But Sashenka caught a new note in that voice and instantly realized she had done something wrong, she had given way too completely to her impulse and lost her power over her mother.

"You clear out too," Sashenka shouted at her mother, but mostly out of inertia. "This is my father's home ... He went to the front from here... How dare you... How dare you, with a lover..."

Sashenka knew that she had to contort her face as furiously as possible, so that her eyes would roll up and back and her cheek would start twitching—her mother was terribly frightened when Sashenka's cheek started twitching—but just at this moment Sashenka sensed that her spite was coming out off-balance somehow, it wasn't frightening, and her mother clearly sensed that too. She took a step toward Sashenka, then swung and hit her so hard across the face with the back of her hand that Sashenka dropped to her knees. Sashenka immediately jumped up and started running, hunched over, along the wall of the kitchen, but her mother blocked her way and hit her a blow that set Sashenka's ears ringing. Despite that, Sashenka deftly avoided the third blow and smartly jumped in behind Vasya and Olga. They were sitting there, soaking wet, dull-wittedly huddling against each other, like puppies during a fire or a flood. It was harder for Sashenka's mother to reach her here, behind them, and then in addition the tank-crew master of ceremonies came in and grabbed her mother's hand from behind. Sashenka's mother stood there for a while, trembling all over, as Sashenka had a few minutes earlier; then she went limp, lowered her head onto the master of ceremonies' shoulder, and started crying loudly.

Their neighbor, who lived straight ahead and on the left along the corridor, the mechanic Drobkis, glanced in at the half-open door. He was wearing quilted trousers, felt house slippers, and a sleeveless fur jerkin over his undershirt.

"What's wrong, Katya?" the neighbor asked Sashenka's mother. "Maybe I should call an ambulance?"

"No need," Sashenka's mother said, sobbing. "It's nothing, just a little quarrel . . ."

"These things happen in a family," said the master of ceremonies.

Sashenka saw that her mother had gone limp, and that lent her strength.

"It's not true," she shouted loudly at Drobkis, "she was beating me . . . With her lover . . . This is my father's apartment . . . How dare she . . . She's a thief . . . That's who she is . . . A thief . . ."

Sashenka jumped out from behind Vasya and Olga, darted past her mother, pushed Drobkis aside and ran down the steps. Fortunately, her purse and her shoes were still lying in the snowdrift. Sashenka picked up everything and walked hurriedly to the end of the side street. She was almost running, and her heart was pounding in her throat. It was awkward to go to Maya's place in the middle of the night, and Sashenka decided to walk to the railroad station to warm herself up a bit. She thought over everything as she walked along, and even calmed down. She didn't have a mother any longer. She was going to live on her own. She would leave school and get a job at the glove factory or the post office, delivering mail . . . her mother was a thief, a mean, nasty woman, and a prostitute . . . And Vasya was a *polizei* . . . Ah, if only the master of ceremonies turned out to be a spy . . . A saboteur in disguise . . .

It was noisy at the station, but warm. Demobilized men were lying in rows on the benches or simply on the floor. The air was bluish-gray with cheap tobacco smoke. There was a delicious smell of stewed pork and bread. Sashenka sat down on a windowsill behind an aspidistra in a green tub overgrown with moss and opened her purse. She took out the mandarins, sniffed at them and sat there like that for a while, with her eyes closed. Then she put the mandarins away and tore open the paper package of her present. Inside it were two nuts, one honey cake, and three mint cakes, several hard sugar candies, and a little bag of delicious roasted sunflower seeds. Sashenka ate the rock-hard honey and mint cakes first; it was such hard work that the muscles in Sashenka's chin, and even her neck, started aching. Then she started on the sugar candies. There were lots of young soldiers about, and Sashenka was afraid they might start making passes at her. She shrank down behind the aspidistra and even stopped gnawing on the candies so the noise wouldn't attract attention. But the clock hanging in the middle of the hall showed that half an hour had gone by, and then forty minutes, and still no one had made a pass at Sashenka; she started feeling resentful and bored, then she glanced out from behind the aspidistra and froze in stupefaction. An air force lieutenant was sitting quite close to her, and Sashenka had never seen any men as handsome as him except in the captured color movies. The features of his olive-skinned face were finely chiseled, his thick eyebrows met above the bridge of his nose, his hair was as black as a gypsy's, and the glance of his gray eyes gave her a sweet, melting feeling in her heart. The airman only looked in Sashenka's direction once, and even then he probably didn't notice her, because she was concealed by the aspidistra. He leaned back against his kit bag, set it lower under his head and stretched out to take a doze. His long, up-curving eyelashes quivered occasionally.

"My sweet darling," Sashenka thought with quiet joy, and imagined herself combing his black hair, which was probably silky to the touch, and his head touching her breasts, delightfully tickling the erect nipples.

"My dearest Vitenka," Sashenka thought. "You're my wonderful one, all mine." She invented a name for him in order to feel closer and not be a stranger. "What a fortune I have," Sashenka thought, "all this is mine . . . These eyelashes, these hands . . ."

When Sashenka was dreaming about something, her face tilted back, her eyes became large, and a tremulous, mysterious smile appeared on her lips, as if from unappeased passion.

"My darling boy," Sashenka whispered. "My darling little boy . . ."

If she reached one hand out from behind the aspidistra, Sashenka could have touched the lieutenant's black gypsy hair, because he was perched on the very edge of the bench, and his head, with the chin propped on the kit bag, was even hanging over the edge. Sashenka crumpled up the colored paper wrapping from one of the nuts in the New Year's present and tossed the wrapper into a wastebasket standing nearby, and her hand glided across the lieutenant's hair, as if Sashenka hadn't intended it, but so lightly that the lieutenant didn't even stir. His handsome face was sunk in deep sleep. It was the first time Sashenka had ever seen someone's face remain so handsome while they slept—because a sleeper's face usually displays all the defects that people cunningly manage to conceal when they're awake, and handsome men were especially good at concealing their defects. Sashenka sat there without moving for one hour, and then another. There was a draught from the window and her back turned stiff from the cold; to warm herself a bit, Sashenka huddled up with her knees bent. Her feet set on a ledge that they had found and her head lowered onto her legs. She dreamed about a big cat trying to creep under her blanket; Sashenka tucked the edge of the blanket under herself, but the cat found Sashenka's hand and started tearing at it with its teeth. Sashenka jerked her hand away, and fortunately there was only a little wound left on her wrist, the skin was only slightly puckered, and the cat ran off to one side and watched Sashenka with brown, uncatlike, all-knowing eyes.

Sashenka woke up instantaneously, with a jerk. She straightened out her spine with an effort. Her calves ached as if she had been climbing a mountain, and her back hurt. Demobilized men were walking about in the hall, coughing and yawning. Hardly anyone was still sleeping. The edge of the bench where the handsome lieutenant had been sitting was empty.

"He's left me," Sashenka thought ruefully. "I'll never see him again."

And immediately the spite awoke in her, but it wasn't spite for the handsome lieutenant, it was the old, forgotten spite for her debauched mother, for her mother's lame lover and the two paupers for whose sake Sashenka's mother had sacrificed her own daughter. Sashenka got up off the windowsill, came out from behind the aspidistra, went out into the street and set off hurriedly, certain of her destination and not hesitating for a second.

It was already dawn, the custodians were scraping away the snow, and the bread vans were driving up to the kiosks. The smell of fine snow dust raised by spades mingled with the smell of freshly baked dough. Closing her eyes, Sashenka imagined she was eating warm slices of bread for breakfast and cooling her throat after them with delicious gulps of water so cold that it made her teeth hurt.

Sashenka walked up to the three-story building with its top story clad in sheet zinc and the bottom-floor windows blocked off with metal gratings. Just at that moment a shaggy little horse, covered in hoarfrost, walked up to the building, hauling a sleigh with a large cauldron standing on it, swathed in coarse burlap. Two prisoners in quilted jackets came out of the gates, escorted by a militiaman, also wearing a quilted jacket and a round astrakhan hat, with a German rifle slung over his shoulder with the barrel pointing downward, partisan fighter-style. The prisoners took hold of the cauldron's looped metal handles and carried it away. The cauldron gave out steam and a delicious smell of boiled rutabaga, rye flour, and vegetable oil. Sashenka gulped and swallowed, pressed one elbow against her gurgling stomach, waited for the gurgling to stop, and walked up to the sentry.

"I want to see the commander," Sashenka said.

"Speak to the orderly," the sentry said with inveterate boredom, "there's a porch on the left . . . where people wait . . ."

O3

On the porch, a lot of people with bags and sacks were jostling together, but there were even more of them in the orderly's reception area, a large, cold room divided by a partition. The orderly, a blond-haired young man, was sitting there with a tanned sheepskin jacket thrown over his shoulders, leafing through some papers. The people in the reception area shoved each other on the sly, trying not to squabble loudly among themselves, so they wouldn't attract the orderly's attention: he had obviously called them to order already and warned them. They were mostly country people, but there were also a few dressed in town style, even one fashionable woman in a gray astrakhan fur coat with a matching muff and an astrakhan hood. It was strange to see her jostling among the quilted work jackets and short, fur-trimmed coats, trying to squeeze through closer to the counter, where a clerk and a militiaman were accepting the sacks and bags. A massive peasant had taken the place beside the counter. Easily pushing back the people pressing against him from behind, he unloaded pieces of fatback, thickly sprinkled with salt, onto a piece of cloth in front of the clerk, and the clerk made a note of something in a document. The woman in astrakhan fur grabbed hold of the partition with one hand, pressed her shoulder into the peasant's monolithic, quilted back and squeezed her way desperately, inch by inch, toward the cherished counter, holding out at arm's length a basket tied with silk ribbons, with a bottle of milk glugging in it and an appetizing chunk of roast beef, spiced with garlic, peeping out. Her hood had slipped down onto the nape of her neck and rivulets of sweat were trickling down her young face.

"A black marketeer," Sashenka thought spitefully, drooling. "She got all that astrakhan from thieving."

Just as the woman was getting close, the peasant gently shifted his backside, without even turning around. The blow carried the woman a long way from the counter, behind the other visitors, and flung her hard against the wall. The basket tied with ribbons, which the woman had already managed to set on the very edge of the counter, fell off, the milk ran out under the feet of the jostling crowd, and the woman went diving down, soiling her astrakhan fur on the tarpaulin boots.

"Serves her right," Sashenka thought with malicious glee, "damned black marketeer..."

"What's this now?" said the orderly, raising his head. "I warned you, I'll halt the reception of parcels . . . Why, you people . . . Stepanets," he said merrily, spotting an old woman at the back of the line, "you're here again..."

"Yes, master," the little old woman mumbled through her gums, bowing.

She had three shawls peeping out from under each other, crisscrossed over her quilted vest, and rags with straw poking out of them wrapped around her feet over her felt boots.

"I've told you time and time again, Stepanets," the orderly said with patient insistence. "No food parcels will be accepted for your son... He's guilty of extremely grave crimes... The mass murder of Soviet citizens, do you understand... The people will judge him..."

"I walked four miles," the old woman said, wiping her watering eyes. "The frost is scorching... What do I want, after all... It's not like I want to give him much . . . He has a weak stomach . . . And a weak chest too . . . Here . . . Thanks to the kind people who gave me advice . . ."

With her frozen, bluish-gray fingers, the old woman began hurriedly untangling the knot of a shawl embroidered with cornflowers. The shawl contained a yellowed piece of paper with scuffed folds, which the old woman carried forward, deftly maneuvering between the other visitors, and held it out to the orderly . . .

"What's this?" said the orderly. "What tatty scrap of nonsense is this, then . . ." He fastidiously took hold of the piece of paper with his finger and thumb and started reading, struggling to make out the faded scribble.

"Doctor's note. The patient P. N. Stepanets suffers from deposits of urate salts in his joints and also inadequate kidney function; he requires a milk diet with a large content of vegetables and fruit. Spa therapy is recommended . . . Hydrogen sulfide and radon baths, mud poultices, in combination with the consumption of mineral water. A visit to Essentuki, Zheleznovodsk, Sochi-Matsesta, or Tskhaltubo is recommended. Doctor Vurvarg. 1940."

While the orderly was reading, the old woman stood in front of him, blinking hopefully and wiping her eyes with her blue-gray fingers.

"Everything written here is the truth, master," she said, "written in honest conscience."

"I don't have any time for this," said the orderly, bending over the low partition. "I've got a horde of people here, and you're back here jostling every day! You'd be better off staying at home . . . You walk four miles to get here and four to get back . . ."

"That depends, now," said the old woman. "Sometimes I get a lift . . . Sometimes there's a collective farm cart or a truck . . . It's all written here in the paper, he has to take . . ."

"This is worthless scribble," said the orderly, angry now. "Take the paper. Come back again tomorrow, and I'll detain you . . . Arrest you, understand?"

He gave the paper back to the old woman, who carefully wrapped it in the shawl, hid it away on her chest and walked away to the windowsill, obviously settling down for a snack. She took out an onion and a rag containing salt and bread.

Taking advantage of the confusion caused by the old woman, the woman in astrakhan fur dashed to the counter through the passage that had opened up, holding out in front of her the basket smelling deliciously of roast beef, which, having been impregnated with spilled milk, had acquired an especially delicate aroma. And tickling Sashenka's nostrils, that smell redoubled her strength, arousing her malice. Sashenka darted into the passage with equal adroitness, and she and the woman bumped shoulders right at the counter.

"I don't have a parcel," Sashenka said hastily, straight into the orderly's face. "I'm here on special business . . ."

Sashenka firmly set her elbow on the counter so that it not only prevented the woman from pushing her basket through, but also blocked off the woman's face from the orderly.

"I've got special business," Sashenka repeated, suffering pain because the woman was pressing her knee hard into Sashenka's leg from below, and on the counter she was scratching the skin just above Sashenka's wrist with some kind of sharp metal spike protruding from the basket.

"What kind of business?" the orderly asked, looking Sashenka up and down.

"Special business," Sashenka said for the third time, struggling to keep her hand on the counter.

"Come on through," said the orderly, lifting a hook and opening a little gate in the partition.

Sashenka took her hand off the counter in relief and walked in behind the partition. The woman watched her go with hate in her eyes, and then the woman was squeezed aside again by the tall peasant, who started laying out hard-boiled eggs on the counter in front of the clerk.

"Come in here," said the orderly, opening a door and letting Sashenka go ahead.

It was a small, quite empty room. There wasn't even a desk in it, nothing but two stools, a telephone on the wall, and a portrait of the People's Commissar of Internal Affairs.

"Sit down," said the orderly.

Sashenka sat down on a stool and the orderly remained standing under the portrait.

"I'm listening," said the orderly.

"I know where a *polizei* is hiding," said Sashenka, licking her lips that had gone dry for some reason and remembering with absolute clarity the way that Vasya and Olga had sat huddling against each other, like puppies caught in a house fire.

"You take your time," the orderly said briskly and gave her a friendly wink, "and don't be afraid . . . Come on, tell me all the details . . ."

"He's hiding in my home," Sashenka said in a flat, firm vice. "My mother feeds him stolen food . . . Stolen from the state . . . I hate her . . . My father was killed at the front, he died for the motherland . . . and she and her lover . . ."

The orderly gave Sashenka an intent look, he put his hand on her hair and stroked it . . .

"Don't worry," he said, "you've done the right thing . . . If your father was alive, he'd approve . . . I saw all sorts of things with the partisans for three years . . . So, your mother's living with a former *polizei*?" the orderly asked in a different, for-the-record voice.

"No," said Sashenka, with mist floating in front of her eyes and her lips wet from tears, "Olga's with the *polizei* . . . my mother's with a culture worker."

"What culture worker?" the orderly asked, taking out a notepad. "Which Olga, let me have the surnames . . ."

"I don't know," said Sashenka.

"The address then," said the orderly.

Sashenka gave him the address.

"And where does your mother work?"

Sashenka told him.

"I ate that food as well," Sashenka added.

"Never mind," said the orderly, "It's good that you've confessed . . . Do you go to political studies classes? The son is not responsible for the father. Which classic of Marxism is that quote from?"

Without waiting for an answer, the orderly went over to the phone, picked up the receiver, and spoke a few words that Sashenka couldn't make out. Then he hung up, sat down on a stool, put the notepad on his knees, dashed off two phrases in sprawling writing, tore off the page, and held it out to Sashenka.

"Go and see the commander," he said, giving Sashenka the note and opening an inconspicuous door, covered over with wallpaper, to let her out into a corridor. "Go straight on," he said. "Show them the note."

Sashenka walked along the corridor and found herself in a bright room that was very warm, so that the typist sitting in the corner was wearing a short-sleeved blouse, as if it were summer. And sitting beside the typist was the handsome lieutenant. Sashenka even ran her hand over her eyes at first, unable to believe in such an amazing coincidence. The lieutenant was feeling hot too; he had unfastened the hooks on his uniform tunic, and his neck was cut across by a faint, reddish streak where the tight collar had constricted it. His eyes were not gray now, as they had been at night, but blue. There were three doors in this room, one upholstered with leather, another upholstered with felt, and the third plain wood. A thin man came out through the wooden door, wearing a jacket and black cotton sleeve protectors, like an accountant. He was holding several folders.

"This is what there is in the archives," said the man, walking over to the lieutenant.

The typist stopped tapping away and looked up. The lieutenant looked up too. The thick eyebrows met at the bridge of his nose, the blue eyes turned darker and he became even more handsome, so that Sashenka just stood there, not even breathing. She had forgotten what she came here for and was thinking only of him.

"So, on Ravine Street there are 960 citizens who were tortured and killed, and we have lists of almost all of them, since they passed through the secretariat of the *feldgendarmie*," said the man in the sleeve protectors. "And then those in the area of the former airfield. And in the village of Khazhin . . . Four miles, the quarries of the porcelain factory . . . And in addition there are a number of small, unregistered graves, since in some places the killings were carried out spontaneously . . . Mostly by local *polizeien* in an inebriated state . . . We have a report from the doctor of the municipal sanitary epidemiological service and a statement from one of the custodians. They'll be here straightaway now . . . We still have the doctor under preliminary investigation, and we've summoned the custodian . . ." At this point the man noticed Sashenka. "What do you want?" he asked.

Sashenka showed him the note.

"I see," said the man in the accountant's sleeve protectors, "come through here, describe everything in detail and sign it."

He pushed the felt-covered door and let Sashenka through into a room with an office desk, a sofa, and a window that was blocked off with a metal grille, while the glass had been whitewashed halfway up, like in toilets.

"Write it down," he repeated.

Sashenka was left alone. On the desk in front of her there was a heap of white paper and a marble inkwell in the shape of the folktale-villain Chernomor's head, at which Ruslan was charging on horseback with his spear. Sashenka took off the helmet-shaped lid, picked up one of the pens lying on the desk, and dipped the nib into Chernomor's skull. The penholder was thick, standard office-issue; Sashenka put it down and picked up a more familiar, slim school pen.

"My mother," Sashenka wrote, "is a pilferer of Soviet property. I repudiate her and now wish to be only the daughter of my father, who died for the motherland . . ." Sashenka tried to write force-fully, but the pen splashed and scratched, and although the paper was lined, like in school exercise books, the letters jumped about and the lines of writing either crept upward or curved downward. Sashenka simply couldn't think of what to write about Vasya, Olga, and the master of ceremonies. She thought it would be a good thing to put something in about Batiunya, and Markeev, and Zara with her gold pendants, and in general everyone who had laughed at Sashenka and mocked her. She put down the pen and started pon-dering. In addition to the felt-covered door, the room had another one, painted white like in a hospital. And from behind that hospi-tal door she could hear dull voices and someone coughing harshly and painfully, as if he were really sick. Sashenka decided to ask what she should write next: she got up, tiptoed across to the white door and gently pushed it. The door yielded slightly, and in the crack that opened up Sashenka saw the lieutenant. He was sitting in an arm-chair, leaning one arm on the armrest and resting his head on his palm. An emaciated, pale man, obviously a prisoner, was standing beside him. The prisoner's scrawny neck was bound around with a scarf, and the skin was stretched so tight over his bluish, shaved scalp and temples that it seemed about to burst at any moment, especially now, when the man was shaken by a painful, hacking cough. The custodian Franya was standing beside this man and crumpling his cap in his hands.

"Go on, Shostak," said a voice that was quiet but frightening.

Sashenka suddenly felt scared, but she didn't dare to close the door, because she was afraid it would creak. She took one step to the left on tiptoe and saw a major in glasses sitting at a desk, reading some kind of document.

"Is this your signature, Shostak?" the major asked.

Shostak pulled the end of his dirty scarf out of his quilted jacket, wiped his mouth, took several hoarse breaths and said:

"I need a drink . . ."

"Is this your signature?" the major repeated.

"Permit me," said Shostak, taking the piece of paper. "Yes . . . As the public health physician, I was obliged to alert . . ." The major took the paper, lifted his glasses up onto his forehead and read out: "The bodies of individuals of Jewish nationality are discovered in sewers and drainage channels, and also in a number of cases at points in courtyards used by the public: individual local residents eliminate them without authorization within the city limits, making use of metal rods, knives, rocks, and other means. These actions, in contravention of the instruction requiring that such individuals be gathered together at strictly defined points for subsequent onward dispatch, threaten the city with an epidemic, which is especially dangerous, bearing in mind the large number of German army hospitals that are located here. Rotting corpses attract stray dogs and cats, and also facilitate the propagation of flies and horseflies, and this increases the danger of an epidemic spreading among both the local population and the army. The municipal council's sanitary and epidemiological service does not have at its disposal either the transport facilities or the labor force to deliver the corpses to the places stipulated in advance. Therefore, I hereby request that you petition the military authorities to prohibit such violations of the instruction forthwith, and I likewise request that means of transport be allocated for clearing the territory of the municipality of sites of infection. Senior Physician of the Municipal Sanitary and Epidemiological Service Shostak. August 17, 1941."

"They refused to give me any vehicles," Shostak said in a dull, hollow voice, the way people speak in a state of delirium. "We tried using two-wheeled handcarts, but the shipment point was in the order of three to four miles away, and in addition many of the corpses, especially in order to transport them through the town, and especially in the summer period, required sacks and burlap, since it sometimes happened that the limbs had been separated, and in a number of cases the skin and cutaneous tissue had been damaged, so that the viscera had become extracted, and subjected to an even greater degree of oxidation than the external integuments, increasing the danger of an epidemic. This clearing work was absolutely urgent, insofar as the water main had been blown up and the inhabitants of the town were using natural, exposed sources of water . . . Owing to the intense physical effort and health hazard involved, the work needed to be well paid in meat and milk ration coupons . . . They refused to grant me that too . . . Therefore I gave instructions for custodians to bury the corpses where the individuals had lived . . . That is, making use of secluded spots in courtyards or in nearby vacant lots. Until September 24, the day when it was announced that all individuals of Jewish nationality must assemble together, they lived in their own apartments and had not been removed to separate districts . . . But we had cases of killing in the open street . . . In this connection difficulties arose regarding cleaning up . . . We experienced difficulties even with simple agents for disinfecting an area, such as slaked lime . . ." Shostak sometimes spoke more loudly, and sometimes switched to a whisper, and his eyes glittered feverishly like someone who is seriously ill. He was in a kind of semidelirium and could barely stay on his feet . . . "I need a drink," Shostak said again.

The major poured some water from a carafe into a tin mug. Shostak grabbed it eagerly and set it to his mouth so abruptly that

Sashenka heard his teeth scrape against the tin, but he immediately started coughing, dropped the mug and doubled over, clutching at his stomach. The veins on his shaved head swelled up and every little blood vessel was as clear as on an anatomical teaching aid.

"Sit down," the major said and moved up a stool with his foot. Shostak slumped down heavily onto the stool and wiped his face again with the ends of his scarf.

"Now you," said the major, turning to Franya. "In the case file here we have your report about the dentist's family . . . This is their son who has arrived." The major nodded toward the lieutenant, sitting in the armchair. The lieutenant's face was pale and he kept fastening and unfastening the hooks on the tight collar under his throat. Without saying anything, he took out a photograph glued onto cardboard. Sashenka glued her eye to the crack of the door and got quite a good look at the photograph, because Franya was standing rather close to the door and he was examining the photograph thoroughly. The photograph showed a man and a woman dressed up in their finest. The woman was holding a baby. Standing behind the man and woman were an adolescent boy and a girl. The girl was wearing a frock with an open neck and bare shoulders.

"I recall them," said Franya, who had drunk a glass of red-beet moonshine first thing in the morning, despite having received notice to attend this interview. "Of course I do, they all looked the same, like peas in a pod. A handsome family they were . . . They're still there . . . In their yard . . . If they'd gone to the mass grave, you'd never find them . . . There's about ten thousand there, but only four here . . ."

"Be more specific, Voznyak," said the major, raising his voice.

"Shuma the Assyrian whacked them," Franya gasped, "the shoe-shine man. He wrapped a brick in a newspaper, smashed their heads open in broad daylight and dragged them into the garbage pit by their legs . . . The sixteen-year-old daughter, and the mother,

and Leopold Lvovich, and the five-year-old youngster too. And
he threw his bloody clothes in the garbage pit . . . He put on old
clothes specially, so he wouldn't mind throwing them out . . . Torn
breeches and a canvas work jacket all smeared in boot polish . . .
That family lay there heaped on top of each other for four days,
and Shuma wouldn't let anyone drag them out of the pit; he said it
was so the neighbors would pour slops on them and dump filth on
them . . . And people were afraid of him, he'd gone to work for the
police . . . It was hot weather, the air was rotten, with flies buzzing
about . . . I told him: Your own daughter Zara's breathing this air.
He took no notice . . . Well, I went to the municipal council, and
they explained everything to me: Don't listen to him, they said,
and don't be afraid, there's instructions from the authorities to
stop an epidemic. So take them to the quarries out at the porcelain
factory . . . But where will I get a cart, I said, that's four miles . . .
You're the custodian, that's up to you, he said . . . Well, I dragged all
of Leopold Lvovich's family out of the pit at night and buried them
beside the sheds . . . And I wrapped the little one in burlap and car-
ried him to the graveyard . . . I gave the watchman two pieces of soap
and some warm long johns. And he let me bury him by the wall . . .
You mustn't offend a little child, it's an innocent soul . . . I don't know
what Shuma had against Leopold Lvovich—let God be the judge of
that—but I told him, you'll suffer eternal penance in hell for the
child . . . I took a drink for courage and I told him . . . He belted
me in the face, almost knocked my teeth out . . . But he's paying his
dues in the Ivdel camp now. They didn't catch him here, it was in
Poland, and they gave him twenty-five years. He'd have been better
off if they'd topped him. This man who was released came here . . .
He'd seen Shuma in the transit camp. He's sick all the time, with the
sort of incredible diseases you can only catch in hell . . . The flesh on
his legs is bursting open, his body's all ripped and torn, so he can't
sleep on his back or his stomach or his sides, he goes to sleep on his

knees, leaning his forehead against the wall, and the moment he falls asleep, he tumbles over onto the bunk, his carbuncles start bursting and he jumps up screaming . . . The other convicts don't like him for that; he stops them from sleeping . . . And they don't like the way he eats everything quickly when they give out the food—he licks out the bowl like a dog and goes around asking to lick out other people's bowls . . . He coughs up blood, but he just doesn't die . . . That's his penance for the little child . . . I feel ill will for him, comrade major, although he's a man, too . . . I told him: do Leopold Lvovich in, if you've got the urge, do the wife and the daughter in, but don't touch the little child . . ." Franya sobbed. He wept in an unruly, drunken manner, wiping his face and cheeks and neck with his elbows and the palms of his hands in a way that left stripes on his skin.

The room was quiet for a while, the major sat with his head bowed, while the lieutenant looked straight ahead, and for the first time his face turned pale and changed, so that Sashenka didn't even find him attractive any more. The entire time they were talking, Sashenka stood there in a kind of stupor. It wasn't that she didn't understand what they saying, it was all clear, she could make out every word, but after this conversation, she felt as if she had eavesdropped on some kind of dreadful secret, as appalling as a nightmare, that had left her feeling dizzy, and it had nothing to do with the words that had been spoken here—it reminded her somehow of the three candles in the mirror during the fortune-telling session— but it wasn't a matter of the candles or the mirror, but of something else that had set the dark air trembling, of strange faces glimpsed approaching through a silvery twilight, as if everything habitual and familiar had disappeared and Sashenka's skin had been touched by a gentle breeze and the damp, earthy smell of a different world. But as soon as Sashenka felt it, the fright disappeared, and she thought in relief: "Well, you already knew that, didn't you? Yes, that's how it is." And now it seemed to her that, on the contrary, the sight of trees, snow, the sun, or a piece of bread could plunge her into terror. Sashenka didn't know how long all this went on; she was brought to her senses by a shout from the next room.

"I'm sick," shouted the prisoner who was like an anatomical teaching aid, "I've got cramps in my intestines, I've got spasms in my stomach."

The major picked up the phone and made a call, and Sashenka thought that she was ill too, she must have caught a chill when she was running about in just her marquisette blouse.

A man in a white coat walked into the next room and began feeling the prisoner. He threw the man's head back and pulled down his lower eyelids. Sashenka tiptoed back to the desk, where her unfinished statement was lying.

"... I renounce her," Sashenka read again. "Now I only want to be the daughter of my father, who was killed at the front ..."

Suddenly Sashenka realized that she didn't have her pumps with her. She had either left them at the railroad station or dropped them on her way here. And Sashenka felt so aggrieved that she forgot about everything and her tears simply started flowing of their own accord. Sashenka began rapidly blinking her wet eyelashes and carried on blinking like that for about ten minutes, until she suddenly sensed that someone was watching her. The major was standing in the doorway, and the door was wide open. No one was left behind him in the next room, as if it had all been a vision that had melted into thin air.

"What are you doing here?" the major asked. He walked over with his boots squeaking, took the statement, and read it. "What are you crying for?" he asked. "Do you feel sorry for your mother?"

And suddenly Sashenka thought that perhaps she really did feel sorry for her mother. But then Sashenka remembered her mother standing there with that invalid and beating her, and driving her own daughter out of her home, instead of those louse-ridden paupers. And Sashenka felt furious with herself for suddenly feeling pity. Sashenka looked at the major angrily and didn't answer. And she finished writing quickly: "And the *polizei* Vasya and the *polizei* Olga, his wife, are living in our apartment." She signed the paper with a flourish and handed it to the major.

"You don't know how to write papers like this yet," the major laughed, "you write too sketchily . . . And apart from that, we need the date and the address . . ."

04

Sashenka spent three days in bed with a high temperature at Maya's place. She woke up at dawn and looked at the ceiling, luxuriating on her clean sheets and waiting for the custodian outside the window to start scraping the sidewalk with his spade. Then Sashenka closed her eyes and fell asleep to the monotonous, scraping sounds, and woke up again in the late morning, at about ten o'clock. Sashenka loved to spend the night at Maya's place. Maya was a pale, unattractive girl with a poor metabolism, which meant that her face was always covered in little pimples, smeared with green antiseptic. Maya was a kind and well-read girl, but she had no friends and she was afraid of boys. And so Maya's parents were very pleased that she was friends with Sashenka. Maya's father worked as a lecturer, and her mother taught literature in a vocational school. The father was small, with a bald patch and comically pouting lips, as if he were constantly playing an invisible reed pipe from a folktale. The mother, by contrast, was tall and bulky, with a woman's sparse sideburns and mustache. In this home Sashenka felt calm and comfortable, and she was well fed, but something awkward had happened that had made Sashenka try to avoid coming around recently, and she had even made friends, although not for long, with Irisha, a colonel's daughter. In fact, nothing had really happened, it was just a stupid idea that Sashenka got into her head, and she cursed herself for it and eventually decided that every time this nonsense came back into her head, she would pinch and scratch herself in a way that no one would notice. Two months earlier, Sashenka and Maya had gone to the movie theater and watched a captured movie filled with such passionate and tender love that when they came back out, Sashenka was so stunned, she walked along the middle of the street, stumbling along rapidly, as if she were hurrying to get to a date, and the Mexican Frank Capra was waiting for her by the sparkling water kiosk on the corner of Makhno Street and Isaac Street. Maya didn't like the film.

"Sheer naive mediocrity," Maya said. "Read *An Adventure in a Sealed Pullman Car*; one of our secret agents loves a female agent in that . . . And, of course, he dies for the motherland, but for him the motherland embodies everything: the birch trees, and the Kremlin stars, and the female agent . . ."

"Maybe you'll advise me to read *Eugene Onegin* too?" Sashenka asked with a scornful laugh.

Maya was an outstanding student and good at writing synopses, whereas Sashenka had stayed back in the same class for two years and was actually planning to leave school altogether, but Maya couldn't possibly know anything about love, she probably didn't even dream about boys at night. It made Sashenka feel furious that Maya, with her pimples, could even talk about love at all.

At Maya's place there was a good lunch waiting for them. Sashenka was given a bowl of pearl barley soup filled right up to the brim, with fragrant spots of melted pork fat floating on top of it. There was a large marrow bone lying in the bowl, covered in little pieces of meat and sticky gristle, which Sashenka liked even more than the meat. For the main course, there were rye-flour dumplings with meat gravy. The dumplings had been browned on a griddle and saturated with pork fat—you only had to press a fork down on them and the fat started oozing out, mingling with the gravy and making it thicker. And there was even a third course—tea with pieces of fruit jelly. Sashenka ate it all, her heart was filled with exceptional gratitude to Platon Gavrilovich and Sofya Leonidovna, and she felt guilty for making fun of Maya on the way back. Not long before this, Sashenka had quarreled with her mother, and now she thought how outsiders could sometimes be better than your own mother. After the meal, Sashenka sat down on the plush sofa and decided to think about something good or funny, because she felt calm now and she had a warm feeling in her stomach. She started thinking about the film again and remembered the way Frank Capra had hugged the blonde so tightly that Sashenka, sitting in the hall, had actually felt a sweet aching in her own joints and body, although it was only faint, nowhere near the intense, sweet feeling she got at night. Now, sitting on the plush sofa in a drowsy, well-fed state, Sashenka experienced that feeling again, even more powerfully, so that her breasts started tickling and she pressed her cheek against the back of the sofa and closed her eyes, but something jangled and Sashenka gave a start and jumped to her feet. Sofya Leonidovna was picking up the broken shards of a plate that she had dropped. Her hair escaped from under her scarf and her housecoat came open, revealing her yellow, dangling breasts, and just for a joke Sashenka imagined Platon Gavrilovich embracing Sofya Leonidovna when they were alone, kissing her cheeks with their covering of sparse, curly hairs, and suddenly, instead of feeling cheerful, Sashenka felt sick, so that little pieces of the fruit jelly that Sashenka had eaten rose up into her throat. She put her hand over her mouth and sat there like that for a while, until she felt better and the pieces of fruit jelly crept back down, but she got a little pain in her stomach. Sashenka had this feeling again several times, and she tried not to look at Sofya Leonidovna and even declined supper, a genuine omelet made with American powdered egg, and that evening she made up with her mother. After that, Sashenka didn't go to Maya's

56 \   Redemption

place for about two weeks, and when she did go, she felt ashamed to look Sofya Leonidovna in the eye, as if she were hiding some secret, disgusting vice of her own and Sofya Leonidovna might guess what it was. Sashenka hadn't had these feelings for a long time; she had even begun to forget them, but the problem was that now, when Sashenka had come here exhausted and ill, they reappeared and even grew stronger. So when Sashenka woke up in the morning and listened to the voices in the next room, she waited nervously for Sofya Leonidovna to appear, anxiously running her nail across her wrist several times and scratching the skin as a punishment. Sofya Leonidovna came in washed and fresh, with her hair woven into a braid, and lit up by the frosty morning sunlight from the windows. She put her palm on Sashenka's forehead, then slipped her hand under the blanket and felt Sashenka's shoulders and chest.

"You're soaking wet," Sofya Leonidovna said, "you need to change your shirt..."

Maya came in, also washed and fresh, with hardly any patches of green antiseptic on her face today. She brought her own night-shirt, a silk one with lace around the collar. Maya was taller than Sashenka, almost as tall as Sofya Leonidovna, and Maya's nightshirt came down almost to Sashenka's heels.

"Your mother hasn't even asked about you this time," Sofya Leonidovna said. "Usually she comes to see me in the school when you're with us, and asks... But this time she isn't even interested in knowing if her daughter's unwell..."

"I hate her," Sashenka said in a low voice, like a man's, because she had a cold. "She's not my mother... I only acknowledge my father, who died for the motherland..."

"You can live independently," said Platon Gavrilovich, showing his soapy face in the doorway because he was shaving. "You'll get a pension for your father for another two years. You can finish seven-year school and go to the vocational school."

Maya carried a steaming cup of broth into the room. It was genuine chicken broth, strong and heady, made from chickens that Platon Gavrilovich had obtained in some distant village shop after giving a lecture on the international situation. With every swallow, Sashenka felt her body growing stronger, or so it seemed to her, but it was still hard for her to hold the cup, since it was heavy, filled right up to the brim with strong, rich broth, and Sashenka's hands were weak after she'd had a temperature for three days. The cup tilted over and greasy drops of broth fell onto the blanket cover. Sofya Leonidovna took the cup from Sashenka and set the edge of it to Sashenka's lips. Sashenka drank, feeling exceptional gratitude, and she wanted to hug and kiss this kind woman, but at the same time the familiar old anxiety was still prowling around in Sashenka's head, and she suddenly found herself wanting to shout to Platon Gavrilovich: "Don't, don't stand beside me, don't come close . . ." But Platon Gavrilovich walked over and took Sofya Leonidovna by the arm, his bald spot touching her dusty shoulder, and Sashenka spitefully surrendered to her own absurd imaginings, which she was afraid of and didn't know how to get rid of. She imagined everything that Frank Capra did with the lithe blonde, but instead of the hotheaded Mexican there was Platon Gavrilovich, with his bald spot and juvenile body, and the lithe blonde's place was taken by Sofya Leonidovna. This vision was so funny and so appalling that Sashenka pinched her leg hard under the blanket as a punishment, and almost gagged on the broth.

"Drink it in little sips," Soya Leonidovna said sternly.

"All right," Sashenka said and started laughing; she couldn't help it.

"What's wrong?" asked Platon Gavrilovich

"She's got a fit of the giggles," Maya said, starting to laugh too.

"That means she's getting better," said Sofya Leonidovna. "She won't go running about in marquisette in freezing cold weather again."

Fortunately, someone knocked on the front door. The visitor hammered with his fist, and it was obvious immediately that a stranger was knocking.

"Who could that be first thing in the morning on the weekend?" Platon Gavrilovich said. "Perhaps it's a messenger for me from the district executive committee, to go and give a lecture at the Khazhin village Soviet . . . But then, yesterday they postponed that until Thursday."

Platon Gavrilovich was dressed in breeches that would have suited a fourteen-year-old boy perfectly well, and over them he had a warm, juvenile-sized undershirt, with the little buttons on the chest unfastened, revealing his puerile chest, covered in curly gray hair. He pulled on a Soviet functionary's semimilitary tunic over the undershirt and walked into the hallway, fastening on a broad officer's belt on the way.

"It's for you, Sasha," he said when he came back a little while later. "Someone's here to see you . . . It's Olga," he added, turning toward Sofya Leonidovna, "the woman who used to wash our floors . . . And there's someone else with her . . ."

For some reason Sashenka suddenly felt afraid, and she huddled into the corner of the sofa bed, pulling the blanket up under her throat. When Olga walked in, she gave Sashenka a frightened look too. The tank-crew master of ceremonies walked into the room after Olga. Their faces were red from the frosty air. There was an awkward silence for a while, and then the master of ceremonies spoke.

"Hello, Sasha . . . I've come around to see how you are . . . Olga showed me the way here . . ."

"And who might you be to Sasha?" Sofya Leonidovna asked, glancing suspiciously and jealously at the master of ceremonies.

"He's no one to me," Sashenka suddenly shouted out furiously, "I don't know what they want. What they've come for . . . They want to find out something from me . . . They want to do something to hurt me . . ."

The moment Sashenka shouted, Olga backed away to the door in fright, the master of ceremonies gave Sashenka an astonished look, and Sofya Leonidovna quickly moved in between the visitors and Sashenka, putting her hand on Sashenka's head.

"Don't you be afraid, darling," said Sofya Leonidovna. "You're at home here, no one will hurt you here . . . This is obviously more of your mother's tricks . . . Only she ought to have come herself, and not sent strangers . . . You're her daughter, after all . . ."

"I'm sorry, of course," the master of ceremonies said, clearing his throat. "Your mother would have been glad to come, but she can't, she was arrested two days ago . . ."

"I just knew it," Platon Gavrilovich shouted out neurotically, "I could tell that a woman who can't bring up her own daughter would end up as a criminal . . . A woman who has no motherly feelings has no moral foundations either . . ."

"I'm sorry, of course," said the master of ceremonies. "It's not really much of a crime . . . She was detained with foodstuffs at the checkpoint where she works . . . I don't approve of her actions, of course . . . Only she didn't do it for herself . . . her daughter's high-strung and she needs a nourishing diet . . ."

"I asked her not to, I asked her," Sashenka shouted. "I told her she was disgracing . . . She was disgracing my father . . . His memory . . . She didn't do it for me . . . She gave away half . . . More than half . . . She didn't do it for me . . ."

"Calm down, Sashenka," said Sofya Leonidovna, "your temperature will go up . . . Your eyes are feverish."

"That's true enough," said the master of ceremonies, "and what's the point now . . . I went to see her today . . . She asked for you to come and see her before she's sent away . . . They're going to be transferred to Gaiva. They'll try her here at the local court, I spoke to the investigator . . . But they're sending her to the prison there in the meantime . . . The prison here is in ruins, and they won't keep her in the detention cell for long ... They're going to let people see them on Friday ..."

"Sashenka's not well," Sofya Leonidovna said hastily.

"I see that now," the master of ceremonies replied.

"And who might you be to her mother?" Platon Gavrilovich asked sternly, moving right up close to the master of ceremonies and standing on tiptoe.

"He's her lover," Sashenka shouted with a shudder. "She's shaming my father's memory ..."

Sashenka was trying not to look at the master of ceremonies, but suddenly she glanced at him and caught her breath, as if everything that she knew about herself had become known to him in a single instant, every last little thing, even the things that she sometimes hid from herself, and now Sashenka was entirely in his power, sitting there naked and defenseless in his gaze. It didn't last long, perhaps only a minute, and then Sashenka recovered, but she didn't shout any more, she just sat there quietly, huddling in the corner.

"Please, sit down," Maya said unexpectedly, and moved up chairs for the master of ceremonies and Olga. They sat down, the master of ceremonies leaning firmly against the back of his chair and Olga perching sideways, right on the very edge of hers.

"Your mom sent you this note," the master of ceremonies said quietly, shifting to a formal tone of voice. He leaned across and handed Sashenka a piece of paper folded into a triangle, like the letters from her father at the front. Sashenka took it, unfolded it, and started reading the crooked lines written in indelible pencil.

"My darling little daughter Sasha," her mother wrote, "your mother Ekaterina sends you greetings. See what misfortune I've suffered, my dearest daughter. But don't you worry, the investigator says they won't give me a long sentence if I frankly confess everything, they'll choose a good charge, like petty theft, and not theft of government property at a military establishment. God grant they will. And perhaps they'll take into account my being a widow and my husband, your father, being killed at the front. Little daughter, I can't sleep here at night when I wonder how you're going to live without me. You need to study, and you're frail, you need to eat well. My thanks to Sofya Leonidovna, she's like a real mother to you, even better, be grateful for that, because after all she's a stranger to you, and she takes care of you. My dear little daughter, I hit you before we parted. Forgive me, my heart stopped dead after that and ached for a long time and it's still aching now. Don't be angry, and come on Friday, I want to see you very much. Your mother Ekaterina."

Sashenka spent a long time reading it—starting, stopping and rereading parts, reaching the end and reading the first lines again. Mist drifted in front of her eyes, she had a heavy feeling in her chest, and there was nothing in the world she wanted except to sit there like that with that mist in front of her eyes and the heavy feeling in her chest.

"What has she written there?" Sofya Leonidovna asked angrily. She tried to take the letter, but Sashenka hastily, even abruptly, pushed her hand aside and hid the letter on her chest under the nightshirt. Seeing that Sashenka had turned quiet and was sitting there sadly with her cheeks wet from tears, Olga became a bit bolder.

"They arrested Vasya too," she said pitifully . . . "He was considerate, and quiet . . . With him I would have got by all right . . . But who needs me apart from Vasya?"

"Come on, Olga," said the master of ceremonies, "we've done what we came for . . . And perhaps we're out of place here now . . . In the sense that perhaps people want to get a bite to eat, or perhaps we've harmed the patient's health . . ." He turned to Sofya Leonidovna. "Thank you, ma'am, for looking after Ekaterina's daughter, nevertheless . . ."

He walked to the door with Olga, but immediately came back with something: he must have left the large, greasy, appetizingly fragrant package out in the hallway.

"There," he said, "this is some rations . . . a gift . . ."

Platon Gavrilovich, standing behind the master of ceremonies, made a fierce face and shook his head, as if to say: don't take it.

"No, no, no," said Sofya Leonidovna, nodding briefly to Platon Gavrilovich and pushing the package away with both hands, "we don't need it . . . You'd better . . . Better use it for a food parcel . . ."

"It's all right," said the master of ceremonies, "we've arranged a food parcel too."

He put the package down on Sashenka's legs, on top of the blanket, and walked out. Sashenka heard Olga and the master of ceremonies putting on their coats and Olga winding string around her galoshes to fasten them on. Sashenka could guess what it was from the wheezing and stamping of feet. Then the front door slammed and everything went quiet.

Sashenka lay there all day long, facing the wall in a semiconscious state. She felt hot, and she pulled the quilted blanket out of its cover. Then she felt cold, but to stuff the blanket back into the cover, Sashenka would have had to sit up on the bed and make more movements with her arms, and she decided to get warm by pulling her knees up to her stomach. When the doctor came, it was very difficult to get Sashenka up; although it wasn't exactly painful, it was irritating, because she had finally found a comfortable position, with her knees bent up and her palms grasping the soles of her feet. The edges of the blanket, covering Sashenka's head, formed a cloth canopy between the pillow and the wall; there was a snug, gray twilight in front of Sashenka's face, and she could stroke her heels and the hollows of her feet with her fingers. But when they fished Sashenka out into the light, into the pitiless, frosty sunshine that flooded the room and hurt her eyes, Sashenka's legs ended up in an uncomfortable position that made her hips and middle hurt and her heels ache, and her hands ended up flung far away across the blanket, not able to do anything to help her aching body. Sashenka saw the doctor's face, frozen and red from the frost, like the master of ceremonies' face, but she had no strength left to get furious with him, she only had enough strength to make the doctor and Sofya Leonidovna feel sorry for her.

"Doctor," Sashenka said in a weak voice, "doctor, my dearest, wonderful doctor ... what can I do ... who can I ask for advice ... Sofya Leonidovna, my dearest, wonderful..." But Sashenka couldn't say any more than that. She had misjudged her strength and spoken too many words that she could have easily managed without, and she'd had enough time, hadn't she, when she was lying under the cloth canopy, in the twilight, to find two or three words that would have made everything clear to her and everyone else. And Sashenka was so annoyed with herself that she burst into tears.

The doctor examined her, then walked away to the table and started talking in a low voice with Sofya Leonidovna and Platon Gavrilovich, and meanwhile Maya wiped Sashenka's face with a handkerchief.

"A chill and emotional trauma," said the doctor.

"Yes," said Sofya Leonidovna, "the girl has been though a very harrowing experience..."

"Never mind," said the doctor, writing out prescriptions, "her body's young, it will pass."

And indeed, by early evening Sashenka was feeling better: as she lay there, her head felt sound and clear and her body felt well, neither cold nor hot. At night Sashenka slept well, with light, pleasant dreams, and in the morning she ate a delicious piece of cold chicken for breakfast. After a few days of living like this, Sashenka had completely recovered her strength and she told Maya, who hadn't been going to school because of her: "You can go to school ... I'm leaving today..."

"But you're still pale," said Maya, "and you have a cold... And it's freezing outside..."

"You know, Maya," said Sashenka, "maybe I'm a fool, of course, and I'm sorry, but it seems to me that you all have some kind of designs on me . . ."

Then Maya suddenly started crying and said:

"It's true . . . I'll be honest with you . . . I once heard mom talking to dad, and she said that with you I'd be able to make friends with boys too, because you're beautiful . . . And the hurtful thing, really hurtful, was that dad disagreed with that as well . . . But you know, Sashenka . . . Komsomol word of honor and a gun salute to all the leaders, I just love you . . . I won't find any other friends . . ."

"You'll find some," said Sashenka—together with her strength, the pleasurable, ticklish yearning in her bosom had returned, and it made her words firm and strong again, and every word Sashenka spoke inflamed the yearning that she had already begun to miss. "I'll go home," said Sashenka, "and you'll find some friends . . . There's Irisha, she's a colonel's daughter . . . Or Zara . . . But I'm a prisoner's daughter . . . Don't cry . . . What have you got to cry about . . . Your dad's alive, and your mom hasn't been stealing from the state . . ."

The yearning made Sashenka's head start aching again; she hurriedly put on her marquisette blouse, skirt, and boots, all the things she was wearing for New Year's Eve and still had on when she arrived here. Looking beautiful, Sashenka sauntered past Maya, whose face today was especially thickly dotted with green antiseptic, and then she put on her fur coat and walked out into the street. It was a very clear day, the snowdrifts were gleaming brightly, and the white smoke hung vertically above the chimneys of the buildings, because there was no wind, with not a single cloud to be seen in the blue sky. It wasn't very cold, only about 19 degrees. A column of Romanian prisoners was being led down the center of the roadway. Prisoners usually walked along hunched over and shivering, with their noses tucked into the collars of their greatcoats. But these were tall, strapping men, with healthy faces, and although they were being escorted by several soldiers with submachine guns, they strode along cheerfully, and the standard-bearers at the front carried a red flag and their national flag, and two of them were carrying a banner written in Russian and their own language.

"Down with reactionaries," Sashenka read. "Down with boyars and monarchists."

Sashenka turned off into her own side street and almost ran into Zara. Sashenka recoiled and got stuck in a snowdrift, but Zara didn't even notice her—she was standing with her back to Sashenka and peeping around the corner into the courtyard, in the direction of the sheds. Sashenka had actually been quite friendly with Zara during the first few months after she got back from evacuation, and then they had quarreled over Markeev and become enemies. It was strange, but Sashenka and Zara always fell in love with the same person; for instance, they had both secretly been in love with the military instructor at school, and they had managed it so deftly that no one had noticed, not even the military instructor; only Sashenka had noticed Zara's love and Zara had noticed Sashenka's. And so, just by looking at Zara, even though it was from behind, Sashenka realized that Zara was in love, and not simply in love, but forever and ever, until the end of her life, with sweet musings lasting long into the night and the kind of dreams that thrilled your heart and set your cheeks burning at the mere memory of them in the daytime. Markeev and the military instructor had obviously been forgotten. Zara was standing there, stroking an ice-covered downspout with her mitten, and now her big, black eyes, which the boys liked so much and Sashenka hated, were watching in a way that wasn't contemptuous and scornful—they were full of meek entreaty, they were summoning someone and promising everything in return. At the back of the courtyard the handsome lieutenant, Franya, and the buildings superintendent were walking around by the sheds. Franya was holding a spade and clearing away the snow, knocking on the frozen earth to make some kind of marks on it and measuring the distance in strides from the wall of the shed or from the wall of the burned-out ruins, and obviously getting confused and arguing with the buildings superintendent. Sashenka stopped too, peering into the yard and pressing up against a tree, so that the tree would hide her from Zara, but so that she could watch Zara, and laugh at her if necessary. Lit up by the afternoon sunlight, the lieutenant's face was especially handsome, and the light, silvery hoarfrost lay like gray streaks on the gypsy-black hair escaping from under his fur cap with earflaps, and his eyes were such a dense blue that there were bluish shadows lying on his cheekbones. As he talked with Franya and the buildings superintendent, he walked past very close to Zara, almost right beside her, so that Sashenka saw the little pinkish cloud of his breath touch Zara's face. Without noticing Zara, he got into an army Willis automobile, covered in hoarfrost, said something to the soldier at the wheel, and they drove off. Franya and the building superintendent walked toward Sashenka, dousing her with a scent of coarse tobacco, homebrew and frozen dung.

"I buried Leopold Lvovich twice," Franya said. "It was hot . . . I buried him, the dogs sniffed him out and dug him up . . . The sanitary inspector Shostak came . . . He's a goner now, coughing up blood in the lockup . . . But back then he started waving his fists around in front of my face . . . And I told him: I'm a buildings custodian . . . I'm not going to stand guard over dead bodies. I get the lowest rate of pay there is, and you have a meat ration and milk coupons, and you have the Jews' stuff, too . . . Well, naturally, I didn't actually say all of that back then, but I thought it . . . And I thought: just you wait till our boys get here, you groveling toady . . ."

"The commissariat is providing the lieutenant with coffins, manpower, and transport," the buildings superintendent said, listening absentmindedly to Franya's drunken babbling, "and the bodies will be taken away during the night . . . There are neighbors here, and

children . . . It is only permitted to carry out the work at night . . ."
They turned a corner and for a while their voices and the squeaking
of snow underfoot could still be heard.

Zara stood there, slumping against the downspout. As he strode
around the yard, the lieutenant had been holding a long twig, with
which he drew on the snow, probably unthinkingly, and as he
walked away, he dropped the twig quite close to Zara. Sashenka
saw Zara glance around and set off as if reluctantly, as if the thought
had come to her purely by chance; she leaned down, picked up the
twig and went back into her hiding place, then suddenly pressed
the thick part of the twig, which the lieutenant had been holding in
his hand, against her lips. And at that point Sashenka couldn't help
herself—she laughed out loud, remembering the way the lieutenant
had walked past Zara without even noticing her. At the sound of
laughter, Zara darted away, as if she had been caught doing some-
thing shameful. When she spotted Sashenka, she shouted out:

"Lousy bitch, they've arrested your mother . . ."

"And your father's a *polizei*—they're going to hang him," Sashenka
shouted in spiteful glee. "A Soviet lieutenant won't ever have any-
thing to do with you . . . Find yourself some Hitlerite *gauleiters* . . ."

"I couldn't give a rotten damn," Zara shouted, snapping the twig
and flinging it into the snow. Two black-eyed urchins, Zara's broth-
ers, ran out of the old, ramshackle outbuilding at the back of the yard
and started throwing snowballs at Sashenka. One of them was about
five, with a round, jolly face, and the way he threw was very funny,
panting solemnly, not throwing very far and showering himself with
snow, but the other one was already about thirteen, he was nimble
and adroit, and he threw skillfully and ruthlessly, knowing that he
had to aim a bit higher—at the eyes or the teeth. He hit Sashenka
so hard on the nose with a freezing lump of ice that for a moment
the air blurred and rippled in front of her eyes and Zara's laughing
face started drifting off to one side. The name or the nickname of

the second boy, the nimble one, was Louty. Everybody in the yard called him Louty, even his own mother. Sashenka clenched her fists and dashed at Louty, but his mother, the wife of Shuma, who was dying in the Ivdel camp, also came running out of the outhouse, with her black eyes, large nose, and gold teeth. She grabbed Zara and her two sons and dragged them back along the path into the outhouse, looking around in fright. Louty resisted furiously, trying to break out of her grasp and savagely trying to reach Sashenka with his foot from behind his mother's back. After the entire family had disappeared into its outhouse, Sashenka stood in the middle of the path for a while, feeling the salty taste of blood on her lip and breathing tiredly. Then she bent down, put some snow on her bruised nose, felt for the keys in the pocket of her fur jacket, and plodded off home. She climbed heavily up the stairs and put the key in the keyhole. But the door was locked on the inside with the hook. Sashenka remembered about Olga and knocked.

05

O lga, joyful and cleanly washed, met Sashenka with her
long, wet hair hanging loose, and wearing Sashenka's
mother's robe.

"Vasya's come back," she whispered to Sashenka, as if inviting
Sashenka to rejoice with her at news that Sashenka had been wait-
ing for impatiently for a long time. "They let him go, the Lord be
praised..."

The kitchen was intensely heated, several tubs of dirty water
were standing on the floor, and there was a smell of household soap;
clearly someone had been bathing here just recently. Some new
kind of little paper napkins with scalloped edges, cut out of news-
papers, had appeared in the kitchen. The old household table with
its familiar notches—on which Sashenka's mother prepared food,
and which Sashenka loved to sniff because it smelled so delicious,
like ground meat for patties—that little table had disappeared, and
in its place was a new table, stoutly assembled out of fresh wooden
boards. And in general things had changed imperceptibly somehow,
as if Sashenka had come to a stranger's apartment. Vasya wasn't sit-
ting behind his screen in the kitchen, he was at the table in the room,
and when he saw Sashenka he gave her a welcoming smile without
any fright in it, not like before. On the contrary, it was Sashenka
who felt something like timidity. She walked in and sat down on the

bolster of her sofa bed, which she had pounded shiny with her sides on sultry nights filled with dreaming and desires, but now even this sofa seemed unfamiliar to her.

"Sit at the table," Olga said, and she put a blue bowl down in front of Sashenka, the one that Sashenka's mother usually ate from. Two large, black dumplings were lying in the bowl, and Sashenka started eating them greedily, although she knew that Olga had gotten them on the church porch as charity. The filling in the dumplings was a hotchpotch of anything and everything. There were poppy seeds, rice, prunes, carrots, and onions, and it all seemed very tasty to Sashenka, and she thought about Olga gratefully, and every time Olga went out into the kitchen and then came back in again, Sashenka looked hopefully to see if Olga had brought her something else to eat. But Olga didn't give her anything else, she just took away the bowl and wiped down the table. In the middle of the table was a bread bin with pieces of stale church Easter cake, and Olga put it away in the sideboard, to which she had the keys now. Olga noticed that some little bags of Olga's were already standing on the shelves of the sideboard, with wooden spoons carved by Vasya propped up beside them, and a fresh, uncut loaf of bread was also lying there.

"They let me out," Vasya said, smiling and showing his gums, "said I was completely free to go . . ."

Vasya was wearing a fresh striped shirt, which Olga had probably found in the special section of the wardrobe where Sashenka's father's things were kept. Yet neither Vasya nor Olga displayed even the slightest embarrassment about that, and for some reason Sashenka didn't feel indignant; either she didn't have the strength for that, or she sensed that her life had suddenly changed, so that now she had no right to be indignant. Olga and Vasya looked at each other, stroking and patting each other, and smiling at Sashenka, as if they were inviting her to share their joy. And Sashenka suddenly smiled, to make Vasya and Olga feel good, although she didn't really want to smile, and after the two dumplings she was feeling hungrier than ever. It was only now, after she'd started coming to terms with the new situation and her own position, that Sashenka noticed how much Vasya had changed in the last few days. Before, he used to be a big, strong peasant, with a powerful barrel chest and a stupid, constantly frightened face. But now he was sitting there in front of her, an exhausted man with a shaved head, with circles under his eyes and sunken cheeks, the skin on his head was bluish and he looked like the prisoner Sashenka had seen in the major's office. Vasya's neck had gotten a bit thinner and a bit paler too, so that the collar of Sashenka's father's shirt was too big for him; even though the top button of the shirt was fastened, she could see Vasya's scrawny collarbones. But along with its unhealthy look, Vasya's face had also acquired a kind of calmness and a certain insightful expression, as if during these few short days in a jail cell he had understood something and could even look down on other people and teach them a thing or two, the way that sometimes happens after a grave illness or a disaster that has turned out well: a man suddenly starts thinking what a great fellow he is and that he has grasped the essential nature of everything that happens.

"You go and see Kaigorodtsev about your mother," Vasya said. "They'll try to send you to his deputy, the major, but don't go... Tell them you'd rather wait a while... You'd rather come back later... I wasn't a free man, I was obliged to do what they said, but I took one glance and I realized... No, no way... Don't end up with that one... He's a badass, real bad... But he's got an edgy kind of job too, sorting out the likes of us... So I thought, the important thing here is to be patient... Some other boss, higher up, will come and figure everything out... And he figured everything out immediately, God grant him good health... a learned man, obviously... A colonel... You, he said, are not guilty, the only thing you're guilty of is not showing up for the hearing at your local militia station, since a complaint was submitted against you . . . You tell me you didn't trust the Soviet authorities . . . Guilty, I said, you're right there . . . But it was Anna who reported that I was a *polizei* . . . I lived in her apartment . . . she used to treat me the way a drunk treats a woman . . . I told the village Soviet chairman: excuse me, but why didn't anyone tell me what kind of person she is, why did you put me in her apartment? It was that Anna who reported that I was a *polizei*, but all I did was drive a water cart at the commandant's office . . . I found out by chance, God grant them good health . . . There are good people everywhere . . . Yes . . . The Colonel, he figured things out immediately . . . God grant him good health . . . You go to him about your mother . . ." Suddenly Vasya stopped with his mouth slightly open and his eyes staring, and he pressed his hand against his throat; his face contorted and he started coughing, as if he were gagging on the air. He coughed for a long time, straining violently and dropping sputum with little red threads in it out of his mouth onto the fresh collar of Sashenka's father's shirt. He hastily unfastened the button below his throat with his gnarled fingers, as if it were choking him, although the collar was too large and it was sagging down. Olga started fussing around Vasya and hammering him on the back with her fist as if he had swallowed a bone, and she shouted angrily and demandingly at Sashenka.

"Run to the kitchen and get some water, don't just sit there . . ."

Sashenka jumped up and meekly ran into the kitchen. When she came back, Vasya's coughing fit had already passed and he was sitting there, smiling and wiping away his tears, and Olga was sitting beside him, already calm.

"There's no more need," she told Sashenka affectionately. "Our Vasya here's taken sick,' she added, as if Vasya were just as dear to Sashenka as he was to her. "Never mind, we'll cure him . . . You put the mug in the kitchen . . ."

"It's all right," said Vasya, "I just had a little fit there, what's important is that now I'm as free as a bird . . . Completely acquitted . . . I'll go to work now . . . I'll get a job at the glove factory . . ."

Olga had a curved comb stuck in her hair at the back. Vasya pulled it out and started combing Olga's hair, carefully lifting up the damp, rye-colored strands from below with his left hand and running the comb through them, tracing out a white, washed part in the middle of Olga's scalp. Olga narrowed her eyes in pleasure, and rubbed her pockmarked cheek against Vasya's chin, looking like a shabby old cat that hasn't been petted for a long time.

"If they hadn't let me go," said Vasya, "they'd have sent me to Gaiva today . . . Did you say goodbye to your mother? They're sending them off at twelve . . ."

"I was ill," Sashenka said. "I'll go now . . ."

She hastily put on her fur coat and ran outside. Shuma's sons were lying in wait for Sashenka beside the steps, with snowballs. Thirteen-year-old Louty's eyes were blazing with stubborn fanaticism. His snowballs were well compacted, first slightly warmed in his hands and then frozen again, so that they had turned into round lumps of ice that whistled through the air. Shuma's younger son, the five-year-old, made his snowballs clumsily, they crumbled into dust, and he found that amusing. The younger boy's face was round and pink, and his eyes weren't ferocious, but mischievous. Sashenka was in such a hurry that she had no time to fend off Louty. He chased after her all the way to the end of the side street and hurt her twice with hits from his icy snowballs, once on her leg and the second time on the back of her head between her collar and her hat. Louty obviously threw with deliberate thought—not one of his snowballs hit the fur jacket with its quilted lining—he aimed at spots where her body was exposed or least protected.

When Sashenka ran up to the three-story building with its upper floor clad in zinc, the gates were already standing wide open and the relatives, who were standing on the other side of the street to see people off, were agitated; obviously the prisoners were about to be led out at any moment. Sashenka recognized the woman in the astrakhan coat. She was standing there, craning her neck impatiently, peering in through the gates, and once again she was holding a delicious-smelling basket. The tall peasant was here too. He was standing propped against the wall, calmly smoking. The old woman whose parcels had not been accepted was here too; her eyes were watering and she kept taking the shawl tied in a little bundle out of her bosom with her bluish fingers, checking that it was still there. The master of ceremonies was standing right at the very edge of the crowd, in his fur-lined tank helmet. Sashenka almost bumped into him and hastily hid behind his back. The orderly whom Sashenka knew walked out of the gates. He was wearing a short sheepskin jacket, with a Mauser pistol in a big holster hanging on his belt. The orderly gave the crowd a worried look and said:

"Citizens, I warned you that no parcels will be accepted . . . There was time for that during the set hours, all in due order . . ."

"Comrade commander," the woman wearing astrakhan said in a voice trembling with respect, "but I cooked some food for my husband . . . What can I do . . ."

"You can send the food by post . . . They'll tell you the address at the visitors' pass desk . . . Sharp items and alcoholic beverages are not accepted," the orderly replied in a humdrum, bored voice. "So I'm warning you, citizens, if you create a disturbance, the guards will use force . . . In your own best interest . . . Is that clear, in general?"

There were a few seconds of silence.

"Yes, it's clear, of course it is," the tall peasant answered for all of them.

"Well, all right then," said the orderly, and turning back toward the gates, he shouted:

"Didenko, let's go!"

First to come out of the gates were two militiamen in quilted jackets and round astrakhan hats. One of them still had a red partisan's ribbon set slantwise on his hat and he was holding a Mosin-Nagant rifle with no bayonet at the ready, while the second militiaman had a heavy German submachine gun hanging on his chest. Then the prisoners trailed out in rows of four. One part of the building was occupied by the militia, and the other part by the ministry for state security, where they kept the former *polizeien*, major bandits, and political cases. But when prisoners were sent to the railroad station, they all shared the same armed escort. The prisoners were young and old, tall and short, mostly men, although there were a few women, but all of them looked the same in some way; maybe it was the bluish color of their faces, or the way they maintained order and distance and observed the rules of behavior during transfer, with which free people were not familiar. The prisoners were surrounded by a dense escort in greatcoats of various colors: gray army coats, blue militia coats, and some made of green English cloth. There were also militiamen in partisans' sheepskin jackets and quilted jackets. The members of the escort were armed with Russian Mosin-Nagant rifles, Shpaginsubmachine guns with round disks, and German submachine guns with heavy cylindrical housings, like a full-sized machine gun's, and slim barrels. The orderly walked at the front, waving his Mauser pistol about and keeping the barrel pointing downward. One group among the prisoners was led along separately, not in a row, but in a bunch, and they were accompanied by two large German Shepherds in addition to the armed escort. This group included a tall, broad-shouldered man with a square jaw, a jagged crimson scar beside his ear, and dull, lackluster eyes. His arms were tightly bound together behind his back with thick rope at two points: the wrists and the elbows. Walking beside him was a small, skinny young man with a hollow chest, pale face, and narrow shoulders, but he was bound just as tightly. Shostak was walking in this group too; he wasn't bound but he held his hands behind his back, obviously in accordance with the regulations for prisoners. Shostak's face was a lifeless, sallow color, he coughed and gagged continuously, and every now and then he wiped his wet, slimy lips on his shoulder. The fourth individual walking in this group was an elderly man with a pince-nez. He was wearing a good-quality beaver-fur coat, but on his head he had a small, torn fur cap with earflaps that obviously wasn't his and looked completely incongruous together with the coat: it stuck up comically on his dark hair with broad gray streaks, right on the very top of his head, and it didn't cover his frozen ears. He tried to keep as far away as possible from Shostak and turned away in disgust, so that the spray from the other man's coughing wouldn't hit him in the face. He was also holding his hands behind his back. Squinting around, he thrust thems into his sleeves, warming them as if in a muff, but a young militiaman in the escort noticed this and shouted:

"Come on, get them out . . . Up to your tricks again . . ."

It clearly wasn't the first time. The man pulled out his hands and wiggled them to warm up his fingers. In fact, he was wearing perfectly decent gloves of double-knitted wool.

Sashenka's mother was walking in the third row, at the left edge, on the far side from the sidewalk where the people saying good-bye were standing. Walking in the same row as her were two swarthy women in long skirts that trailed over the snow—obviously gypsies—a young boy of about fifteen or sixteen, and a peasant who looked very much like the tall peasant, only a bit shorter. This peasant was distinguished from the other prisoners by his healthy complexion, and his calm air of discipline and skillful, hard work suggested that he was in good standing with the wardens, and after his trial he wouldn't be banished from the republic, but sent to one of the nearest camps, perhaps even to work on building a local railroad station that had been destroyed by a bomb.

Sashenka's mother wasn't wearing her ragged old coat, but the warm army peacoat that Sashenka had seen before on the master of ceremonies. She had tarpaulin boots on her feet, the same boots in which she used to carry frozen lumps of porridge, patties, and doughnuts, and sometimes a little bag of rice or sugar, all the foodstuffs that Sashenka's mother hid when they were being added to the general pot or complete items that she took by reducing the individual portions of personnel.

Sashenka's mother had a shawl bound low around her head, like an old woman, and that made her face seem unfamiliar to Sashenka, especially the sharper-looking cheekbones. And it was strange for Sashenka to see the disciplined skill with which her mother obeyed a command from an escort, staying in step when the column turned and maintaining her distance. However, when the column had completely emerged from the gates and the two militiamen at the back came into sight, the prisoners began acting anxious, looking around to see if they could spot their relatives, and Sashenka's mother looked too, ignoring the shouts from the escort. Elbowing his way through the people around him, the master of ceremonies made his way right up to the cordon, although his injured leg made it hard for him and he struggled to stay on his feet, since the others were all pushing too. Sashenka's mother noticed him and her face immediately lit up, even becoming young and beautiful, despite the old-womanish headscarf, and she looked at the master of ceremonies with a love that triggered a painful twinge of spiteful jealousy in Sashenka's heart.

Sashenka hastily hid behind the other people and, to encourage her bitterness, she started thinking about how her mother had hit her and how she had shamed the heroic memory of Sashenka's father, and given the apartment to two paupers and driven her own daughter out into the street. These thoughts used to set the blood racing through her entire body, especially her head, making it boil with fury, so that her heart struggled to keep pace and she felt its pounding reverberating everywhere—in her temples, in her legs, just below her throat, and in her ears. But now Sashenka thought about all this feebly and drearily; she didn't even know what she wanted, and her leg and the back of her head hurt where Louty had hit them with his icy snowballs.

At the sight of Sashenka's mother, the master of ceremonies' face changed too, becoming comically soft and tender; on his forehead, beside his eyebrows, there were marks left by splashes of molten armor plate, frozen forever where the skin had puckered into spongy patches with open pores. But now wrinkles appeared around the patches, like the wrinkles of a man with dimples in his cheeks when he wants to laugh.

"Katya," the master of ceremonies said tenderly, although his neck had turned red from the strain of using his elbow to hold back the tall peasant, who was also trying to squeeze his way forward, and his left side was being squeezed by the astrakhan woman, who had turned desperate now, and with his chest he was holding back the pressure of an escort, who was bent over double.

"Katya," said the master of ceremonies, "don't you worry, every-thing will be all right . . . I'll write to my general . . . I'll put in a petition . . . A petition for leniency . . . In consideration of your . . . in general . . ."

The master of ceremonies was struggling hard to stay up, with his wounded leg sliding on the trampled, slippery snow.

"How's Sashenka, my Sasha?" Sashenka's mother shouted, rising up on tiptoe because her view was blocked by the well-fed peasant prisoner.

"All right," the master of ceremonies shouted, almost falling under the pressure from all sides, "she's with that Soviet official's wife . . . I forgot the name . . . She's all right . . ."

"If you see her," Sashenka's mother shouted, raising herself up even higher and craning her neck, "tell her, ask her to forgive . . . Ask her to forgive her mother . . . For bringing her into the world, but not providing for her and disgracing her . . ."

Tears ran down Sashenka's mother's face, and it instantly turned pale, looking old and unwell.

"Momma," Sashenka suddenly shouted out impulsively, and started forcing her way forward so fiercely that she immediatelyran into the official-smelling back of a militiaman and stopped there with her fur coat hanging open and its buttons torn off.

"Sashenka!" her mother shouted despairingly. "Sashenka . . ."

"I'm here," Sashenka babbled in fright, trying to reassure and calm her mother, like a little child. "I'm here, I'm all right . . . You'll come back . . . You'll atone for your guilt . . . I'll work . . . I'll get a job at the glove factory . . ."

"Sashenka," her mother carried on shouting, "Sashenka . . ."

That was all she kept repeating, as if she had forgotten all the other words at once or she didn't want to waste precious seconds on any other words, on long phrases, on the subordinate clauses, predicative clauses, and verbs that Sashenka had never been able to memorize at school either . . . But here there was everything in a single word: all her fear of not returning from imprisonment and not seeing her daughter again, because she hadn't slept for six straight nights already, there were thirty people in the cell, it was stifling, her thoughts gave her no peace and her heart hurt all the time, so that she had already gotten used to it. And every now and then, especially just before morning, her joints ached, and the skin was flaking off her hands that were swollen from washing the kitchen vats, and after the trial there would be heavy work on the land, the kind that all the convicted prisoners with no qualifications did. It would be good if she managed to get work in the kitchen. And who else should she want to tell about her unlucky life, if not her own daughter . . . About how she had wanted to love, how wearily she had pined alone at night for so very long, how her youth had deserted her, how her figure had been ruined by the heavy vats, how she had forgotten the smell of face powder, lipstick, and eau de cologne, how her legs had turned heavy in the tarpaulin boots, and bony projections had appeared by the soles of her feet, so that the big toe on her right foot was driven completely inward and now she couldn't even dream about high-heeled shoes. And her daughter had grown up beautiful, but spiteful and high-strung, and there was no way that she, her mother, could be forgiven for that. And there was another thing she wanted to share, because it was oppressing her heart but it was something she couldn't share with her own daughter, it would be better with some chance acquaintance who was understanding, best of all with an elderly woman, that would make things easier for her, but she hadn't found a single person like that in the cell, someone with whom she could talk about this. For the first time since Sashenka's father died, she had a man, and now it was hard for her without him. She had waited five years after her husband, restraining herself, groaning at night, squeezing her withering breasts against the pillow, but now she had poured out everything in two months, she felt miserable and ashamed at the intense desires that had awakened and were tormenting her ailing, rapidly aging body, and it was frustrating that she hadn't managed to satiate it before the end, before it finally sputtered to a complete halt and grew old, because at her age every second was dear, and her months and years would be spent all alone on a prison bunk. She couldn't tell Sashenka about this, but she wanted her daughter to understand her yearning, even though it wasn't clear to her; or rather, precisely because it wasn't clear to her, so that she could forgive her mother and feel sorry for her.

When Sashenka's mother stopped walking and shouted out, breaking step, the lines of prisoners fractured and pandemonium broke out. The old woman, Stepanets, suddenly darted in between the prisoners and the line of escorts with agile precision, taking no notice of the German Shepherd lunging toward her. She grabbed hold of the skinny young man with his arms bound, and started wailing. The woman in astrakhan fur tried to toss the delicious-smelling basket to her husband in the beaver-fur coat, but a young militiaman in the escort kicked the basket aside, and as Sashenka dashed toward her mother, she stepped on a boiled calf's tongue, seasoned with garlic, pressing it into the snow with her heel. The blond-haired orderly ran past her, shouting something, and two members of the escort grabbed hold of the tall prisoner with the lackluster eyes and bound arms and hung on him. The tall peasant was the only one who wasn't sucked into the pandemonium, and behind a militiaman's back he deftly handed his brother chunks of fatback wrapped in greased sackcloth, two round loaves of home-baked bread, and several packs of Belomor cigarettes. All of this instantly disappeared into the well-fed prisoner's rucksack. Sashenka wasn't able to squeeze through to her mother; the prisoners were forced back into the courtyard and the gates were locked. The old woman, Stepanets, was locked in the guardroom. The major in glasses came out onto the porch. The pale-faced orderly gesticulated as he said something to him.

"Draw up a list," the major said in a loud voice. "Cancel their right to receive food parcels, by hand or by post . . . And identify the ringleaders . . ."

He swung around and went back in, without looking at the jostling relatives, who were now feeling scared by what had happened.

06

When the master of ceremonies came up to Sashenka from behind and took hold of her shoulder, she tried to jerk free and run away, but he was holding her so tight that the iron grip of his fingers made Sashenka's collarbone ache. And as he held her, the master of ceremonies said in a gentle voice:

"Don't you avoid me, Sashenka . . . I haven't done you any harm, but if you don't like me, then spurn me later on . . . Meanwhile we have to help your mother . . . I know this orderly a little bit . . . He was at the front line too . . . We have to wait a little while . . . One front-line veteran has to respect another . . . The major's got no heart, and the commander's away. The orderly's the only decent one there . . ."

"Where are you taking me?" Sashenka asked angrily.

They walked along narrow passages, along fences, between vegetable plots dusted with snow, with the remains of last year's dry corn rustling on them here and there.

"He lives over there," said the master of ceremonies, nodding toward a low, entirely rural wattle-and-daub house with white walls and a thatched roof. Wattle-and-daub houses like this could be found all over the place, not only in the streets on the outskirts, but even in the center, in courtyards behind the brick buildings. And here, about ten such houses with two or three windows were scattered among the vegetable plots and cherry trees. Shaggy mongrel dogs strained at their chains to get at the strangers and rushed along the low, woven lattice fences. On one side these little houses ran up to the yard of the recently restored two-story municipal hospital, and on the other side to red buildings erected in the 1930s, where the workers of the Chemapparat chemical equipment factory lived.

"Let's sit down a while," the master of ceremonies said, lowering himself onto a crudely made bench beside a gate, not in front of the orderly's house but slightly to one side of it, so that they had a good view of the approach to the house.

"He has to come for lunch . . . I had a talk with him here once before . . ."

"Let go of my shoulder," Sashenka said spitefully.

The master of ceremonies relaxed his fingers with an embarrassed air and Sashenka twisted her arm about, stretching her cracking joints. She had a premonition of trouble ahead, and the illness, her unexpected apprehension about facing up to Vasya and Olga, and the sudden pity, grief, and even tenderness she had felt for her mother, had completely drained Sashenka's strength, and she realized that she needed to harden her heart to become stronger.

"Look," the master of ceremonies said suddenly, "what a sly bitch, she's sniffed him out too . . ."

In the distance, the woman in astrakhan fur was making her way between the fences, shying away from the straining dogs.

"She's a black marketeer," said Sashenka, "and her husband's a black marketeer. Their kind should be clamped down on hard . . ."

"No," the master of ceremonies replied, "she's not a criminal case . . . Her husband comes under Article 58 . . . An enemy of the people . . . He was a teacher of literature at the teachers' training college . . . I don't feel sorry for them . . . We laid down our bones for the motherland at the front, and they trade the motherland for foreign currency. You know the kind of rumors that are going around . . . A friend of mine told me, a frontline veteran . . . A bright young guy . . . Nine classes of school . . . Our allies are up to no good . . . I don't care much for the English myself . . . The Americans are decent guys; I received some of the equipment they gave us . . . But the English really dislike Soviet power . . . This good friend of mine, he knows the score, if he says something, you can believe it . . ."

In the meantime, the woman in astrakhan fur had crossed a little bridge laid over a ditch, snuggled up against a latticework fence and started peering along the path winding between the snow-dusted vegetable plots; her feet were clearly freezing in their fashionable felt boots and she kept knocking the back of one boot against the other foot.

"She'll intercept the orderly," the master of ceremonies said in alarm. "That's our people for you . . . Sly, foxy rascals . . . You could sit here for a while and maybe I could go around and outflank her . . ."

But just at that moment they heard the sound of last year's cornstalks rustling; it was the orderly coming home for lunch, only not along the path, but across the vegetable plots behind them, which put paid to the prospects of the astrakhan-clad wife of the enemy the people. The orderly wasn't alone, though. He had already been intercepted somewhere, obviously quite near, by the old woman Stepanets. The orderly had an expression of weary dismay, and his eyes were shifting about fretfully.

"Stop bothering me, granny," the orderly said in a hoarse, strained voice. "What can I do . . . They'll put him on trial . . . I'm not the judge . . ."

"But he's so thin, my little son is," the old woman wailed, "you can see every bone in him . . . He's sick, through and through, he is . . . And he coughs blood . . . even before the war he coughed blood . . . They took him off to the district center . . . The purfessor said as he had to be kept in the warm . . . And drink warm milk in the mornings and before bed . . . With honey . . ."

"What are you filling my head with all this nonsense for?" the orderly asked, turning angry. "Go and see the commander . . . Go and see the major . . . Your son's a murderer, do you understand? He killed innocent civilians . . . There's signed testimony against him . . . Do you understand? . . . When they shot the children from the orphanage . . . The gypsies and the Jews . . . And he was involved in executions near your village . . . There's testimony on that too . . ."

"If they'd just let me in to him," the old woman Stepanets wailed, standing her ground as if she couldn't hear what the orderly was telling her. "I don't need a place . . . I'd sleep on the floor beside him . . . He's not well. Maybe just to tidy things up or hand him something . . . "

"Come tomorrow," said the orderly, overwhelmed and obviously eager to get rid of her. "Come to the chancellery at one o'clock tomorrow afternoon . . ."

"And should I bring the doctor's note?" the old woman asked, encouraged, and even brightening up a bit.

"What note?" the orderly asked in surprise.

"The one about his sickness," the old woman replied.

"All right," said the duty officer, giving in. "Bring the note as well . . ."

"Thank you," said the old woman, bowing and crossing herself, "you're a kind man . . . Everyone says that about you . . . God grant you good fortune . . ." She set off back along the path.

It had gotten noticeably colder, and a wind had come up, blowing the snow off the cherry trees and the dry stalks of last year's corn. It as if a stormy, frosty night was approaching, as if there hadn't been any afternoon and the late morning was merging directly into the early evening twilight.

"What are you doing, Stepanets?" the orderly shouted after the old woman. "Are you going to trudge four miles now?"

"Yes, four," the old woman replied, looking back.

"On foot?"

"I won't find a cart," said the old woman. "It's too late . . . Maybe someone would have given me a lift a bit earlier . . ."

"Through the fields all the way?" the orderly asked.

"It's open fields as far as Raiki," said the old woman, "after that it's forestry land and downhill . . . Then fields again after that . . . It's easy walking out of town, but into town is harder . . . It's uphill, not downhill. Before you reach the top, you're in a real lather . . ."

"I tell you what," said the orderly, "better not come tomorrow . . . Come in three days' time . . . I'm afraid the commander won't be here, and what can you settle without him . . ."

"No," said the old woman. "I'll come . . . Just in case he's here . . . Maybe he'll let me send a food parcel . . . I baked lots of spice cakes for my son, with honey . . . And if the commander's not here, I'll go back home again . . ."

She crossed herself and set off along the passage between the fences, hunched over and hobbling along with rapid, old-woman's steps in her huge felt boots, neatly tied onto her feet with rags that were stuffed with straw for extra warmth. Hobbling in those boots, she would reach the outskirts of the city, set off across the fields through the night blizzard, through the sleeping village of Raiki, rousing the dogs, downhill through the frozen forestry land, slipping on the snow packed hard by sleds and on like that for four miles, all the way to Khazhin . . . And in the morning, back into town, to her son . . .

The old woman had long ago disappeared from sight, but the orderly still didn't go for his lunch, although his wattle-and-daub house was close by. He just stood there, thinking about something.

"We could approach him now, maybe?" the master of ceremonies whispered to Sashenka.

But the woman in the astrakhan fur coat beat them to it. Dashing along, stumbling, and once even falling very comically, so that the astrakhan hood slipped over onto her ear, the woman rushed through the vegetable plots to the orderly. She caught one of her magnificent puffed sleeves on a rusty roll of barbed wire hanging from a post, and tore it, leaving the astrakhan dangling in tatters. For a brief instant Sashenka's heart leapt with joy, because she hated the woman for being beautiful too, perhaps even more beautiful than Sashenka, and she had a kind of fur coat that Sashenka didn't have, and also for something else vague and indefinite, but Sashenka sensed that this vague thing was the main reason she disliked this woman so much. This time, however, Sashenka's joy was short-lived, because her heart was oppressed by ominous premonitions. Perhaps one part of Sashenka's vague feeling was that somewhere in her subconscious, she had begun to sense that this woman had known and lived a life that was not merely beyond Sashenka's reach, but one that Sashenka was not even capable of dreaming about, although perhaps there were dreams of a light, formless kind, which Sashenka had had very rarely, dreams in which there was just as much breathtaking happiness as in her physical yearning at night, when it concluded in her dreams in a wild, sweet ecstasy that led to calm. In those rare, formless dreams, so very rare that in all her life Sashenka only remembered perhaps two or three of those happy states, and apart from the state she didn't remember anything, not a single detail, although there was one time when she had remembered the landscape of some region where she had never been, flooded with moonlight; in those rare dreams, too, there was ecstasy and there was sweetness, but there was no ferocity and yearning, and the whole thing didn't end in a calm that soon turned to boredom, or even into aversion for the recent sweetness, because in those dreams the calm was constantly present, and the ecstasy and sweetness in those dreams were filled with calm all the time; and it wasn't possible to touch anything there, neither the objects around her nor herself, and that was the only thing Sashenka definitely remembered.

Meanwhile, the woman in astrakhan fur had run up to the orderly where he was standing pensively.

"Comrade commander," the woman said in a respectfully trembling voice.

The orderly raised his head and gave the woman a dumbfounded look. The orderly was young, and the woman, deciding that he was examining her beautiful face, lowered her eyelashes flirtatiously and hid her left arm, on which the sleeve was torn, behind her back, tightly clutching her shopping bag in that hand.

"I'd like to talk to you alone," the woman said in a whisper that had perhaps set more than one man's heart pounding. "The important thing is, let me finish what I'm saying . . . I've been trying to get to meet you for a long time . . . You in particular . . ."—she thrust her right hand inside her astrakhan fur coat and drew out several notebooks bound in calico.

"What has happened to my husband is a misunderstanding," the woman began hastily, afraid of being interrupted. "Perhaps he is brusque, perhaps sometimes he does express himself vaguely, but he's a very talented man . . . Believe me . . . He's been misunderstood . . . I don't mean to say that he was deliberately slandered . . . He's been misunderstood . . . We have a lot of acquaintances in Moscow . . . highly respected people, Stalin prizewinners . . . I wrote to them as soon as it happened . . . I'm sure they've sent references . . . Or they will send them . . . Pay attention to them . . . My husband is a difficult man, I know . . . Sometimes even I can hardly bear him . . . But he's a talent . . . He's erudite . . . He knows four languages . . . He has translations from English . . . He's translated Byron . . . And Lorca . . . That's from Spanish . . . Here, look, listen . . . This is talent . . ."

She awkwardly opened the top notebook with her chin, because her left hand was occupied, and started reading in a low voice, obviously at random, the words that happened to be in front of her eyes:

" 'You'll have a child more beautiful than the stems of the breeze.' . . . 'Ah, Saint Gabriel, joy of my eyes! Little Gabriel my darling! I dream of a chair of carnations for you to sit on.' . . . 'God save you, Annunciation, sweetly moonlit and poorly clothed. Your child will have on his breast a mole and three scars.' . . . 'Ah, Saint Gabriel, how you shine! Little Gabriel my darling! In the depths of my breasts warm milk already wells. In amazed Annunciation's womb the child sings. Three bunches of green almond quiver in his little voice. Now Saint Gabriel climbed a ladder through the air. The stars in the night turned to immortelles!' "

The orderly gazed at the woman in mounting amazement, then his face darkened, and then it flushed an intense red, and he fell into the appalling fury that comes over kind and placid people only extremely rarely, but which is especially terrible at those moments in such people, and the true causes of which are not entirely clear either to them or those around them. Moreover, when she finished reading, in order to intensify the impression, the woman had in fact permitted herself several ambiguous glances and movements, which might, if one so wished, have been taken for an attempt at seduction . . .

"Bitch!" the orderly shouted, smashing the notebooks out of the woman's grasp and stepping on them. "You're trying to take advantage of me . . . Trying to impress me with this worthless gibberish . . . Trying to buy me . . . In forty-two I wouldn't have thought twice . . . In the partisans . . . I'd have just riddled you with bullets . . ."

As if she had also lost her fear and gone crazy, the woman went down on her knees and started tugging the notebooks out from under the orderly's foot. For a while they presented a strange sight, the orderly pinning the notebooks to the ground with all his strength, and the woman pulling so hard that her eyes bulged out of her head and the eyebrows painted on top of her plucked ones were washed away by sweat, and the color ran down her face. Eventually either the woman managed to tug the notebooks free, or the orderly came to his senses and stepped back. The woman hurriedly put the notebooks away in her coat and, obviously having completely lost her grasp of the situation, held out the basket to the orderly.

"This is for you," she babbled, "there's roasted meat with garlic... And home-baked cookies... With powdered egg..."

"Trying to give me a bribe!" shouted the orderly, who had just begun to calm down a bit. "Why, I'll stick you away... With your husband... You'll be slopping out toilet buckets..."

The woman didn't shout, so much as squeak, like a bird caught in a snare, and ran off through the vegetable lots, then crashed into a fence and disappeared from sight. The orderly was breathing as hard as if he had been carrying heavy weights; he unfastened his sheepskin jacket, unbuttoned his tunic, and turned his sweat-soaked singlet toward the freezing-cold wind. The master of ceremonies walked up to him from behind and cautiously slapped him between the shoulder blades. The orderly gave a start and looked around, then when he saw the master of ceremonies, he said calmly:

"Ah, it's you, my frontline comrade-in-arms... Come on, let's go to my place... I live just here. My wife's made borscht... We'll have lunch..."

"I'm not alone," said the master of ceremonies, nodding at Sashenka.

The duty officer glanced at Sashenka and seemed to recognize her, but he didn't say anything.

They walked into a small yard, and from there into a low wattle-and-daub house with a dirt floor, where there really was a delicious smell of freshly made borscht.

"Ganusya," the orderly said affectionately to his wife, "pour us a little glass before lunch... A really little one, because I've got to go back to work..."

The duty officer's wife, Ganusya, was so like her husband, she could have been his sister, with the same bright-blond hair. She laid the table easily and quietly, gently set out the aluminum bowls, and skillfully cut the bread into identical slices, and the orderly watched her with an affectionate smile, his eyes glowing with the boundless love that endures as long as life itself, which was confirmed by the lettering in thick, indelible war-trophy ink on his wrist; the name "Ganna" was written in capital letters, so that the top of the "G" touched the blue veins where they bulged up from under the skin, as if the name of his beloved was impregnated and tinctured with the living blood.

"I'm going to leave this job," the orderly said after clinking glasses with the master of ceremonies and drinking. "I haven't slept for the last three days . . . And yesterday I went into the Raiki Forest, after a gang . . . My buddy got sliced in half beside me with a submachine gun . . . His guts tumbled out . . ."

He rolled up the soft center of a slice of bread, used it to pick up the bread crumbs off the table, and swallowed it.

"But that's not the problem . . . You understand me . . . In three years we've seen plenty of deaths, and guts . . . That's not the problem . . . I'm too kindhearted for this kind of work . . . I don't know who started the rumors about me . . . But people just keep on coming to me . . . They bring all their petitions to me . . . Not to the major, not to the commander . . . That old woman Stepanets comes every day . . . But her son's looking at twenty-five years at least . . . Although I don't think he'll even last a year . . . Consumption . . . He had consumption, but he still went and joined the Nazi death squad . . . We have testimony to that . . . Some joined out of cowardice, but he volunteered, they even wanted to reject him because of his illness . . . But he kept on trying . . . He wrote a complaint about the local police to the gestapo commander . . . We have that document attached to the case file . . . And today was a really terrible day . . . Then this woman showed up, and she tries to seduce me . . . With her painted eyebrows, reading something that might just be Russian, or might not . . . We've got a prisoner, held under Article 58 . . . Betrayal of the Motherland . . . Although people write a lot of nonsense too, to tell the truth. Some out of malice, trying to settle accounts, some just haven't figured things out properly . . . And then this mess today. We didn't get the prisoners to the station . . . Now we'll have to send them off at night . . . I earned a reprimand, and that's my third already."

Ganusya took a cast-iron cooking pot out of the oven. The steam it gave off smelled absolutely wonderful, delicious enough to make you drunk. This was Ukrainian borscht, which was cooked only in a cast-iron pot and in a village stove; it was the color of venous blood, dark and viscous, and a spoon stood upright in it didn't fall over, but got stuck between the vegetables confiscated from black market traders, the greatest part of which had doubtless gone to the orphanage, and a lesser part to the security agencies' canteen or, if so desired, as rations for those who had families. The potatoes in this borscht weren't slippery after being frozen, but soft and oily; the cabbage didn't have the taste of bitter leaves from autumn trees, but was imbued with the juices of well-manured private vegetable plots; the beets weren't pale pink and tart, but dark cherry-red and sweet; the meat wasn't rubbery, with bones in it, but succulent, it easily tore into slices and was saturated with fat. It had been concealed from German requisitions and obviously raised on the finest lumps of stolen collective-farm silage. After eating a bowl of this borscht, you could easily go all day long feeling satisfied, only every now and then drinking water to dilute the fat and ease the process of digestion. Sashenka had eaten really well at Sofya Leonidovna's apartment, but never before had she felt so agreeably full as this. This state of satiety left her totally relaxed, and she realized that she was done for, because she vaguely anticipated some kind of trick, and she even had a premonition about which direction it would come from.

"Ganusya," said the orderly, burping soundlessly into his hand, "call them and say I'll be there by early evening . . . I was on a raid yesterday, and a bullet tore the sleeve of my jacket . . . It needs to be patched, and now that I come to think of it . . . There's no work to be done right now. I'll be there in time to ship out the prisoners at 12:30 tonight." He turned to the master of ceremonies: "Let's have another one." He poured two full shot glasses and filled one halfway up for Sashenka. "Ganna," he called, "you have one too . . . I've met a friend, a frontline veteran, a regimental comrade . . . You're from the Third Ukrainian Front, right?"

"No," said the master of ceremonies. "I was on the First Belarusian."

"Never mind," said the orderly, "the main thing is, we have a common enemy, external and internal . . ."

Ganna came over, red and flushed, with her breasts high and firm under her embroidered blouse. She picked up her shot glass with her finger and thumb, jutting out her little finger. The orderly clinked glasses with everyone, drank, and instead of following his drink with a snack, gave his wife a resounding kiss on the lips.

"That short-ass almost did me in yesterday," the orderly told the master of ceremonies resentfully, "in the Raiki Forest . . . He obviously got a clear bead on me, with his sight trained on my left side . . . Only when he squeezed the trigger, he jerked it, rushed things . . . But I got so infuriated, I gave him a gentle pat on the head with my gun butt . . . The major cursed, we couldn't even interrogate him . . . And he never came around. But I was infuriated, you understand . . . It's not my life that I mind losing, what I mind is leaving behind a woman like this . . . I just can't get enough of her . . . I've been drooling for over a year now."

"Petrik," said Ganna, blushing to the roots of her hair, "don't you go talking such nonsense."

Ganna raised her little white hand, loose and relaxed, and first touched the orderly's dry hand with her wrist, then ran her palm across it, with the tips of the fingers trailing gently and the little nails scratching.

"It's out of the question for me to be killed," said the orderly, bursting into laughter. "I'm still a newlywed, only one year . . . Listen, my frontline comrade in arms, get married. What are you dragging it out for . . . You can't find a woman? I don't believe it . . . Men have become more valuable now . . . The dead have driven up our price."

"That's what I wanted to talk to you about," the master of ceremonies said, "about my woman . . . You haven't forgotten, have you?"

"Hang on, hang on," said the orderly, straightening up as if he were sitting at an office desk at work, and not in his own home. "Right then, Ganna, you go, I've got a serious conversation here."

Ganna got up with a sigh and went out.

"Right," said the duty officer, "you've come about that woman . . . And I had you mixed up with someone else . . . But not to worry . . . You're a frontline veteran, the genuine kind . . . And I remember about you now . . . I recall that business of yours . . . I haven't slept properly for three days, my head's a total mess." He moved his shot glass away and suddenly glanced intently at Sashenka, and her heart faltered as her premonitions started coming true.

"I understand," said the orderly, "I remember it all clearly now . . . Well, what did you expect?" he said, turning to the master of ceremonies. "We've had instances when complainants retracted their statements and we closed the case . . . Now, though, the accusation isn't based on her daughter's statement, but on material evidence . . . Your woman was caught with the foodstuffs right there at the checkpoint. She hid them in her boots and in a few woman's places too, sorry to have to say that . . . There's a report, and witness's signatures . . . The statement can even be retracted now, it doesn't make any difference . . ."

"What statement?" the master of ceremonies asked in surprise.

"Come on now," said the orderly. "Don't play the halfwit with me, I hate that . . . Didn't you two get your story straightened out?

I took a shine to you, as a frontline veteran, you just bear that in mind. My simple advice to you is, don't go petitioning for her at all just yet . . . Then it will come out that she's the widow of a decorated airman . . . A hero of the battles for Warsaw . . . His heroism was specially singled out in the central press . . . We've got all of that . . . And for the legal documentation it's best not to emphasize that she's sleeping with you . . ."

"Aren't you ashamed, you great big men?" Ganna suddenly shouted from the doorway, "Saying things like that in front of her daughter . . . You're plastered on the moonshine . . ."

"Ganna," the orderly said as sternly as he could manage, turning his body toward his wife and holding his palm out toward her with the fingers splayed, as if fencing her off from the conversation taking place in the room. "Ganna, don't you interfere in my official business . . ."

"How can you say that sort of thing about a mother in front of her daughter, no matter what kind of thief or speculator she might be?" said Ganna. "The girl's gone all green."

"I don't give a damn," Sashenka shouted, jumping to her feet.

The robust meat borscht, mingling with sips of sugary moonshine, no longer lulled and weakened her, but had precisely the opposite effect, somehow instantly cuing up a new series of pictures in her mind, and these pictures buried the hesitations and doubts about her mother, who had never given a thought to Sashenka's future. Sashenka's mother was a coarse, lecherous woman, who had already forfeited any right to the memory of Sashenka's heroic father, and any connection with her could deprive Sashenka of the right to that memory too. Sashenka didn't have a mother any longer, but she did have Sofya Leonidovna, and Sashenka could give her the pension from her father, so she could live there in peace and have her meals there.

"I don't give a damn," Sashenka shouted, "I won't retract the statement . . . So there . . . That woman had me, but she didn't raise me . . . And a mother isn't the one who has you, just the opposite, in fact . . . Your mother is the one who raises you . . . I don't want to know her . . . My father died for the motherland . . . He fought . . . He gave his life . . ."

Suddenly the tears started flowing of their own accord, and so abundantly that it wasn't just Sashenka's face that got soaked, but her chest, her arms, and the tangled tresses of hair cascading onto Sashenka's cheeks. Ganna took Sashenka by the shoulders, her warm hands smelled of dried cherries, but Sashenka only found the whiff of this aroma pleasant for the first brief moment; an instant later Sashenka started feeling sorry for herself, and Ganna's warm, appetizing hands only inflamed this self-pity and resentment against life even more. Sashenka pulled herself free and cast a sideways glance at the orderly, who was frozen in amazement, but she didn't look at the master of ceremonies, she turned her back to him, and then stepped into the porch, grabbed her fur coat and fluffy beret, ran out into the freezing-cold air and set off into the total darkness that had descended in the meantime. Sashenka couldn't remember such a black night for a long time, although in fact it was still evening, and not very late, only seven or eight o'clock. But everything was already sleeping, with only a few feeble little lights glimmering here and there, emphasizing even further the remoteness and desolation of a place that was now completely unrecognizable.

07

Sashenka ran fearfully through the dark vegetable plots, which went on endlessly, and it wasn't especially her face that she felt afraid with—she could touch that with her hands—but she felt afraid with her back, which was completely unprotected, exposed to the chilly, snowy wind. Not only mustn't Sashenka touch her back, she mustn't even think about what was happening behind her, where the infinite darkness of night began immediately beyond her fur coat. She caught a sudden glimpse of something white to her right, either the wall of a little house or a snowdrift, but quite a high one, so that even a grown, strong man could easily hide behind it. Sashenka realized that, and ran around the snowdrift in a wide semicircle, peering hard into the darkness, but not a single familiar form emerged ahead of her or on either side, and Sashenka was afraid to look back to where she had probably passed the hospital, from which she knew the way. Something like frozen tussocks started skipping about under Sashenka's feet, and it got brighter, but it wasn't because the moon had sailed out from behind the clouds, it had simply run into a cloud that was thinner and more tattered by the wind and was shining through it as a white patch. By this light Sashenka saw a ditch close by, evidently dug just recently, after the snowfall during the afternoon, because the clay along the parapet of the trench was fresh and only slightly frozen.

Sashenka decided to go around the ditch, since it was deep enough for a man to hide in, if not at full height then by squatting down on his haunches. However, the curiosity that had been aroused together with Sashenka's fear drove her to approach the ditch, instead of recoiling from it, and glance inside. It was strange that if the clay parapet was fresh, the lumps of clay hadn't actually frozen to each other yet, as if they had really been extracted the day before. The bottom of the ditch was covered with hoarfrost and seemed to be strewn with a thick layer of snow. The snow was soft and clean, slightly blued, as if it had been starched, and lying there stretched out at full length on the snow was a young Jewish girl, the dentist's daughter, wearing the light frock in which Sashenka had seen her in the photograph. She was a girl of rare beauty, and she clearly knew that she was beautiful, because she had flirtatiously exposed her beautiful arms, rounded shoulders, and pure, graceful neck. Except that the head, smashed with a brick, had been artfully covered over with colored ribbons woven into the hair, and the skin beside one little ear had been lightly powdered with hoarfrost, in the same way that Sashenka concealed the scar from her operation on the back of her neck. Sashenka didn't know how long she stood there, leaning over the ditch without breathing. All she remembered was suddenly crying out, as if she had abruptly woken up, and staggering back; and immediately dark, rustling shadows hurtled up past her from the ground, almost touching her face.

"Mommy," Sashenka shouted. "Mommy..." The shout reminded her of everything that had recently happened; she took a gulp of air so cold that it stabbed at her shoulder blades, and to lift her spirits she shouted even more loudly: "Sofya Leonidovna ... My dear ..."

And then she realized she ought to have shouted at the very beginning, for her voice changed this place, making it less deserted, silent, and strange. Dogs started barking beside low wattle-and-daub houses that sprang up around her. The moon sailed out from behind the clouds and started shining at full power this time, and someone came out into a yard nearby.

"What do you want?" the shadowy figure asked, warily keeping its distance, clearly afraid of robbers.

"How do I get to the hospital from here?" Sashenka asked, clenching her jaws shut and trying to stop her teeth chattering.

"There's the hospital," said the dark figure, "it's right there in front of you . . . Don't you play stupid games with me . . ."

And it was true, the moon that had sailed out lit up a flock of crows just as they were landing on the hospital fence, the same crows that Sashenka had startled and driven off the vegetable plot. It turned out that the hospital wasn't behind Sashenka after all, but in front of her, so Sashenka had managed to get her bearings in this place even without realizing it.

Forgetting even to say thank you, Sashenka set off at a run along the hospital fence and soon found a passage that she followed until it brought her out onto a familiar street. With her heart pounding, Sashenka ran past the familiar ruins of the main post office, past the municipal movie theater—where the final show was still in progress and she could see light in the projectionist's booth—past the glove factory, where the shift hadn't finished yet either and the lights were still burning.

"My illness has started up again," thought Sashenka, "I went out too soon, got chilled again, and exhausted my nerves . . . Dear Sofya Leonidovna, Dear Mommy Sofya, how I'd love to see you really soon . . . Forgive me . . . I'll love you more than your own daughter . . . Calm my nerves, I'm afraid, life is hard for me, I'm completely alone . . . Be a mother to me . . . I've caught a cold, I've got a temperature, and I keep seeing all kinds of pictures . . . Help me . . . Your mother isn't the one who has you, but the one who raises you . . . Dear momma Sofya . . . I've got no talent for school, why should I waste my young days for nothing . . . I'll get well and go to work at the glove factory, I'll buy myself some shoes, and a marquisette dress . . . Maybe a fur coat . . . And I'll give away everything that I'm wearing now . . . I don't want anything from my former mother, the thief . . ."

Musing in this way, but not loudly, only in a whisper, so that people who came walking along toward her wouldn't hear, Sashenka reached the end of the street, and now the apartment building for Party and Soviet functionaries was just around the corner. Sashenka rang the bell for a long time, and she had just thought anxiously that Maya and Sofya Leonidovna could have gone to the movies and Platon Gavrilovich could have gone to the Party office, when the door abruptly opened, although Sashenka hadn't heard any steps in the hallway, and her heart skipped a beat, because she realized that someone had tiptoed up to the door and peered through the peephole, wondering whether to open up. Instantly mortified by this event, which had never occurred before, Sashenka walked into the dark hallway, and a shadow in a robe stepped aside without giving any indications of being glad. It was Sofya Leonidovna.

"Come in," Sofya Leonidovna said in a quiet voice.

She invited Sashenka into Platon Gavrilovich's study, where the walls were lined with bookshelves displaying the red spines of the classics of Marxism-Leninism, and asked Sashenka to sit down in a chair, like some visitor for whom she felt no pity because the visitor's back was shuddering with the cold, or her throat was dry, or her face was pale. In any case this wasn't a place where they would take fright and start scurrying about, this wasn't a place where they would put her to bed and feed her nourishing broth, but a place where, at best, they might hear her out and sympathize out of politeness, or perhaps even sincerely, if they were well-disposed.

"I've always treated you like my own daughter, haven't I?" Sofya Leonidovna asked.

"Yes," Sashenka meekly agreed.

"But you say that we have some kind of designs on you," Sofya Leonidovna continued, "that we want to use you . . . You hurt Maya very badly, and me, and Platon Gavrilovich . . . Don't think I hadn't already noticed how you feel about me . . . You don't like the way I look and you don't like the way Maya looks . . . You're a grown-up already, and I'm talking to you like a grown-up . . . Maya is an affectionate and trusting girl, she has a good character, she could give her heart to her friend . . . or someone she loves. She's a devoted girl . . . But you're ungrateful . . . Yes, you can take offense at what I'm saying . . ."

Sashenka listened to Sofya Leonidovna at first, but then her concentration wandered. Sashenka stopped shuddering so much, perhaps because there was no one here to feel sorry for her, and no one would have taken fright, even if right now, with this cold in her chest, she had started eating snow to moisten her dry throat. And Sashenka realized that Sofya Leonidovna had never been a genuine friend, because she defended herself and wouldn't let Sashenka hurt her. All the sneers and humiliations with which Sashenka had gratified her own feelings, not even openly, but in secret, had been gathered together in a folder by Sofya Leonidovna, like documents, not in a spirit of suffering, but out of righteous wrath; she hadn't forgiven Sashenka for a single leering glance or a single one of the unjust thoughts with which Sashenka had repaid her concern and nourishing food.

Sashenka stood up and walked into the hallway. She heard Platon Gavrilovich sigh in the kitchen and Maya start crying in the dining room. But Sashenka wasn't thinking about them now. She was thinking about how to evict Vasya and Olga, or at least move them back behind the screen in the kitchen so that she could start living an independent, adult life, since Sashenka's childhood had come to an end a few minutes ago. It had ended at the moment when Sashenka realized there was nobody left to take any notice of her misery, and without anyone else's attention and concern, this misery was insipid and tedious, and it brought no sweetness, for one of the attributes of childhood is the ability to torment someone and ravage their feelings. Sometimes this ability is absent even in infancy, sometimes it stretches on into old age; in the course of a life it can disappear and return: childhood is the ability to delight in one's own helplessness . . .

The apartment was intensely heated again, although perhaps Sashenka's temperature from her uncured cold, which had risen as evening approached, was responsible for that: Sashenka could feel that temperature in her soaking wet temples, in her burning ears and the shudders running up and down her spine. Sashenka was so hot that even her fur coat was soaked, and the wet squirrel fur stroked her neck disgustingly. Olga was bustling about performing household chores, dashing between the kitchen and the room. In the kitchen she had a brew of herbs, garlic, and some other ingredient that smelled a lot like urine, on the boil for Vasya's chest, and the suffocating smell was enough to set Sashenka's head spinning.

"It's a piece of advice a woman in the choir gave me . . . She can be trusted . . . For Vasya . . ." Olga started trying to convince Sashenka, as if Sashenka were just as concerned about the chorister's reliable advice and just as anxious about Vasya's health as Olga was. "The woman's son was ill," Olga carried on explaining, without noticing that Sashenka was feeling dizzy and wanted to have a cold drink made from the fruit concentrate that her mother sometimes brought home in her boot.

"They gave him a bad beating," Olga said in a leisurely voice, yawning as she stirred the brew with a silver spoon from the set that Sashenka's mother had kept ever since her wedding. "They kicked her son, obviously, although he didn't tell anyone about it. They beat his kidneys off his spine and his stomach came away from his bowels . . ." Olga scooped up some murky-yellow brew with the spoon and tried it, setting the very end of the spoon to her lips in order not to burn them, "... but the food, it moves, the nourishment does ... It doesn't get into the stomach and it builds up around the heart ... That's why he was coughing and he felt so bad, and he had stabbing pains in his heart." Olga buzzed away monotonously, like a fly, lulling Sashenka and driving her into the drowsy, sweltering heat, so that Sashenka didn't have the strength to raise the question of eviction right now, she just stood there agreeing with everything and listening to Olga's babble for some reason.

"But the woman in the choir told me," Olga went on, "I've got a remedy, she said, they used it in the old days, and this remedy completely cured my son ... Only people are too proud these days, not everyone will accept it ... But I said all I wanted was for Vasya to be well ..."

Olga grasped the cooking pot of boiling brew by the lugs with a rag and carried it into the room, wafting a salty, astringent smell through the air. Sashenka followed her in. Her mother's former bed had been made up with the fresh linen sheets that Sashenka's mother hadn't used even once since her father left for the front. Vasya was sitting on the bed cross-legged, Tatar-style, wearing her father's white, freshly laundered underwear, which had always lain in a neat pile in the section of the wardrobe where all her father's things were, and which Sashenka's mother had never allowed her to poke her nose into. Vasya's eyes were glittering feverishly, and a fit of coughing had obviously only recently ended, because his chest, which could be seen in the slit of the shirt, was heaving fitfully, and his lips were wet, and Vasya was wiping them with the palm of his hand, then dabbing his palm with the edge of the sheet afterward. When he saw Sashenka, he smiled at her, exposing his gums, and nodded at the cooking pot.

"There it is, my sugar-sweet moonshine," Vasya said. "God grant, Sasha, that you never have to cure a hangover with moonshine like that."

"Never mind," said Olga, "you drink it up, Vasechka, it's a sure remedy . . . And you'll get well . . ."

She poured the brew into the sky-blue china mug from Sashenka's early childhood. Vasya drank it, wincing, wiped his lips, crossed himself, and smiled again.

"Not too bad," he said. "Heady moonshine."

Olga took an entire loaf of bread out of the sideboard, and not a solid brick of bread from a shop, heavy and wet, but a round, home-baked loaf that could only be gotten at the market, with a crunchy crust and springy, gray crumb. Vasya made a little hole with his fingers in the top of the gleaming crust, forming a little pit in the crumb, and Olga poured vegetable oil into it and sprinkled salt on it.

"He likes it like that," Olga said, "the oil soaks into the bread . . ."

"I've caught a cold," Sashenka said and took off her fur jacket.

"You lie down, then," Olga said. "Drink some hot water with a bread roll."

Sashenka set up the folding bed by the wardrobe with the mirror in the small room, and started getting undressed. Her movements were rounded and lingering; she removed her clothes with hands that had no weight, and she couldn't care less where the clothes disappeared to after that, she didn't put the marquisette blouse on its hanger, and she simply dropped her only smart skirt. Olga came in and gave her a cup of hot water with a sugar candy and a stale piece of church bread.

"Thank you," Sashenka said, for even though she was so unwell, she had no right to anyone's concern and she had to say thank you for everything. The bread smelled of icon-lamp oil. Sashenka decided to dunk it in the hot water to kill the smell and make it easier to swallow, but she dunked it clumsily and almost all the hot water spilled out onto the floor. Olga went out to the kitchen, came back with a rag and wiped the puddle dry, and she brushed the crumbs off the blanket with her hand.

"Thank you," Sashenka said.

After that she lay there quietly on her own for a long time. She heard Olga pump up the oil lamp and Vasya start fondling Olga, but everything was beyond Sashenka's grasp now and her joints didn't tense up, and her breathing didn't quicken, and her bitterness now was lifeless, not the kind that generates spite and self-pity, but on the contrary, Sashenka felt quite indifferent about her fate, because no one pitied Sashenka and no one loved her.

The desire to be loved is inherent in everyone, but there are strong, high-strung, sensitive natures, in whom the longing for someone else's love is so great that they lose the ability to love anyone themselves, and in order to constantly feel the strength of the other person's love for them, they make that loving person suffer. These unfortunates don't become like this in a single instant, all of a sudden—one vivid example of such a character is Judas, the Hebrew youth who was misunderstood or maligned by the four evangelists—Christ's most handsome, most passionate, and most beloved disciple. The reason he hanged himself was not at all that he repented. Judas did not feel sorry for Christ, since the love between two people is never equal on both sides, and Christ's love for Judas was so strong that Judas could not have had a grain of love left for Christ. Judas suddenly felt terribly lonely when Christ was no longer there beside him, for only Christ, with his all-consuming, unearthly love, was capable of slaking the thirst of this frenzied, passionate need to be loved that consumed Judas, never abating even for a second. This always happens when someone loves extravagantly, as Christ loved everyone, and most of all the unfortunate youth Judas, for in love too, if some take a great deal or everything, then only a little, or nothing but the longing, is left for others. Such also is maternal love, the closest in nature to Christ's love, and therefore children cannot love their mother, and the feeling that they experience is a different feeling altogether . . .

Sashenka lay like that until deep in the night, when the wind outside the window died down and the moon rose. She felt sorry for Vasya now, because she had stopped feeling sorry for herself, and every time he started up with his loud, hacking coughing, she wanted to walk into the room barefooted and beg his forgiveness. Even now Sashenka didn't feel sorry for her mother; on the contrary, her mother was the only person for whom Sashenka felt hostility, because of her own illness, and other people's mockery and her mother's weakness, Sashenka's mother was now the only person in the world compared with whom she felt as strong as before.

"Yes, my dear young man," said the prisoner in the pince-nez. As often happens in a dream, Sashenka saw him in an unnatural position, cut in half, and the lower half had disappeared. He was wearing a soldier's tunic and over the tunic a jacket that was made of expensive material, but worn and threadbare ... "Yes, my dear young man," said the prisoner, "such an interpretation of Judas does also exist ... However, it is purely literary, enjoying no support among either theologians or atheists ... Christ and Judas are the only example of a great love in its pure form, that is, sexless, not based on the instinct of reproduction. Judas betrayed Christ when his need to be loved, and therefore also his weakness, which is the same thing, exceeded all the a priori bounds established by us earthly creatures ... It is paradoxical that such an interpretation has something in common with the biblical parable of Job, but strangely enough, this is perhaps the only instance in the Bible in which the Supreme Being was weaker than the earthly one. The theologians interpret this parable incorrectly. At that time, the Lord by no means felt that he was almighty; on the contrary, he was weaker than he had ever been and yearned for love. That was why he condemned Job to suffering, so that Job would love him even 'in his suppuration' ... Do you catch the affinity? In exactly the same way, Judas betrayed Christ to his crucifixion ... perhaps this is blasphemy, but the commergence of

Christ with Judas and that of the Lord with the insignificant Job, living 'in his suppuration,' *is* the idea of the great primeval chaos with which everything began and to which everything will return, the chaos that reigns over both human beings and God, where there is identity of small and large, good and evil, loving one's neighbor and tormenting one's neighbor . . . We find this disagreeable, we shall always try to fend this off, as we try to fend off death, which nonetheless exists independently of us, for the overwhelming majority of people are, in purely physiological terms, incapable of living beyond the bounds of their own passions, just as no one can live beyond the bounds of the atmosphere. But it is the struggle with death that has made man precisely what he is: he has distanced himself from animal existence, developed science, religion, art, philosophy . . . Yes, in exactly the same way that man required an understanding of his mortality in order to construct the civilization in which you and I have the good fortune or misfortune to live, for the coming civilization, concerning the nature of which we can as yet merely surmise, it will be equally essential for him to possess a clearer understanding of the universal chaos that sets in beyond the bounds of our passions. For universal chaos is universal death and the universal womb, which both repels and attracts . . ."

The speaker coughed to clear his throat, which had tired of words, and took a drink of something.

"I could only agree with you on one point, professor," said someone else's voice. "The fear of death is extremely necessary and it serves to equilibrate an as yet still low level of morality . . . I cannot agree with the rest; it seems to me that you wish to impose on Christian chastity ancient Greek perversions that are alien to it . . ."

"Ah, young man," said the prisoner, who was clearly visible down to the midpoint of his torso, "chastity itself bears within it the most powerful passion and the most powerful call of nature . . . The tantalizing depravity of chastity can be seen especially clearly, not in philosophy, but in poetry . . . for these thoughts I was purged from Sverdlovsk University before the war . . . And I didn't even express them to an audience from a university lectern, but at a friendly party on the occasion of the silver wedding of the head of the department of mineralogy . . ."

"You shouldn't drink any more, Pavlik," said the beautiful woman whom Sashenka used to hate but now regarded with indifference, appearing in the opening of the door. "You have already disinfected your stomach; in small doses it is healthy . . . But after drinking too much, you become heated, and the cell is damp."

Having said that, the woman walked into Sashenka's room together with the handsome lieutenant about whom Sashenka had dreamed earlier, when she was still entitled to everything that was best, but now she wasn't even surprised to see him, she could only look at him from the outside, without feeling any jealousy, like Maya or some other plain creature.

"I'm very grateful to you," the woman whispered to the lieutenant, "I know that my husband had no chance of being selected to work on this detail . . . You need two strong prisoners, sound diggers . . . I know everything . . . I heard you making the request at the chancellery . . . You were helpful, you insisted that they send my husband . . . Two nights outside the cell and good food . . . You helped him, me and, perhaps, the fatherland . . . We must preserve him . . . Believe me, the time will come when men like him will be needed more badly than a pauper needs food and a warm bed . . . But do be consistent; Pavel Danilovich cannot dig graves at night by lantern light . . . In the snow . . . Not for that have we dragged him out of the cell for at least two days . . . I'll arrange things with the escort . . . He is eating in the kitchen. It is better if he stays where it's warm . . . Naturally, the second prisoner will also have to be kept here, or else he will inform on us . . ."

"I don't have much time," the lieutenant said quietly. "The sanitary inspection service forbids the graves to be dug up in the daytime, and I have to get back to my unit . . . They've given me the prisoners for two nights . . . In that time I have to find my relatives and transfer them to the cemetery . . ."

"The custodian is in agreement, and so is the man whose apartment this is; he invited us himself," said the woman. "They want to earn something for it . . . He is even willing to accept ordinary stewed meat and bread . . . The custodian, however, is more demanding, he wants milk and household soap, but I'll obtain them, believe me, I'll definitely obtain them . . ."

"I agree too," Sashenka said out of the darkness, "I could do some work for a jar of stewed meat."

She felt afraid lying there alone, as if she were in a grave at the side of a road, along which life flowed, without touching or fearing her.

"There seems to be someone here," the woman said with a start, pressing up against the lieutenant.

"This apartment is mine," Sashenka said as firmly as she could manage, "go out and I'll get dressed . . ."

The lieutenant and the woman hurried out, and Sashenka started getting dressed. She had thought her body and head were heavy with night, but her fears proved groundless: her body was as light as the dawn, especially when Sashenka pulled on her sweater and wide flannelette trousers.

"Hello," said Sashenka, walking into the large room, which was full of strangers and brightly lit by two oil lamps. Vasya was already dressed, standing there in his greasy greatcoat, tightly tied around with Olga's scarf, so that he wouldn't chill his weak chest.

Franya was there too, dressed up for work and holding a spade.

"You won't be able to work, young woman," the lieutenant said quietly, "the frozen ground out there has to be broken up . . . In the wind . . . And you don't look well to me . . ."

After he said that, the lieutenant looked at Sashenka, and Sashenka realized immediately and simply, in a way that rarely happens in this world, with no doubts and no oaths, that she was born and had grown up for the sake of this man, trying to eat as well as possible, so that her stoop would disappear and her hips would round out, and it was for this man's sake that she hadn't died of typhus three years earlier.

"I can dig the ground," Sashenka said, not feeling lonely any longer, and tears sprang to her eyes at this chance she had finally been given to feel sorry for herself. "I need to earn something . . . My father was killed on the front and my mother has been arrested as a thief by the Soviet authorities . . . I don't intend to hide that . . ."

She put on a quilted work jacket and wrapped her head in a shawl.

08

Two prisoners and one armed escort were sitting in the warm, brightly lit kitchen, eating warmed-up meat with bread. As the arrested professor ate, he pensively contemplated the pieces of meat skewered on his fork, while the other prisoner—a strong, robust man—and the escort chewed firmly, for they had understood with the essential being of their succulent, healthy bodies the wisdom at which the most lucid minds arrive only late in life and at the price of sacrifices and continuous nervous stress and strain.

The professor's wife prepared additional portions of meat in the frying pan, making such skillful use of seasonings—vinegar, onion, pepper, and breadcrumbs—that at first Sashenka felt something like gratitude to her, for the smell of luscious meat on such a blizzardy night rouses hope and allays fear. It really was a terrible night, a night from which all living things should hide: biting wind, searing frost, a black, starless night that oppressed even strong souls. It was still the same night that had frightened Sashenka among the snowbound vegetable plots, but even more desolate, lending even more strength to a diseased imagination, and disfiguring the land on all sides.

Franya walked at the front with a railroad lantern that he had signed out from the building superintendent's office. First of all,

Franya walked over to the burned-out, one-story ruins of the house in which the dentist's family used to live: he almost fell and smashed the lantern against the surviving iron porch with its various twirls and flourishes, and swore in his heart, on his liver, and on the soul of the mother of God, then started measuring out with unsteady strides the distance from the porch to the cesspit and on from there to the shed. Sashenka, the lieutenant, and Vasya crowded close together. Olga had come with Vasya, to help him work and to keep an eye on him. All around it was quiet, everything was sleeping. Only in one dirty, crooked little house on the edge of the yard the windows kept lighting up and going dark again—in there the atrmosphere was restless and sleepless.

"The little boy was killed," Olga said with a sigh. "Yesterday Louty found a bomb behind the old bathhouse and started screwing something on it . . . He's all right, he's not hurt, but his little brother was killed . . . Five years old . . . A fine boy he was, lively . . ."

"There's so much of that junk still there under the snow," said Franya, walking over and also glancing at the restless windows, "it's the third case in my section . . . The executive committee's passed a resolution to set up patrols . . . But what can you do?" he asked with sigh. "Life's not so pleasant for the people and why's that? . . . A new priest has come to our church from Estonia . . . Well educated . . . I ask him: why is life so unpleasant for the people, why do they live in enmity like this? Because, I told him myself, man is tired of perpetuating the human race . . . Father Georg almost threw me out of the church."

Franya set off toward the shed again, measuring the distance with his strides, and eventually stuck his spade into the snow near the cesspit. They started digging. First they cleared away the snow and then Franya, Vasya, and the lieutenant started breaking up the top layer of frozen ground with a crowbar, resting by turns. Sashenka and Olga cleared away the frozen earth with round-pointed shovels.

They came across pottery shards, stones, iron fragments of some kind, lumps of bad-smelling rotten wood, frozen flypapers speckled with flies. They found Leopold Lvovich's remains close to the surface; he was lying face down, and the body had already been affected by decay, but it was not yet a skeleton. He was lying there completely naked, but his head had been bundled up in a shirt that had turned reddish. Suddenly the professor appeared in a quilted work jacket; he had obviously relinquished his beaver fur coat to the stronger prisoner.

"You don't feel any pity for what now only distantly resembles a human being, do you?" the professor said to Sashenka for some reason. "You are consumed by a different feeling: horror at the thought that this hideous thing could once yawn pleasurably, laugh, eat . . ."

"He's either putting ideas in my head," Sashenka thought, "or he's guessing my own thoughts, which are unclear and frightening, even to me . . . What a mercy it is that I never saw my own father dead."

"You can love a dead person's memory, but not the body," the arrested professor continued. "The dead should be buried by strangers . . . Why do people long to see their dead loved ones . . . It's monstrous . . . Great grief, like great love, should be like a dream . . . A man disappears together with his life, and what's left is the most terrible mockery of him: his dead body . . . Remember what it says in one of the wise books: 'Leave the dead to bury their dead.' "

"Go back to where it's warm, professor," the lieutenant said quietly, although he was gradually getting more and more agitated. "Perhaps you don't entirely understand the situation . . . This isn't an Etruscan mummy . . . This is my father, killed by a blow to the head with a brick and buried in a cesspit. You're terrible scum, professor, believe me . . . You're worse than a child molester . . . You should be put away . . . I'd gladly smash in your face, pardon my rudeness . . ."

"Ah, young man," the professor said sadly, "the true persecutors of philosophy are not bigotry and vice, but human suffering and human tears, for philosophy renders this suffering and these tears comical."

"Forgive him," said the arrested professor's wife, dashing up to the lieutenant. "He's always getting tangled up in his thoughts and saying absurd things . . . My God, how hard it was to drag him out of a damp cell for just two nights . . . He suffered himself, when our daughter died . . . He suffered so much . . . He didn't leave the graveyard for three days . . ."

Turning to her husband, she grabbed him tightly by the sleeve of his quilted jacket and pulled him off to the side.

"I've paid with the finest quality food for you to sit in a warm room," she told him in an angry whisper. "You are not only affronting this kind young man at a tragic moment for him, but also annoying the escort, who is obliged to loiter out in the frost with you, and the second prisoner too. You are a detestable man. Perhaps a character reference will arrive from Moscow . . . I wrote to two members of the Academy . . . I have arranged . . . At the cost of repeated humiliations I have arranged for you not to be sent to the regional center, but to be kept under preliminary investigation for the time being . . ."

She hissed all of this like a snake, pressing her lips to her husband's ear and squinting sideways at the escort, sullenly stamping his felt boots off to the side, next to the morose prisoner. They had been bought with meat, bread, and a warm room, in order to preserve the professor for literary scholarship, but with his absurd behavior the professor could oblige them to follow the instructions, according to which they had been sent out on a night shift, one to dig the frozen ground and the other to supervise him. The escort had been given this task as special extra duty by the master sergeant, who was goading him. And therefore, he had calmly savored the meat and the warmth, rejoicing in his good luck. "Throw me in a river, and I won't drown, I'll swim out with a fish in my teeth," he could well have thought. And suddenly the master sergeant had triumphed in the most unexpected manner, at the most inappropriate moment and, moreover, not thanks to the major or the orderly, but to an insignificant individual, who was obliged to obey any instructions he was given and for some reason had absurdly rebelled, in the sense that he had violated his own interests, purchased at a high price, and was ruining everybody else's opportunity. Since the prisoner's behavior was incomprehensible, it aroused a fury in the escort that piqued his vanity, and when vanity is piqued, comfort is relegated to the background.

"That's enough," the escort said harshly, "you've had your fun . . . take a spade, old man, and you too," he said, shoving the morose prisoner on the shoulder, "follow your instructions according to the letter of the work detail . . ."

"We can do everything," said the woman, darting over to him, "he can't dig, he has a bad heart . . ."

"Well, what of it?" said the escort. "And I've got a shrapnel wound in the upper section of my ankle joint . . . Not to mention the advantage of not having betrayed the motherland . . . And I'm carrying out instructions according to the letter of the work detail."

"Quiet," said the lieutenant, "come on, quiet . . . I want total silence . . ."

He was standing, slumped back against the wall of the shed and breathing as if he had run several miles. Sashenka walked over and stood beside him. Despite his angry shout, the lieutenant looked helpless just at this moment, as if he were searching for protection. He was a broad-shouldered young man, an airman who had fought right through the war, he had been injured three times in his burning plane and wounded twice on the ground, but now he felt afraid, like a child, and he needed a woman's hand; that happens even to very strong, experienced men, and God only knows what female instinct, developed over thousands of years, made Sashenka reach out her hand and caress him, without feeling any shame in front of the people around them. She stroked the hair that had escaped from under his cap with the earflaps, wiped his damp forehead, carefully straightened his scarf, and for the first time in her waking life she felt a strange sweetness below her heart, reminiscent of the sweetness of those dreams that had no form, dreams in which there was just as much happiness as in physical yearning, but which did not end in a wild ecstasy that was followed by calm and later by disappointment, for the ecstasy and sweetness in these dreams were always replete with calm. Sashenka did not realize that she had been visited for the first time by the feeling of motherhood—the highest wisdom to which a woman can ascend in love, a love that not only does not demand reciprocity but, by virtue of its own completeness, entirely excludes it, a bottomless, blind love with none of the torments and doubts intrinsic to sensual love. This love is immanent in every woman. But it is not always roused and it arises suddenly, sometimes in a very strange way; it can arise in an eight-year-old girl for a forty-year-old man, so that a complete child feels stronger and older than a grown-up, and a man sometimes even subconsciously feels the need to seek protection from a little girl. This love can also be dispersed through the ordinary sensual love accessible to all, like precious flecks of gold, appearing at moments of complete spiritual unity, something which does not occur so very often in earthly life. Just as this love is dependent on age only to a very slight degree, neither is it dependent on intelligence and upbringing, nor does it depend on morality and decency. However, once it has arisen, it can completely transform and change a person, and it always leads only to improvement. Perhaps the instinctive search for it, which is so difficult, and in which success is so rare, causes a person to suffer, to become bitter, betray, and hate. Mystics may explain this by the searching of souls which were closely related thousands of years ago, and say the very greatest happiness, which is rare, occurs when the soul of an ancient mother transmigrates into the body of a modern young girl, and the soul of her son transmigrates into the body of her beloved... The materialists, naturally, repudiate all this, especially since there is a whiff of ancient Greek perversions about it, but recently some of them nonetheless do acknowledge the existence in the matter of happy marriages of the dark areas pointed out by the sociologists...

Many, if not all, of these thoughts were expressed by the arrested professor that night in these very same words, or at least similar ones; he carried on talking, regardless of the fact that his wife was trembling with fear and indignation, and the second prisoner and the escort, completely frozen through after the warm kitchen, had long been ready in their hearts to beat him skillfully in the prison style, without leaving any bruises, and even the lieutenant abused him, because the professor continued with his glib rhetoric at the very moment when a man felt a need for silence. To the professor, however, these words did not seem to be blasphemous and vulgar, his heart had been oppressed for a long time by words that had accumulated over the years, incoherent and absurd words, full of contradictions, but living words, one never knew where they would lead and what they would combine to form. It seemed to him that for many long years he had used words that resembled stuffed birds, packed with sawdust, and moreover without accusing anyone or anything, apart from his own insipidness and pragmatism, but the consequence of his own cowardice had been that the living words had flapped and fluttered in his soul as if in a cramped, narrow cage, and now he was releasing them into the night, gesticulating feverishly. His skinny figure in the quilted work jacket, peasant fur hat with earflaps, and pince-nez would have appeared comical, if not for the blizzard, the gloomy faces, one or another of which was occasionally lit up by the lantern hanging on the remains of the iron porch beside the ruins, and the dead body that they were lifting out of the pit by raising it up with a spade to create a space underneath, so that a rope could be slipped through. All this made the professor look like an insane wizard, reciting a prayerful incantation over the deceased, who, moreover, was not being buried, but extracted from the ground, which gave the sight a completely different significance. The escort walked up close to the old prisoner, glanced into his rapidly darting eyes and thought, with no malice now, but rather in a cheerful, kindly way, as a healthy country man often thinks when looking at a harmless madman: "The old man's not right in the head . . . I ought to report it."

Franya opened one of the sheds, where the four empty coffins were standing: they had been supplied in advance by special order from the carpenters' shop at the woodworking plant. Leopold Lvovich's remains were laid in the largest coffin. The lieutenant tore off his greatcoat and covered the terrible naked bones and body.

"I didn't think of that," said Franya, turning away, blinking and blowing his nose, "I ought to have got some burlap or clothes ready . . . But I wrapped up his head back then . . . It was smashed very badly . . ."

Olga walked away, sobbing and crossing herself, and came back with a large woolen shawl that Sashenka's mother had never worn even once.

"You should take that for yourself," said Franya. "Yours is all full of holes. One like that's good enough for the grave . . ."

"Never mind," said Olga, "I'll earn myself another one . . . And he's frozen through . . . Let it lie there . . . Forgive us, Lord . . ."

"Help me carry it into the shed," the lieutenant told Vasya . . . "I want to see my father's face . . ."

They carried the coffin into the shed and the lieutenant stayed there, but Vasya came back out, also crossing himself rapidly, without his cap on, and suddenly he started coughing, with his eyes bulging out terrifyingly. Olga dashed over to him, and he carried on coughing on her shoulder, slowly calming down. The lieutenant had taken the lantern with him, and it was completely dark now, with only a solitary star twinkling right above Sashenka's head: God only knows how it was able to force its way through the blizzard, although it had quieted down a bit. Everyone standing there quieted down too; the escort stopped drawing devils' faces in the snow with his rifle butt, which he was doing simply in order to busy himself with something. The morose prisoner, who had been slyly chewing a stale piece of rye-flour pie, hid it in his pocket and wiped his lips; the professor, drooping and exhausted after his diatribe, looked at his energetic wife, who was endeavoring by all means, fair and foul, to preserve him for literary scholarship. He looked, blinking rapidly and meekly, yielding himself up to her judgment, the way that good-natured dogs who have done something wrong look at their masters. The silence stretched on for longer and longer, becoming more and more impossible to bear, and Sashenka's heart ached as she languished beside the shed, inside which the son's meeting with his father was taking place.

Meanwhile the blizzard died down completely, the sky cleared in many places, and stars scattered right across the broad vault of heaven; the wind had obviously subsided just above the earth, but was still raging on high, shredding the clouds and driving them away. Soon the number of stars multiplied so greatly that the entire breadth of the sky wasn't enough for them, and they were densely crowded together, which rarely happens in winter, but only on sultry August nights. In the moonglow the snow blazed into life where it was now calmly lying on the ground, and this light, following immediately after darkness, this calm after the blizzard, far from lightening their hearts, only intensified their anguish; for hope had disappeared, the hope that had been cherished in man's heart, over and above his will, since the age of pagan barbarity, that nature is the cause of his sufferings, a hope which, as it happens, is not entirely senseless, even according to the latest scientific hypotheses, and therefore it is particularly oppressive when nature calms down but fails to calm the soul, stripping man of protection and leaving him alone with his own sins. The longer this calm lasted amid the festive glow of the snow, amid the swarms of stars and the air that had warmed slightly in the moonlight, the more agonizingly Sashenka's heart ached. And she was also oppressed by the strange, sepulchral calm inside the shed, from where not a single rustle or sigh could be heard, nor any evidence at all of human life. The shed was as silent as the oblong pit, darkly yawning open amid the pure snow. The moon illuminated this pit and the layers on its walls were clearly visible: the upper layer, about twelve inches of fibrous rotted material and humus, densely packed with shards, stones, and glittering pieces of glass; after that came seams of sand, and a pure, yellowish layer of clay, in which the imprint of the human body that had lain in this clay for four years was clearly visible. During the flash floods in spring and rainy weather, when the soil came alive, the body that was gradually becoming part of that earth also came alive, in the sense that it began moving, broadening out, and swelling up from the warm water and the sun's rays that pierced through the alluvial soil, and pressing against the walls and bottom of the pit, and the clay had compacted with the kind of champing sound that you can sometimes hear in a cemetery on a spring night after abundant, warm rain.

This, or something like this, was what the professor thought as he, like Sashenka, stared fixedly at the pit, feeling strangely agitated and tempted now, at the age of forty-seven, by new thoughts that didn't consist of words, but of some kind of signals that were hard to translate into human language, welling up rebelliously in his brain and kneading at his temples. Meanwhile, the freakish accidents of nature continued, these phenomena which, naturally, were entirely comprehensible to astronomers, or at least to most of them. After appearing literally before their very eyes from out of a turbulent, blizzardy night, the moonlit starry night was initially so calm and windless, that it seemed not alive, but painted, but then movement began in it too, although of a different kind. It started becoming noticeably brighter, and even warmer, and sheet lightning started glimmering in the distance, so that the horizon, which had been fused with the darkness, became visible, and so did the roofs of the distant buildings amid the sky where it turned green at the horizon, and although there was still a long time to go until dawn, the distant stars paled, while the nearer ones swelled up, starting to glitter in devilish merriment, and so brightly that they seemed to tint the snow with bluish, diamantine fire, shimmering in derision of human torments. And then everyone there without any exception, including even the escort, for the first time in his life, especially during the performance of his official duties, experienced a strange increase in the intensity of their heartbeats, of the kind that only happens during nightmares, and the escort, who slept without dreaming at all, experienced the special terror that comes from ignorance of such properties of the body. To be on the safe side, he tried to force a cartridge from the clip into the bore of his gun barrel, but his hands refused to obey him, also for the first time in his life, and, jerking his chin up a little and opening his mouth slightly, he breathed heavily in unison with the prisoners he was escorting, together with the other individuals who had been caught unaware by this phenomenon of nature. Olga, Vasya, and Franya crossed themselves in fright, Olga and Vasya in the Orthodox manner, and Franya from left to right, in the Catholic fashion. But Sashenka and the professor, as high-strung characters, wanted to shout out or burst into tears, or grab a spade and start filling the pit with earth, in order not to see the clear imprint of the human body in the clay, like the imprint of ancient creatures in a geological cross section. But in reality, the explanation for everything was very simple. Amplified by the collision of a cyclone and an anticyclone, the magnetic charge of the atmosphere had influenced the hemispheres of the human brain, and they, in turn, had influenced the greater and lesser pathways of blood circulation. The rhythm of the flow of blood had been disrupted, in fact accelerated, which instantly affected the tissue fluid or tissue lymph, which sensed a shortage of oxygen and nutrients, as well as an excess of carbon dioxide and decomposition products. This was why the escort was unable to turn the bolt of his gun and why Olga and Vasya fell into a religious ecstasy; an especially appalling calm fell inside the shed, and Sashenka and the professor, sensing a strong internal pressure squeezing their hearts up toward their throats, felt like throwing frozen tussocks at the pit to cover it over, in order not see the clear indentations of the shoulders, legs, and head on the already half-frozen clay. But clearly, even atmospheric magnetism does not affect everyone in the same way; it roots some to the spot while it raises up others, who are frightened or tormented by grief, and sets them in motion. The silence was broken as the door of the shanty right at the back of the yard opened and the mother of the five-year-old child, killed by a grenade at the old bathhouse the previous day, came out onto the well-trampled track. As she walked along with her large nose and gold teeth, with her hair straggling untidily down across her cheeks, she was supported under the arms by two members of this wide-branching family, her husband Shuma's brothers, both as swarthy-faced, gold-toothed, and large-nosed as she was. They both had shoeshine stands, where they sold bootlaces, one by the station, and one by the bathhouse, where the boy had been killed after finding an old grenade under the snow. The stand by the bathhouse had been inherited from Shuma by his younger brother. Shuma had set himself up in that advantageous spot before the war, and in those years he was a man of sound health and a great lover of the joys of life. For instance, he loved to drink beer right there in the bathhouse, sitting on the stone bench with its drainage grooves all awash with hot water, amid the steam and the splashing, blowing off the suds into a soapy stream with his well-steamed lips. The beer was brought to him in the bath chamber by an attendant from the bathhouse snack bar for a modest remuneration. Shuma pampered and loved his body, and cared for it without any help from doctors, but even so, it wasn't really clear why, in his subsequent activities, as soon as he got the chance, he deliberately made the rounds of the addresses of doctors, not people of any other profession, and he beat those doctors mercilessly. In addition to Leopold Lvovich, his neighbor, he killed the pediatrician Laprun and his family; he killed the surgeon Goldin and the neuropathologist Baraban, who was deaf and half blind from old age, but who, despite his age and blindness, employed the age-old natural cunning of his natural character to such good effect that he managed to hide away so craftily with a reserve of food and water that only Shuma, who knew the surrounding area well, was able to extract the old neuropathologist from the basement premises of the knitted-goods factory and kill him there and then in the factory yard, by striking his gray-haired head against the concrete corner of the finished-goods depot . . . But now, Shuma, sick with appalling, unearthly diseases, was dying piece by piece in a hospital barracks hut in the taiga, and the members of his family were trailing across a snowbound yard in a mournful procession, accompanying the mother of Shuma's five-year-old son, who had been killed in an accident. Men and women who looked like each other walked along, male and female, cousins, nephews and nieces, grandchildren. At the back came Zara and Louty. Zara walked with her head lowered, but Louty, on the contrary, looked around proudly and unwaveringly; he spotted Sashenka, and his eyes started blazing with hatred. No old people were to be seen in this procession; following the customs of their ancestors, they had stayed with the boy's body, tidying him up and equipping him for the journey ahead. The members of

the procession talked among themselves in quiet, guttural voices as
they walked around the yard. When the procession was only about
sixteen feet from the shed, the wooden plank door opened and the
lieutenant came out. His face was completely drained of blood, his
heart had sucked it all away and supplied it to his fists of cast iron
and his chest, a burden weighing many tons. Even his blue eyes had
turned pale, and seemed to have difficulty in making out what was
quite close, although they could see something that was no longer
there, but had existed before. The dead boy's mother pushed away
her husband's brothers and stopped. Between her and the lieuten-
ant was the pit, filled to the brim with yellowish, moonlit air, and on
the bottom of that moonlit air could be seen the imprint of the body
that had lain there, sinking into the clay. Seconds passed like this in
total immobility, and then the mother raised her hands and started
tearing and plucking at her face, the way that Middle Eastern women
do in terrible grief. She grabbed the skin, together with the flesh
below the lines of both cheekbones, squeezing it from above with
her bent forefingers, and forcing her extended thumbs into the skin
from below, so that the skin gathered into folds, which the dead
boy's mother clenched, compressed, and tugged on, as if she were
trying to tear them off the bones. She slid her fingers and thumbs
right across her face in this way in silence, wrenching without a
groan, gradually working down from the eyes to the chin, and then
slid up to her ears and started wrenching again under her eyes. Her
nails and pinching fingers left her face bloodstained and bruised,
but she still couldn't feel any pain, as if she were not tearing her own
face, but someone else's, someone else's body. Her husband's and
her own brothers and sisters, grandchildren, nieces and nephews
clustered together, talking among themselves in guttural, anxious
voices. Eventually the two who were leading her before walked up,
took hold of her hands and tore them away from her face. And then
she started screaming wildly and fainted. The brothers picked up

the wife of their condemned brother Shuma and carried her back along the track to the shanty. But Louty, Shuma's son, whose face and figure resembled his father's, ran up to the edge of the pit, shouted something in a guttural voice, and raised his fists in hatred. He was seized by one of his nephews in a quilted jacket and sheepskin hat, and since this nephew was about fifteen years older than his uncle, he easily dragged Louty away, but Louty carried on struggling and threatening until his mother recovered consciousness and struck him on the face, so that his shouts wouldn't disturb the dead boy, whose soul would carry on living an earthly life in his body for another three days, sleeping at night and waking in the morning. Soon the entire procession disappeared into the shanty, and Zara was the only one who didn't leave; she stayed there at a distance, stubbornly and avidly gazing at the lieutenant, transgressing the customs of her forebears, which prescribed that she be modest and diffident, and hate the enemies of her father, and also the enemies of her father's father, and so on to the tenth generation, and never share her bed with them.

"Now dig a bit more to the right," Franya said in a quiet voice. "I noticed... Your mom's there... Or if you like, we can dig up your sister first... She's closer to the fence, beside the bushes..."

"That's enough for today," said the lieutenant, in what he thought was a quiet voice, but in fact it was extremely loud, almost rising to a shout, and that was a defensive measure by his body, which sometimes expended in this way an excess of the special kind of nervous energy known in the vernacular as feeling sick at heart.

"That's enough for today," said the lieutenant, "I've got no more strength for today... We'll dig up my mother and sister tomorrow."

"Sign the work order," said the escort, who, having finally recovered from the effects of the atmospheric phenomena, now set about displaying his sound military gumption even in this matter, to be precise, by ordering both prisoners to fill in the pit from which the body had been extracted, thereby setting about the direct performance of his duties and also tearing himself away from senseless contemplation of the starry sky, which, as everyone knows, cannot lead to anything good, and transforms a man from a hard worker and a craftsman into a neurotic and a dreamer. The morose prisoner obeyed reluctantly, but the professor unexpectedly displayed an exceptional capacity for hard work; he almost tore the spade out of Franya's hands and began showering down frozen lumps so frenziedly, without any break, that soon the imprint of the body had completely disappeared under a layer of soil. The lieutenant signed the work order and walked out of the yard, and, without saying a word, Sashenka set off beside him.

By this time the exceptional atmospheric phenomena consisting of luminescence and sheet lightning had completely come to an end, the sky had turned paler, the moon had disappeared, the snow had dimmed, and storm clouds had started creeping up again, bringing with them the wind and the reawakened blizzard.

09

O nce he reached the hotel, the lieutenant lay down on his bed and Sashenka sat by the headboard. The hotel room was a double, but fortunately the other bed was empty. The furniture in the room was in various styles from various times. Standing beside the khaki-colored bedside locker, to which a candle was attached, were two household chairs with curved backs and a low, light armchair, upholstered with scuffed leather. And the table, which was large and solid, but crooked, had obviously been knocked together out of knotty, unstained planks in the carpentry shop of the municipal communal services department. The bedstead on which the lieutenant was lying was nickel-plated with knobs, while the other was a standard, low, army metal-frame bed that even had a coating of rust. The room felt damp and cold. The lieutenant lay there, having removed his boots, but left his greatcoat on.

"Take off your coat and get under the blanket . . . You can put the coat over the top to make yourself snug," Sashenka said.

The lieutenant meekly did as he was told, like an obedient child, but when Sashenka tried to move away to clear the oiled paper, crumbs, and empty stewed-meat jars off the table and wipe up the puddle around the tin kettle, which obviously leaked, the lieutenant grabbed her by the arm and wouldn't let her leave him. It was strange, but Sashenka no longer felt her own exhaustion and fever, although she had spent the night out in the wind and the frosty air. On the contrary, at this moment Sashenka felt extraordinarily strong and capable. She fluffed up the pillows under the lieutenant's head with deft, frugal movements, caressed him soothingly, cleared the table, wiped the waterlogged planks dry, gathered the leftovers of food on the bedside locker into a neat little heap, found a rag and plugged a hole in the window, since a chink had been left where the window was closed off with plywood and it let in a strong draught. After that, Sashenka took the kettle, went out into the icy-cold corridor and at the far end she found a little kitchen with a water heater, filled with acrid smoke. However, there was no water, either in the faucet or in the big, zinc boiler. Sashenka went down to the ground floor, fastening her quilted jacket snugly and tying her shawl around herself as tightly as she could. She went outside and stuffed the kettle full of snow, trying to choose the cleanest and whitest snow from a drift as far away as possible from the well-trampled tracks. After stuffing the kettle with white snow, Sashenka straightened up and looked round. Although it was still nighttime, she could tell that its end was imminent, not from any glimmers of dawn or brightening clouds, since the nocturnal gloom was as thick as ever, with the blizzard sweeping through it from end to end, but from the fact that lights were glimmering in windows, occasional passers-by had appeared, and an immense, war-trophy Fiat bus that brought workers from the surrounding villages to the chemical equipment factory went creeping and clattering by. Sleepy, nodding heads in caps, fur hats with earflaps, and shawls could be seen in the bus. Sashenka sighed, shivered and went back into the hotel lobby. She put the kettle in the stove, which was being tended by an old female stoker in big felt boots, and raked about inside the stove with a poker, turning the damp pieces of glowing peat on the bars of the grate, and, with her eyes closed, blew on the this peat that didn't burn.

"A little bit of kerosene would do it," the old woman said pensively. "It'd catch in a flash . . . Blow on it, daughter, I haven't got enough puff . . ."

Sashenka leaned down and blew, raising dust that got in her eyes, then wiped it away with her hands and started blowing again until her cheeks ached, feeling the heat on her face. Standing in the oven beside the kettle was a cast-iron casserole with some kind of soup boiling in it; the old woman kept scooping some up in a wooden spoon and trying it. Before Sashenka's kettle boiled, the old woman had already sampled almost half the casserole and she topped it up with water that she kept for her own needs, hidden from the guests in a secret spot behind the stove. Sashenka took her kettle and went up to the room. The lieutenant, who was still lying there exhausted, rose halfway and propped himself up on his elbow.

"I was worried about you," he said wearily . . .

Sashenka poured hot water into a tin mug and found a jar of jam, a few packets of crackers, and an opened jar of stewed pork in the bedside locker.

"You eat too," the lieutenant said, scooping up melted pork fat with a cracker.

Sashenka took a broken piece of cracker and inconspicuously scraped the wall of the jar with it so that the lieutenant wouldn't notice, taking advantage of the fact that he was tearing open a packet of crackers. And so Sashenka felt perfectly satisfied, because there was quite a thick layer of fat left on the walls of the jar, and even a few fibers of meat and greasy gristle here and there. She left the best pieces of meat, sealed in the fat, for the lieutenant, who was exceptionally weak and pale. There were still a few jars left in the locker, it's true, but Sashenka realized they were intended for paying Franya, Vasya, and Olga for digging up the graves. After she had eaten, Sashenka lay down beside the lieutenant on top of the blanket, with her cheek pressed against his cheek, without feeling any arousal or sensual desire as she did it, merely tenderness and calm. They lay there like that in the cold room, warming each other with their breathing.

"It's cold for you," the lieutenant said quietly, "get under the blanket."

For an instant Sashenka felt afraid; it suddenly seemed as if something vile could happen now, for, strangely enough, in this moment she felt nothing but disgust for what she had dreamed about, lying on her sofa bed.

"There's no need," Sashenka said, "I'll lie like this . . ."

She recalled her first kiss on the dark balcony—the wet, repulsive way that General Batiunya's son had touched her face, destroying her dreams, and, as she now thought, laying the ground for all her subsequent miseries.

"Don't be afraid," the lieutenant said wearily. "I won't touch you."

"I'm not afraid," Sashenka said, her heart pounding in fright as she threw back the edge of the blanket and slipped under it, frozen through and through, preparing for the very worst at the same time as feeling a gentle, languorous sensation appear in her joints. The strong male body immediately seared Sashenka with its heat, frightening and alluring, but several seconds went by and the lieutenant carried on lying there without moving; only his hand found the nape of Sashenka's neck, cautiously caressing it, and Sashenka hastily jerked his hand away, because she was afraid that the lieutenant might feel the scar from the operation, which spoiled Sashenka so badly. So that the lieutenant wouldn't feel the scar, Sashenka took his hands, put them together, palm to palm, and squeezed them between her knees, in the way that she herself liked to lie, with her hands stuck between her knees, where her skin was absolutely satin-smooth.

"I've taken you prisoner," Sashenka said, squeezing his hands between her knees.

Sashenka trustingly put her head on the lieutenant's chest, and when she felt the regular beats coming from within, she didn't immediately realize that it was his heart, because she hadn't really realized what was happening to her.

"It's a bit frightening for me to hear someone else's heart," Sashenka said, "especially yours . . ."

They lay in silence for a little longer, huddling against each other. The candle was burning down and the lieutenant propped himself up on one elbow and extinguished it. It went dark, although outside the windows and also in the corridor, they could clearly hear footsteps, indicating that it was already morning.

"Let's get a bit of sleep," the lieutenant said, "we haven't slept all night, after all . . ."

"All right," Sashenka said, "I'll just close the door so we won't be disturbed."

She slipped out from under the blanket, ran across the cold floor on tiptoe in her stockings, knocking over a chair, and started groping for the door, but stumbled into a locker and knocked something off it, she thought it was an empty stewed-meat jar. Eventually she stumbled across the door, closed the hook, went dashing back at a run and boldly dived under the blanket, as if she were used to it, as close as possible to the large, moist body.

"I'm sorry," the lieutenant suddenly said in a hoarse voice, "I'm sorry."

"What for?" Sashenka asked in surprise. "What are you saying, you silly thing . . . I'm so happy with you . . ."

"I'm sorry," the lieutenant repeated. "I can't be alone right now . . . Forgive me, little sister . . ."—he was feverish and almost delirious—" . . . you know, little sister, I think that professor is right . . . Your nearest and dearest should be buried by strangers . . . Especially if they were killed by a brick to the head . . . I've been wounded five times . . . I crawled along on burned legs . . . I cooled my legs in swamp water . . . Sometimes it felt as if my legs were enveloped in flames all the time. I wanted to put out the fire . . . Then I crept into a barn. There was grain in there, and rats. I ate the grain, and the rats ate me when I lost consciousness. There was plenty of meat on all sides without me, but they like warm meat . . . They especially liked my roasted legs . . . They gnawed right through my flying boots . . . Even when I was woken up by the rats' teeth, it was hard for me drive the rats away from my legs . . . I beat them with the stick I tried to use to support myself when I walked, but they gnawed the end of the stick . . . There was one gray rat there in particular . . . Completely gray . . . I'll remember its face for the rest of my life . . . It could think, I'm sure it could . . . It didn't gnaw on the stick, it didn't snarl, but calmly and patiently waited for me to pass out . . . Have you ever heard of Greek tragedy, my girl? Well that rat's eyes refuted the cognizability of existence . . . They mocked at the theoretical optimism of Socrates . . . A rat like that could easily get into its head the idea of murdering an entire people out of compassion . . . In order to put an end to its torment and humiliation once and for all . . . Lots of rats darted around me, grown lazy from an abundance of food, with faces wet with human blood, but I summoned up all my strength and all my experience; I outwitted that rat, mastering the pain, trying not to groan, because I was certain it would understand and run farther off, but I tried not to groan. I cautiously crept closer and killed that gray rat with the stick . . . I paid dearly for that success, my legs started bleeding from the excessive effort, but I don't regret it . . ."

"You're soaking wet," Sashenka said solicitously, "you're soaking wet, my darling, my dear heart . . ."

"I'm drained," the lieutenant said, breathing heavily, "completely drained. I don't know if I can dig my mother and sister up out of the ground tonight. They were killed all together with the same brick . . ."

He suddenly grabbed Sashenka tightly by the wrist and moved her face close to his own, which was burning up with fever.

"You shouldn't sell your own blood that cheap," he said in a whisper, "it's bad business . . . There's no profit in trading your own blood that way . . . You have to take a liter for every drop . . . Two liters . . . A bucketful . . . Only then will the number of buyers be reduced . . ."

"What are you talking about, my darling?" Sashenka asked, looking delightedly at his blue eyes. "Don't distress yourself . . ."

"I'm sorry," the lieutenant said, "perhaps just a minute, a moment . . . I want to take a doze . . . Perhaps that's where salvation lies . . . I want something different . . . To immerse myself in something different . . . Forgive me, my girl . . . That drunken Catholic custodian talked about atonement . . . But I'm afraid, and fear hardens the heart . . . I can't imagine myself digging up the ground today and seeing my mother in the clay . . . The only thing I'm dreaming of is that her features have been distorted beyond recognition . . . There are ten thousand lying in the porcelain factory quarries . . . They were killed by fascism and totalitarianism, but my dear ones were killed by our neighbor with a rock . . . Fascism is a temporary stage of imperialism, but neighbors are eternal, like rocks . . ." He fell silent for a moment and gulped several times. "The custodian told me he watched through the window, but he was afraid to defend them . . . First our neighbor killed my sister, because she was young and she might run away or fight back. Then he stunned my father, my mother fainted, and the boot-cleaner's practical reason told him that he could leave her for last . . . He started chasing my little five-year-old brother and couldn't catch him for quite a long while, because he crept under the table on all fours, or ran around and around the aspidistra . . . Our neighbor moved aside the table, the aspidistra, and the chairs, and it was only then that he managed to kill the boy . . . Then he finished off my father and killed my mother. She died an easy death, because my father, he saw everything, he was only stunned as he lay there, but my mother died without recovering consciousness . . . Perhaps he merely smashed her skull when she was already dead, that's what I really hope he did, because my mother had a weak heart . . . Then our neighbor tied all their legs together with the washing line and dragged them out into the yard, then he dragged them into the cesspit like that, into the night soil. He took a spade and smeared their faces with shit, filled their mouths with shit . . . Now he works in a sawmill at the Ivdel camp . . . And you know what I dream about. I dream about him surviving those twenty-five years and being released, so that I can rip open the skin on his neck with my fingernails . . . Old man's skin, but that doesn't matter . . . So that skin will hang down onto his shoulders like a collar, and then I can wait, wait until he bleeds to death from the torn veins in his neck . . . And soak my fingers in his blood . . . I know no one can live long with dreams like that . . ."

"My sweet darling," said Sashenka, badly concerned now by her beloved's hoarse, hasty speech, which was more like raving. "My sweet darling," said Sashenka, pressing his head against her breasts, "I'm alone too . . . My father gave his life for the motherland, and my mother's a thief . . . Things are hard for me . . . But we're together now . . ."

"Yes," said the lieutenant, "we're together . . . I have to think about something else, or my skull will burst . . . I have to feel something else, live for something else . . . Right now, this very moment . . . Mere minutes decide everything . . . You know, I dreamed several times about killing that boot-polisher . . . After I found out the details . . . I only have to close my eyes . . . I had a dream at dawn today too. I was standing up to my waist in blood . . . The walls and the ceiling—they were all concrete . . . A hollow echo . . . There was a hideous moment—I was killing his children . . . I'm done for . . . They talk about universal forgiveness, atonement. But I don't dream just in my sleep, it's when I'm awake too . . . I yield to my heart, I feel an indescribable sweetness at the torment of my mother's murderer . . . I break his fingers, I tear the tendons out of his legs . . ."

The lieutenant started choking. He was soaking wet with perspiration.

"Go to the boiler room," he said in a quiet voice, "find out . . . I want to take a bath . . . Can they heat the water . . . Does the shower work . . . Go and find out right now . . . My body's itching . . . I'd like to be clean . . ."

Sashenka got up and put on her boots. The lieutenant lay there, slumped back on the pillow, calm now; his chest had been heaving rapidly, but now he was breathing regularly. Sashenka went out into the corridor that was flooded with sunlight, but when she reached the first window aperture and saw a section of a bright winter day in full bloom, the glittering roofs white with snow, the calm black crows, the celestial blueness, the kids' shouts coming up from below, obviously from the old bathhouse, where there was an icy slope for sliding down—when she saw and heard all this, Sashenka suddenly felt a terrible, incomprehensible anxiety that turned to fright and she went dashing back and tore open the door of the room. The lieutenant was lying on his side, facing the wall, and his right arm was bent at the elbow, with the hand pressed against his head. Sashenka grabbed hold of that hand with both of her own, trying to unbend the arm and pull the hand away from the head, still not even understanding why, but the hand was made of iron, it was completely still, and through the cloth Sashenka could feel the arm's knobbly, tensed bicep muscle. Then Sashenka hastily and frenziedly sank her teeth into the lieutenant's wrist, the lieutenant groaned and, as he tried to tear Sashenka off, he struck her a swinging, backhanded blow with his left hand. Sashenka's temples started buzzing and rainbow-colored spirals started drifting in front of her eyes, but she didn't let go of the wrist, she clamped her jaws together even more tightly, and something heavy fell onto the floor.

"Enough," the lieutenant wheezed, "enough . . . Let go . . ."

Only then did Sashenka finally throw herself backward and sit down on the bed. She was breathless and sat there with her mouth wide open. Lying on the floor beside the bed was a large army semi-automatic TT pistol. For a while everything was quiet.

"How stupid," the lieutenant said. "I forgot to close the door with the hook . . . Such a small detail . . ."

Then Sashenka started crying.

"You're a fool," she said. "You're a fool, a fool . . . You've got no shame, you haven't . . . You tried to deceive me . . ."

"I didn't survive the war, my girl . . . I was killed . . . I was a student in the philosophy department, but I became an advocate of bloody vengeance after I saw my father's face. Contorted in agony, with traces of sewage on his lips in that shed . . ."

"Sometimes I don't want to live, either," Sashenka said, "I want just to lie there with everyone feeling sorry for me . . ."

"You're a good girl," the lieutenant said and sat up. "None of it's true . . . Despite everything, I want to live . . . Even though that boot-polisher stuffed my father's mouth full of shit when he was still alive . . . Save me . . . I have to think about something else . . . Now, after you've saved me . . . I hit you . . . That's terrible . . . Everything that . . ."

"But it doesn't hurt," Said Sashenka. "Don't worry, my adorable one . . ."

"Something different . . ." said the lieutenant, "I must think about something completely different . . . It will block it out . . . It will save me . . ."

He suddenly embraced her as if he was drowning and had finally managed to set his hand on an object that promised salvation. He pressed her breasts against his lips and Sashenka felt a tingling, languorous sensation throughout her body, a feeling she hadn't experienced for a long time, but this time the feeling was alive, everything that she had felt before was nothing compared with this, in this sweetness there was neither sin nor fright; she felt her beloved's inexperienced and artless hands uncover her body, removing her clothes, but she didn't feel even a hint of shame.

"I'm cold, I'm cold," Sashenka complained in a whisper, and he hurriedly pulled the blanket up over Sashenka's exposed back. Everything was simple and just, and Sashenka, also overcome by impatience, tried to help her tired beloved. The joints of Sashenka's body desperately yearned for the moment she had craved, but which simply wouldn't arrive, and the yearning for that moment was great, beyond the comprehension of those who have already stepped beyond it, for no memories or imagination could possibly reconstruct that apocalyptic thirst after it has been left behind. But then the thirsting ended for Sashenka too and the sweet agony began, the blissful torment in which her strength dissolved deliciously and joyful moans erupted from her chest, and finally came the something never experienced before, a sense of disappearing, of the death of the soul, which she would gladly have prolonged forever, flinging out a demonic, drunken challenge to life, nature, and impotent order, deriding and triumphing over all that was sanctified in this world, thumbing her nose at God, jeering at atheism, despising suffering, acknowledging neither father, nor mother, nor motherland, nor love and all the rest of it, the desires and sensations were so hard to define in this moment of total triumph of the body over the soul, of unreason over reason, of the animal over the human, of the idea of the devil over the idea of God, this moment of conception, the only moment, ambivalent like everything in the universe, when life, deprived of the assistance of fantasy and reason, shows its genuine value, equal to zero, and imparts through this truth an ineffable delight. But this effect, for all its transcendent bliss, is tenuous and inarticulate, having flung out a challenge to reason and fantasy, it finds itself vanquished, for, having forfeited words and thoughts, it is incapable of decoding its own essential nature and seducing man with that and, being chaste, and rapidly fading away, it merely strengthens order and reinforces the purposive nature and meaning of life. Thus does transient, persecuted life, filled with contrived meaning, enter into battle with the eternal, real chaos that reigns in the universe and emerge victorious.

Only at the moment of conception does this eternal chaos of the universe erupt into human flesh, and then only for a single, insane instant.

Helpless and happy, Sashenka lay beside her beloved; at first, perhaps, for a minute, perhaps five, perhaps even longer, Sashenka was so weak that she couldn't raise her arms, and in her legs, which seemed to be lying a long way away, she could only feel her aching knees. Her beloved was also weak and quiet, and even his face had changed, the wrinkles around his eyes and on his forehead had smoothed out and, having lost their harshness, his features had become calmly exalted; this was a face like those of kind, stupid women when they pray, or of men whose sins are not great, and so their prayers are gentle toward both themselves and God, and do not require any shackles or raptures. But gradually this feeling started to pass, and as his strength returned, so did his concern, and the eyes that were pale-blue and naive during those moments of calm darkened once again and acquired a glint of intelligence. However, he carried on looking at Sashenka tenderly, and with his strength, his desires also woke again. He embraced Sashenka and started kissing her so passionately that they both lost their breath and every kiss left them breathing deeply and heavily.

"Again," demanded Sashenka, whose body had also recovered its strength and become engorged, and was insatiably begging for caresses.

And then once again they reached out for each other, and once again there were sweet torments, and again their strength dissolved, and again there came that moment of disappearance, which they would have liked to prolong forever, but which quickly faded away, bringing weakness and calm. They lay there again for a while and suddenly, as if they were now a single organism, they both felt ravenously hungry.

"Look away," Sashenka said, "I have to get dressed and feed you."

He suddenly laughed.

"What's the matter?" Sashenka asked.

"I've remembered that I don't know your name," the lieutenant said. "What nonsense . . . A convention . . . A label . . . We are given names and surnames for telling apart strangers, people who don't need each other . . . I can sense you by smell, the way a wolf senses a she-wolf . . ."

"You're talking nonsense," said Sashenka, "We have to introduce ourselves immediately. If Zara finds out that we weren't even acquainted, she'll start spreading rumors . . ."

The lieutenant was called August.

"A good name," said Sashenka, "but to myself I called you Vitya . . . That was before . . ."

"When?" August asked in surprise.

"It's not important," said Sashenka, "but now I'm going to get up, get washed, and heat up some stewed meat. There's a stoker here, a woman—maybe I'll get a brew of dried flowers with grated carrot from her . . . It tastes better than real tea."

"Even if it's just carrots," said August. "That's a good idea you had, tea . . . Give the stoker some jam in exchange."

"That would be overdoing things," Sashenka said thriftily "For jam you can get flour and bake flapjacks . . . I know where . . . But she'll give us the brew for two crackers . . . And she'll be grateful for that. . . ."

Sashenka lowered her feet, suddenly stepped on something cold, and cried out.

"What a fright I got," she said, holding her heart. "I thought it was a mouse . . ."

It was the TT pistol, still lying there in the same place. August's face darkened; he quickly grabbed the pistol with his finger and thumb and stuck it under the pillow. Sashenka sat down beside August and put her arms around him, and he put his head on her shoulder.

"That's all over with," he said, "finished." And he kissed Sashenka on the neck . . .

Sashenka quickly and skillfully put together breakfast. She bartered two crackers for carrot-tea brew from the woman stoker, and for another cracker she got a heavy cast-iron skillet from her too. August had a piece of stale bread in his rucksack; Sashenka soaked the bread in water, coated it in powdered egg and fried it with the pork fat. That produced a delicious kind of toast with an eggy coating. On August's plate Sashenka put four pieces of toast and a piece of heated-up, marble-veined meat from the jar, and for herself she took two pieces of the toast and a slice of gristle, which she smeared with clarified butter to give it flavor. August gave his folding pocketknife with a fork on it to Sashenka, and he ate with a big SS dagger made by Solingen, with an obliterated swastika on the handle.

10

It was a spring-bright day. After the blizzards and the freezing cold, it had suddenly turned warmer, so that now, in January, March, icicles appeared, dangling from the cornices of the buildings and the ruins, and at noon water even began dripping from the roofs. In many places on the main streets the ruins had been demolished and fenced off, and the burned-out, three-story carcass of the former department store had been screened off almost all the way up to the third floor with a large panel of plywood bearing the production goals due to be achieved in 1950 for crude oil, pig iron, steel, and coal. Members of the local community were strolling back and forth from the movie theater to the plywood panel; there were glimpses of greatcoats, tank helmets, and natty round fur hats. The girls were wearing boots. The ones who were less well-off wore shawls, but the wealthier ones had little caps sewn from greatcoat fabric. Irina, the colonel's daughter, and General Batiunya's son came walking straight toward Sashenka and August. Irina stood out from the general crowd because of her dark-brown war-trophy fur coat. When she spotted Irina, Sashenka pondered for a moment and glanced at her own quilted jacket.

"August," said Sashenka, "excuse me for a moment, I'll just run and put on my fur coat . . . I have a fur coat and lisle thread stockings, I'm not a pauper . . . I'll be back in five minutes."

Before August could even object, she ran off. Sashenka quickly reached her own side street, but just at the entrance her way was blocked by a funeral procession. They were burying the little boy, Shuma's son. Four men with large noses were carrying the little coffin. Behind them the women were leading the boy's mother by the arms. From time to time they let go of her, as if the ritual demanded it, and the mother began monotonously, routinely tearing at her face. Suddenly Louty ran out of the back row of the procession and gave Sashenka a kick. Sashenka was in a great hurry, she had no time to get worked up, and she rubbed her bruised thigh as she ran on. Louty, satisfied with his success and delighted with his strength and impunity, rejoined the procession. Olga and Vasya were having lunch. Steam was rising from a saucepan of gruel: water, vegetable oil, salt, and rye flour.

"You mother's admirer came around to see you," Olga said, "there's a note."

"Sasha," the master of ceremonies wrote, "there's happy news for us . . . I went to see the general, my old commanding officer, and he called the right place . . . It looks like your mother will be brought back from the regional center to the local detention cells. She's very worried about you, but otherwise she's well. Uncle Fyodor."

Sashenka crumpled up the note, stuck it in the pocket of her quilted work jacket, then pulled off the jacket, the shawl, and the old sweater, and dressed up again the way she had for the New Year, in the marquisette and lisle thread, the fur coat, and the fluffy beret: she even touched up her lips. Sashenka ran outside and set off back, running for all she was worth. August was still standing there in the same spot, at the entrance to the broad avenue, but just at that moment the funeral procession was moving past him and Zara suddenly emerged from it. Sashenka was about ten steps away when it happened, but without straining to hear anything, Sashenka could guess what Zara was talking about. She was telling August that

Sashenka had lice crawling over her at the New Year's festivities. Zara's face was spiteful and passionate now, like her brother Louty's face, but at the same time there was desperation and yearning in her expression. Zara was looking straight into August's eyes, and Sashenka knew very well what that meant: she and Zara used to be friends once and they used to fall in love with the same people at the same time. The over-age nephew came out of the procession, took hold of Zara by the hand and led her back, obviously squeezing it painfully because Zara winced, but she still turned her head and, despite the pain, desperately carried on shouting out vile things about Sashenka to August. Standing there a short distance away, Sashenka broke into a sweat of bitter fury. She even felt her first brief flash of resentment against August.

"Well, let him," Sashenka thought, "let him go with Zara . . . I'll be left alone . . . And he'll realize . . . Some day . . ."

When Sashenka walked up to August, he looked at her as if nothing had happened, and that put Sashenka on her guard.

"Where have you been for so long?" he asked. "I was missing you already."

He's pretending, Sashenka decided. But immediately she felt ashamed of her momentary bitterness when he was there beside her. He was all the riches that Sashenka had now, the only reason she had for taking an interest in herself, only for his sake was it worth taking care of her own appearance and her own health. They turned into a side street and walked into a building with a large number of signs on doors; it obviously housed a lot of municipal departments. The more important and cleaner offices were located at the bottom of the building, where the doors were upholstered in thick felt and there was a delicious smell of bread and coffee coming from somewhere—obviously from the departmental staff canteens. But the department that August's document was intended for was located right at the very top; to reach it they had to walk up the stairs, and the upper flights were absolutely filthy, chipped, and covered in gobbets of spit.

"I'm with you," Sashenka whispered, "I'll never leave you again . . . I'm afraid without you . . ."

"Silly girl," August said and kissed her on the lips, although visiting petitioners or municipal Soviet workers could have appeared out of half a dozen doors at any moment.

In the room that August and Sashenka arrived in, the energetic woman sitting at the desk was wearing a field jacket bearing the marks left by military decorations and shoulder straps.

"Tonight," she said as she read the document, "we're transferring several mass graves from the central area of the city to the graveyard. We could include you . . . During the war people were buried anywhere at all, and now it often hinders construction work and the requirements of communal services. Foundation pits keep running into mass graves all the time . . . How many units do you have?"

"Four," said August. "Or rather, three . . . My little brother has already been buried."

"Address?" the woman asked.

August didn't know the address, so Sashenka proved useful there.

"That's fine," said the woman, "it's quite close; we'll come around on our way . . . The transport situation is desperate, as you know . . . The Chemapparat factory is giving us horse-drawn vehicles. They need to expand, and the foundation pit of the new production unit runs straight into a mass grave . . ."

After leaving the burial department, August and Sashenka set off along the street, walking downhill toward the river, or rather, August set off, and Sashenka ambled along beside him, quite unable to walk in step with him. A sense of haste had appeared in August's behavior and in the expression on his face, and Sashenka was frightened by it. There were no ruins to be seen along the river. Everything here was healthy, rosy-cheeked, and fresh: the pinkish snow, the women carrying buckets on yokes from a hole in the ice, the country children on the far side of the river, laughing as they ran along the ice by the opposite bank, the frolicking dogs . . .

This was a simple, clear life, not tormented by thoughts and doubts, a mellow and delicious life that had no past and no future, but only today's sunshine and pink snow on the roofs of the little wattle-and-daub houses. Halting at the very edge of the ice, August starting avidly peering, but even so, the haste in his expression didn't disappear, it only intensified. Nature never calms a soul that is genuinely troubled, and all hopes that it will do so are inevitably futile, often leading to self-deception, for the senses of a profoundly troubled soul are always keen; such a soul is sharp-sighted and intelligent, even if in his or her usual condition the person concerned does not possess any special intelligence; the human soul, with the rational, sensate principle inherent in it, is not a creation of dispassionate nature, but its antithesis, born out of the constant struggle with nature, and therefore, in an agitated, morbid state, this struggle becomes particularly unequal. At such moments illusions disappear, and when someone appeals, whether out of ignorance or cowardice, to his enemy, the blows he receives in reply are especially remorseless, and the pink snow, and the sunshine, and the blue sky— everything that the power of fancy, belief, and prejudices, based on blindness of the soul, would have transformed into something which that person finds pleasurable, and which, in his usual condition, helps him to live, is now, at this moment of Hamletesque old age of the soul and keen-sightedness, transformed, albeit subconsciously for the individual, into a part of the universal, hostile chaos, and it takes a cruel revenge, deriding his sufferings. Not to flee from your own soul to its enemy, but to appeal to your soul, and only to it, no matter how appalling the things that are revealed to you about yourself might be—this is the only path to resistance and healing. At the same time, however, this path is as dreadfully dangerous as major surgery, which might save you, but which you might not survive, especially if the pain is profound and inadequately understood. And therefore it is not easy to resolve upon such a course, even having understood in your heart the inevitability of that which the run-of-the-mill materialists term "soul-searching"—to be sure, out of the very best possible intentions of sifting out unhealthy individuals and cultivating physically healthy progeny—even having understood in his heart the inevitability of soul-searching, an individual tries to procrastinate or flatters himself with other hopes, of which there are, unfortunately, quite a large number.

"Let's go to a movie," August suddenly said. "Let's go right now. Where's your movie theater?"

Very soon, literally only about ten minutes later, they were sitting in a large, cold hall with a ceiling covered over with painted plywood and a screen covered in gray blotches, which for no obvious reason had a grand piano standing beside it. Sashenka was holding August's hand tight. He was acting nervous, because the show was taking a long time to start. The hall was buzzing with the merry cross talk of young voices, the squealing of little girls, and the tramping of feet. Finally, the lights went out and an announcement appeared: "This film was captured as a trophy of war," and then foreign captions in color appeared and a foreign color movie began. Sashenka was actually enthralled by it at first, but August sat there with his head lowered, looking at the floor under the seat.

"Are you all right?" Sashenka asked in an anxious whisper. "What's wrong, my dearest, I'm with you, aren't I?"

"You watch," August said, "I'm listening . . . I like to do that sometimes—not watch, but just listen . . ."

Suddenly the image disappeared and the sound broke off. Immediately, as if they had been expecting this, dozens of feet began merrily stamping, and the beams of little flashlights began darting about over the walls, the screen, and the ceiling.

"Vityok!" someone shouted from the back row, like a gunshot right beside Sashenka's ear.

"Heh-heh-heh . . ."

"Stop horsing around . . ."

"Don't be such an idiot, Borya . . ."

"Venya, they took my hat . . ."

"Heh-heh-heh."

A diminutive woman, already elderly, but with large breasts and painted lips, appeared through a side door. She walked without hurrying, in order not to blow out the candle that she was carrying, shielding it with her hand. The candle only lit up her face and cast a glow on her breasts and hands, so from a distance she looked like someone walking for religious purposes, if it were not for her brightly painted lips.

"We've called the power station," she announced, halting by the piano. "We'll have light in twenty minutes." And she immediately hurried away again.

"I'll stab you to death with a fork," someone shouted, like another gunshot beside Sashenka's ear.

"Yahoo, yahoo . . ."

In the darkness, someone hammered on the piano and someone tap danced. They clattered the folding seats of the chairs. The woman with the candle came back several times to make announcements. The jolly horseplay in the darkness continued. At least half an hour went by. Someone jabbed August in the shoulder blade rather painfully, and in the gloom of the back row a face illuminated by a small flashlight loomed up over August's shoulder. There was something piggy, plump, and pink about the features of that face; everything about it was snub nosed, puggy, upward-creeping—the nose, and the corners of the mouth, and the chin, everything was quivering rapidly, ready to burst, to explode, roaring with laughter, spattering saliva; everything about it was all who-gives-a-shit, go for it, Vanka, God doesn't exist anyway. It was like a mask that appears in a nightmare, and despite its jolly disposition and apparent innocence, it inspired fear and provoked hate.

"Pass it on," said the face, restraining its merriment, "don't let me see you here later," the face said, prodding August in the shoulder again, while its eyes turned into narrow slits, its cheeks inflated and its nose was dragged even higher up toward the forehead, and the chin toward the nose.

August pushed the face away from him in disgust.

"A lieutenant here's bashing our guys," the face instantly shouted, but in a muffled voice, because August hadn't taken his hand away yet and the face's mouth was still covered by his palm.

Immediately, several small, agile figures started creeping toward August, filling the entire hall with jabbering.

"Let's get out of here quickly," Sashenka said and dragged August toward the exit.

They emerged into blue-gray twilight; the winter day was fading rapidly. A knot of small figures came tumbling out after them. The street was deserted, with only a few indistinct figures hovering by the ruins of the post office in the distance. One little urchin had a limp, but he darted along quite quickly, supporting himself with a metal ramrod. Sashenka dragged August along, clutching his arm tightly. They almost ran along a stone wall that went on and on forever. Several little brats ran parallel to them, trying to overtake them and block their way. August was astounded by the effortless determination with which they had come together and ganged up on him, as if they had known him for a long time and been waging a battle against him for years. He was astounded that there wasn't even the slightest hint of hesitation, but the kind of unanimity that is only found in a secret religious brotherhood. If he had been facing a strapping hoodlum, or even several of them, everything would have been simple, but these were scrawny juveniles, and August felt defenseless. The first blow from the ramrod struck him on his right shoulder blade. Then Sashenka shrieked; a metal ball from the ball bearing of a tank, fired from a catapult, had hit her on the leg. A brick went hurtling past her right temple, thrown with such great force that it crumbled against the wall. August looked back and met the gaze of the lame urchin's jolly, gray eyes, and he realized that this cripple could quite simply and easily maim or even kill him or Sashenka, absurdly canceling out their lives and the long and arduous effort that had shaped them. Sashenka shrieked again behind August and the lame urchin smiled merrily; something like inspiration, the joy of artistic creation, glinted in his eyes, and at that instant August was saved by an iron-hard fury that welled up in his chest. He grabbed the lame urchin by the collar of his quilted jacket, easily lifted him off the ground, smashed his head against the wall and flung him away hard, judging the effort so that the limping urchin didn't fall into the snow, but onto the solid icebound slope. Rapidly swinging around, August struck another small figure that was whirling around Sashenka, then grabbed his metal rod and struck out again at something soft . . . After that he looked around. There was more space around him now, and he caught a glimpse of Sashenka's frightened face. The juvenile with a limp was lying by the wall in a pool of blood. His teeth were clenched, he was groaning and crying, struggling to get up; his face was gray— the jolly, carefree cruelty had disappeared from it, and it had even acquired a kind of pensiveness, or so it seemed to August. Breathing hard now, and filled with shame, bitter regret, and contrition, August walked across to the juvenile to help him, and at the very moment when he felt pity for the lame urchin, the little figures, who had run off and were hiding close by in the darkness, sensed his pity and realized that their enemy had weakened. Several bricks came flying from that direction, and one hit him on the head, knocking off his hat with the earflaps. When August recovered his wits, Sashenka was holding him, leaning him back against the wall, dabbing with her shawl at August's warm, wet, sticky ear, and the little figures were already far away, walking along tightly bunched together, carrying the lame urchin, and then they turned into a side street and were lost to sight among the ruins.

In the hotel room, Sashenka washed the abrasion on August's head just above his ear and bound it up with an individually packaged bandage that turned up in a suitcase; she bound it up rather clumsily, but nonetheless the bandage stayed in place. Sashenka's leg and her shoulder, which had been hit with a ramrod, hurt very badly, but she didn't start worrying about herself and caring for herself the way she used to, but went to heat up the kettle.

"You're always fussing about like a broody hen," August said, pulling a wry face, "all your hustle and bustle turns everything hazy in front of my eyes."

But Sashenka didn't take offense; she knew how much pain he was in now and how heavy his heart was.

"Rest for a while," Sashenka said, and sat down at the head of the bed where August was lying. "Rest, my darling boy . . . If they'd given you to me when you were just three . . ."

She embraced him and he calmed down, closing his eyes and laying his cheek on her palm.

"Loolay-loolay-loolay," Sashenka sang, rocking her beloved.

Sashenka's grandma, her father's mother, was from an old Cossack family. In her wooden trunk she kept the chased-silver cradle that had belonged to her own father, Sashenka's great-grandfather, which had been passed down the line of inheritance from some obscure Cossack camp commander or centurion. The trunk also contained a necklace of old silver coins, which Sashenka liked, and the scabbard of a *yatagan*. At the beginning of the war Sashenka's mother had handed in this saber to the militia as a cold weapon. Sashenka had loved her grandma Oksana. This pious old woman could speak only Ukrainian, and she used to tell Sashenka stories about imps, goblins, and witches. One day she told Sashenka that Sashenka's mother had slyly enchanted Sashenka's father, binding him to herself with herbs, celandines, and dawn earth. Sashenka was twelve years old then, and they lived a long way from this place, in Pavlograd, where her mother also worked in the mess at a military base.

"What do you mean, she enchanted him?" Sashenka asked, puzzled.

And her grandma had explained that Sashenka's mother had gone to a wise woman, who had given her a potion, and then Sashenka's mother had gone out barefooted into the open field and gathered dawn earth, wet with the first dew, and slipped all this into Sashenka's father's soup, and after that he was a lost man. Sashenka had listened to her grandma and believed her, because she loved her grandma and felt sorry for her father.

Sashenka's grandma had died three years earlier. She caught typhus at the same time as Sashenka; Sashenka had survived, but her grandma had died.

"Loolay-loolay-loolay . . ." Sashenka sang her grandma's song, comforting her beloved: "Nothing for the other children, but bread rings for my boy, so he will sleep at night."

It was already completely dark outside, night was approaching again, and from the way the windowpanes trembled in the wind, and fine, icy snow sometimes sprinkled against the windows and was suddenly followed by moonlit silence, Sashenka could sense that this night would also be a strange, restless one, full of inexplicable atmospheric phenomena.

"It's time," August said and got up. His earflap hat sat crookedly on his head, squeezing down the bandage, and Sashenka had the idea of putting cotton wool between the lining of the hat and the bandage, so that it would cushion the pressure.

When they went outside, it was a night with no moon and no stars—they were completely concealed by clouds that had crept across them, leaving no hope that they would reappear any time soon; the recent restlessness and the constant changes seemed to have given way forever to a mute blankness. The entire world around them seemed to have frozen, as if it had breathed in and been struck dumb in the anticipation and premonition of something, and the heaviness in its chest left it no strength to breathe out. That was what Sashenka thought as they walked along in the darkness. But it didn't last long after all; it was a deception, for very soon the clouds disappeared and the moon started shining, and even the greenish sheet lightning flickered, as it had the night before, somewhere out on the edge, lighting up the chimney of the chemical equipment factory. However, the sheet lightning also quickly faded away and a blindingly bright, festive moon took this world shrouded in darkness unawares, startling it by lighting up every grubby little cranny and making the snow glitter uneasily. However, the bright moon also failed to hold its own for long and the clouds covered it over again, although they were not as thick as before, and everything was balanced out, with a state of neither light nor darkness prevailing on all sides, a sort of anemic haze, with pale shadows from scantily illuminated objects, and scraggly stars, sparsely scattered with long distances between them; and a greenish, gnawed apple core resembling a moldy slice of cheese was all that remained of the rich, mellow moon that had held sway only a minute earlier.

The entire yard—the two-story building where Sashenka lived, and the few single-story brick houses, and the burned-out ruins, where the dentist's murdered family used to live, and the crooked hovel right at the back, where the murderer Shuma's family lived, and the cesspit, and the privy, standing on a slightly higher spot among malodorous snowdrifts, around which the dentist's family had been buried in ground that was soaked through with rotten sewage—all of this now seemed to be illuminated with a low-glow bulb, so to speak, the way that basements are often lit.

"I'll stand here for a while," said August. "I'll catch the prisoners in the street, otherwise I'll never drag them out of the warm kitchen . . . We have to dig more quickly today, so the coffins will be ready when the carts arrive at three o'clock . . ."

His voice was cool, calm and businesslike, but this very circumstance was what Sashenka found most disquieting of all.

"How are you feeling?" she asked.

She could see that August was feeling bad, but she asked in order to start up a conversation and then to use the conversation to calm him and herself down.

"Go and get changed," August said instead of answering. "And if the prisoners have already arrived and they're in the kitchen, tell the sergeant that I'd like them to get started with the work quickly, in order to be ready by three o'clock . . . Those hired men work too slowly. I'll pay them for yesterday, but they don't suit me anymore."

Sashenka walked up the steps and into the building. The escort, the professor, and the morose prisoner were sitting in the intensely heated kitchen. They had bowls of fragrant buckwheat porridge standing in front of them, flooded with milk—powdered milk in fact, from American aid parcels, since there was a colorful box of powdered milk, already half empty, standing on the table. The professor's red-faced wife was making fluffy flapjacks. Sashenka gave her a hostile look, gulped and said:

"It's time to get to work . . ."

"Yes," said the professor's wife. "Vasya's ready . . ."

"I'm coming, I'm coming," said Vasya, glancing out into the kitchen.

His sick chest was tightly bound up in a shawl, and he had Sashenka's father's fine, expensive, warm, astrakhan fur hat pulled down on his head; Olga had ferreted it out from the deepest corner of the wardrobe and extracted it from under its sprinkled covering of naphthalene.

"No," Sashenka said sternly, "you're not needed today." And she suddenly took a step toward Vasya—a moment earlier she didn't even know she was going to do it—and grabbed her father's hat off his head, so that the ribbons tied under his chin snapped. Vasya's eyes opened wide and round and he started blinking rapidly in alarm. Olga, also alarmed, immediately darted out at the noise, and shielded Vasya with her body.

"What's she doing, giving orders here?" Sashenka shouted from behind the professor's wife. "This isn't her place . . . Take no notice of her, I've arranged things with the lieutenant . . ."

"Yes," said August, who had followed Sashenka in and was standing in the door, "come on, sergeant, lead the men out."

"It's only for the best anyway," said Olga, "I was thinking myself . . . Vasya's got a weak chest . . . And I'll earn some stewed meat myself tomorrow from the colonel . . . His kitchen needs whitewashing."

However, the professor's wife wouldn't give in.

"I'd like to have a word with you alone," she said in a rapid whisper, walking up to August. "You must understand, you're a cultured man, after all . . . It's a windy night, frosty . . . He's come straight from a damp cell . . . If need be, I'll pay for everything myself . . . We have to take care of him . . . He's the future of our literature . . . Our literary criticism . . ."

"All things considered, it's time to go grave-digging," said the professor, pushing away his bowl of buckwheat porridge and getting up.

The escort got up too, giving the professor a look of contemptuous mockery, and the morose prisoner looked at the professor maliciously, choking and burning his mouth as he hastily gulped down his buckwheat.

"All of you did this," the professor's wife shouted despairingly, seeing her plans crumbling, and she clenched her little fists and ran up to Sashenka. "You . . . you hate me . . . I know . . . I can feel it . . . But you, you . . . You're an MFW . . . A Mobile Field Wife . . . He's got dozens like you . . . In every town, in every village . . . They've been all been debauched by the war . . . They've learned to kill . . . And you're hoping . . . You piece of filth . . ." She laughed.

Suddenly she was hysterical; she seemed to come unhinged instantly, as often happens with people who brace themselves for ages, suffering hardships with gritted teeth and then sometimes flying off the handle at a mere trifle . . . Through her laughter and her tears she shouted out many insulting words at Sashenka, but Sashenka didn't answer; she could see that August was tired and weak, he could scarcely stay on his feet, and this shouting was torturing him.

The professor took his wife by the shoulders, and Vasya took her by the legs, and they carried her away and put her on Sashenka's little sofa bed. Olga splashed some water in her face; the professor's wife gave one more squeal and calmed down.

"Shall I take the prisoners to the same place, Comrade Lieutenant?" the escort asked. His lips were trembling and curling up, and it was clear that he would have liked to laugh, but he restrained himself, obeying the regulations and maintaining discipline.

"Yes, take them into the yard," said August. He walked up to Sashenka and said quietly: "Perhaps you have some old things, a dress or something . . . For my mother and sister . . ."

"All right," Sashenka said almost under her breath, and went to get changed.

She put on her sweater, long pants, woolen skirt, and quilted work jacket. Then she rummaged in the wardrobe and chose her own brand-new white frock with the red flowers, mother-of-pearl buttons, and flared hem for August's dead sister. But for his dead mother she chose a dress that was no longer new, in an old-fashioned style, with a zip fastener, but still quite sound and decent. Sashenka put all this into a suitcase, muffled her neck in a scarf as warmly as she could, and walked out into the yard, which was still dimly lit by the moon through the thin clouds.

When Sashenka reached them, the morose prisoner and the professor had already cleared the snow off the marked-out area, and now they were taking turns pounding it with a crowbar. The crowbar kept twisting out of the professor's hands, leaving no more than faint scratches on the frozen surface, and his pounding was done for him by August or Franya, who had marked out the area, but who was extremely drunk and so worked clumsily. The expression of haste that frightened Sashenka had appeared on August's face again. He stood at the edge of the pit and waited impatiently for his mother's remains to appear.

"Go and take a walk," the professor told him, breathing hard from the heavy physical work, "we'll take her out, and you'll see your mother in her coffin, not surrounded by filth and frozen night soil . . . That would be more honorable with regard to your mother . . ."

"Stop that talking," the escort shouted.

"I suppose you're right," August said, and moved off to one side. Sashenka took hold of his hand and they walked out into the middle of the roadway and went quite a long way away through the streets and along the avenue, past fences, past the sleeping hospital, straight to the snow-covered vegetable lots with the little wattle-and-daub houses sparsely scattered among them. What a night lay all around them, what anguish there was in all of nature, anguish—struck dumb, incapable even of groaning to bring itself relief. The dull light glowed through the clouds onto the snow, incapable either of blazing up more brightly or fading away; nothing stirred, nothing sighed in its sleep, or rustled, or barked. There were none of the sounds either near or far, clear or enigmatic, that living nights are so full of. It seemed that if a conflagration broke out now, or hail started clattering down, or human voices, filled with horror, started calling for help, all of that would merely dispel the fear and help the hearer feel like a human being whom nothing apart from death can threaten.

Sashenka kept a firm hold on August's hand and he docilely followed her. Taking advantage of this, she turned off the path winding between the vegetable plots and went toward the yard of the hospital, avoiding the trench in which she had imagined she saw a beautiful girl who had been killed with a brick—August's sister.

It is hard to say how much time went by before Sashenka and August came back to the yard, but a cart was standing in front of the building, and the driver was swearing impatiently, and August's sister and mother still had not been taken out of the ground. There were eight coffins on the dray, lying on top of each other in two layers. These were wounded men and nurses who had been killed during an air raid on the railroad station in 1944, and then buried in the factory square, which was now needed for the foundation pit of the chemical equipment factory's foundry shop.

"There, you see," said the escort, "you see, Comrade Lieutenant . . . And he was going to leave already, the driver was . . ."

After that, everything was all hurrying and scurrying, and none of it left Sashenka with any firm memories. Both pits had already been dug, and all that had to be done was to take out the deceased. The mother had dried up, so that she looked like a mummy, and they didn't lift her out, but chopped her out of the frozen ground that adhered thickly all over her body and her face. It was dangerous to clean the dirt off with spades, since the body was fragile and could fall apart, especially at the joints. It resembled a sculpture molded out of earth, and only the gray hair, growing on the little earthy head, was soft and evoked human compassion, although feelings were also aroused by a scrap of clothesline on a lumpy leg of sand and clay. They raised the body up carefully and placed it in the coffin, ungluing the hair from the wall of the pit and cutting off the clothesline and, naturally, they didn't try to attire it in the dress that Sashenka had brought, but simply covered it with this dress with the zip fastener, as if with a blanket, and nailed down the lid of the coffin. But the sister was amazingly well preserved, which could be accounted for, to some extent at least, by the internal structure of a young body, as well as the structure of the ground and the location of the burial site. Although the two pits were located quite close to each other, the sister had been buried in pure clay, beside the fence, where there was no sewage or other products of decomposition, and also, thanks to the bushes and the shade, the icy, frozen snow had been preserved for an especially long time in spring and then, after being sprinkled over with earth, it hadn't thawed out for a long time, and when it did thaw, it had all soaked into the clay and created propitious conditions around the body, cooling it. And for this reason, the sixteen-year-old girl's body had remained blossoming and attractive, although perhaps that was also partly owing to the diffused moonlight. They raised the sister up, setting her on the greatcoat that August took off, and clothed her there in Sashenka's frock with the flared hem and little mother-of-pearl buttons.

Everything on her face and in her plump, luscious lips and around her plump, girlish breasts, only appeared to be soft, since the tissues had stiffened and sclerotized. Especially on the lips and the breast, there were clear traces of the filth and excrement that Shuma had dumped and poured onto the bodies, abusing and defiling them when they were already lying in the cesspit.

The professor's wife, who had long ago recovered from her hysterics and was now hovering solicitously by her husband, wiped away these smears of sewage on the girl's body with snow. Then both coffins were carried to the dray.

"Professor," said August, "you will stay here until I come back from the cemetery . . . Sergeant, you wait here . . ."

After that Sashenka remembered a dug-up square, soldiers with entrenching tools, a long line of carts loaded with coffins, the cemetery, the frozen river down below at the edge of the cemetery, and all the time that same, dull, wretched sky: neither darkness nor light.

"What should I do?" August asked quite a long time later, standing on the intersection of Yanushpolskaya Street and Paris Commune Street, with the moon that had flared up brightly for a brief moment hanging directly above his head. "It's terrible murder and humiliation, but there is no equality in death and suffering . . . Those who stood on the very lowest rung had no right even to slavery . . . They had no right even to humiliation; with his brick, Shuma was very probably destroying the ideal order of things, for humiliation is at least some kind of mutual relationship that promises a future . . . In the ideal case, which was perhaps understood by a few erudite bureaucrats, who were familiar with ancient Greek paradoxes and were regarded as freethinkers in the Gestapo, in the ideal case the Jewish people should have died quietly and painlessly in places allocated precisely for that purpose, thus fulfilling their international duty to mankind in the name of universal happiness . . . This was also understood in his own way by the owner of a small factory near Khazhin that produced lubricating oils . . . He succeeded in getting the occupying forces to grant him the right to have some of the Jewish children who were doomed to die delivered to him . . . He put them up in a boarding house, in good conditions . . . The children were given milk, margarine, fruit jelly . . . And then they were all given injections, and they died in their sleep, an easy death in clean beds . . . Special, high-quality sorts of lubricating oil were made from their well-fed childish bodies ... After the liberation, several pits were discovered in the factory yard, filled with nothing but children's heads ... The owner regarded his activity as both good and useful at the same time, since otherwise the children would not have calmly gone to sleep forever, they would have died in torment and terror ... That is the problem of ideal service to mankind by an entire people, from whom no one demands exhausting labor, or deprivations, but merely an easy death ... Such is the viewpoint of cultured anti-Semitism, which considers that Hitler's atrocities complicate the problem ... I happen to have read a work of this kind, printed on a mimeograph ..."

"My darling," Sashenka said, catching August's hands as they darted through the air amid the snowflakes sprinkling down from the clouds, "my darling, you need to take a rest ... Your eyes are bloodshot ..."

"Leave me alone," August shouted, "leave me alone, go away ..."

But Sashenka didn't go away, she knew he was being unfair because he was feeling bad ...

After that they sat in the overheated kitchen.

"Professor," August said, "it's not a matter of the killings, appalling as they are ... That's an old sin, and humanity has learned to prolong its kind despite it ... When I first saw my mutilated father and then afterward ... I dreamed of ripping apart the killer's alien flesh ... Tearing his sinews. That night I dreamed I was killing his children ... It was appalling ... I woke in a cold sweat and realized I couldn't go on living like this ... But here was the desperate resistance of my own flesh, the serpentine cunning that makes everything small, that makes any grief and hatred ludicrous ... I'm talking a lot, professor, and erratically, but you know why, of course ... An animal in my situation simply howls ..."

"There's a place in the Bible," the professor said, "do you remember it ... 'How long, Lord, will you tolerate our sacrifices and not strike down our tormentors?' . . . It's not word-for-word, but that's the meaning . . . And the Lord replies: 'Wait until the number of victims increases and becomes such that the predestined limit shall be reached, after which all sacrifices and torments shall be avenged.' "

"You mean to say," August shouted, leaning forward and slumping onto the table with his chest, "you mean to say that it was inevitable, and perhaps even necessary . . . There it is, the vile, serpentine wisdom that creeps into your brain at your temple . . . Just as soon as you drop your guard. You're a vile man with your kopeck-cheap philosophy. I ought to smash your face . . . But you say I'll survive it all . . . I must understand, otherwise it will kill me . . ."

"What I mean to say," the professor patiently explained, taking no notice of the crude outburst directed at him, "what I mean to say is that the limit is already approaching. . . . Retribution and vengeance are available to all, atonement is not only for the righteous, who have the truth on their side. The biblical limit is approaching . . . For centuries, atonement has been continually moving toward this limit; at times the righteousness of the offended could be seen even through the centuries, and now, beyond that boundary, crossed at the price of millions of innocents, retribution and atonement will fuse and become one . . ."

"That's not enough," August said, "that's incomprehensible . . . That's not what I was expecting from you . . . And another point . . . Those who perished in trenches and were burned up in crematoriums were far from perfect . . . But it's too soon to judge the victims when the butchers have not yet been punished . . . However, the time will come and the victims will also answer for the crimes committed against them . . ."

"The time is approaching," the professor said loudly, speaking more to himself than to the lieutenant, "the time is approaching when man will win from destiny the right to possess justice, that is, to establish it at the scale of his own life, just as he won from the gods the right to possess fire . . . Herein lies the Promethean feat, unconscious and unaware of it as they may be, of millions of victims who gave themselves up to be butchered, as Prometheus gave up his liver to be tormented by the vulture . . . That biblical boundary is approaching, the line beyond which lies either universal life or universal death. But eternal glory to those souls who took upon themselves suffering, mockery, and early death in order to exhaust the portion of torments allotted to mankind by destiny and so brought the limit closer . . . I mean to say, who have allowed us to approach so close to the biblical limit that it is already visible, visible in the gloom, in the night . . . The light is visible . . . There will be something new there . . . Perhaps new torments . . . Cosmic, interplanetary, God only knows what kinds . . . But these small, commonplace torments, unworthy even of hate and lamentation, but only of contempt and laughter, these will remain there on the far side of the line . . . Our most appalling tragedies are essentially comical . . . A sixteen-years-old girl is killed by a blow to the head with a brick, smeared with shit, and buried beside a privy . . . Why, that's a vaudeville sketch . . . And the prisons . . . You've never seen how they sleep on the concrete floor in prisons . . . With asthma, cavities in their lungs, and incipient thrombophlebitis . . . No, colleague, spare me that, let's get across that biblical boundary as quickly as possible . . . Perhaps to new torments, even more appalling, but not so comical . . ."

"Every killing is terrible," August said, "but ineluctable, planned murder—this is a new degree . . . The blood of a child who has been found and killed . . . They were absolutely obliged to kill him and any other outcome was excluded here . . . Blood like that washes away any stains that a people has . . . And it renders any fury that its enemies have criminal, even if it is underpinned by so-called just ideas . . . It would at least be understandable to some extent, if not just, if the ineluctable murdering were the lot of everyone who has declared himself a Jew, in the way that people declared themselves protestants, for instance . . ."

"It is particularly hard for our generation," the professor said, "not because the gloom has become a lot denser, but because we have seen the light, approached so closely to the limit, to the end of the tunnel, and this light has aroused our impatience . . . While man was a semi-animal, he lived on authentic ground, under an authentic sky . . . But, on becoming a thinking creature, he entered into a long, dark tunnel, in which not even the sky is authentic, but rather was invented by astronomers . . . Perhaps there are still two or three generations remaining until the end of the tunnel, but the light is already visible . . . That is why it is particularly hard for us. In fact no, there are only one or two generations remaining to the end, no more than that . . . But what lies ahead—that is hard to say . . . Perhaps, once having broken out into open space and found ourselves under an authentic sky, not an invented one, to go back under cover, back into the tunnel, to our petty squabbles, to the possibility of dying at the hand of one of our own kind—perhaps that is what we shall one day regard as happiness."

"After what has happened to me," said August, "after everything . . . After these pits . . . After my mother sculpted out of clay and sand . . . I ought not to have talked to you. I'm fighting for my life, and that's why I'm making myself suffer."

But in the meantime no one else spoke, for the entire heterogeneous group had suddenly realized that these two should not be interrupted just now . . . Each of them, however, was silent in his or her own way. The professor's wife said nothing, even though she was anxious about the dissatisfaction felt concerning her husband's observations by the man beside her, who held power over her husband. However, she sensed that the man her husband was talking to needed him, and so her husband would continue sitting in the warm kitchen for a while, instead of in a damp cell. Sashenka said nothing because she loved August and felt in her heart that just at the moment everything was going as well as possible, and she didn't reply to the professor's stupid words, and in any case this conversation was helping the lieutenant to recover his strength after what he had seen and been through. The escort, observing discipline and also happening to sympathize with the lieutenant—his own cottage had been burned down in the war, with his family in it, and when he saw the smoldering ruins, he didn't go to a railroad station, to spend the night there alone on a bench, he went to spend the night in boisterous company. And the morose prisoner said nothing, because he was gulping down hot flapjacks straight off the griddle, fueling himself for two days in advance, hoping that the half-raw flapjacks stuffed into his stomach would not be digested soon, but be diluted tomorrow and the next day, and still in three days' time by the prison gruel, that they would create a continuing sense of satiety and a belch of baked batter. Olga and Vasya were not even in the kitchen, they were lying down in the room on the fresh linen sheets that Sashenka's mother had been keeping for Sashenka's dowry, and their caresses could be heard even through the tightly closed door.

"I read a thesis on determining the mysterious number," the professor said, "the biblical number of victims, which will be followed by the advent of justice . . . A graphomaniac's work, superficial, but the problem is in the air . . . Possibly it will be called something else . . . There's an element of fatalism in it that even I find repugnant . . . But note the fact that the freer man becomes, the more science develops, the greater the increase in the number of people beginning to respect themselves, their own personality and their dignity—the greater the number of their victims grows . . . The two currents flow toward each other, in order to halt at the covenanted boundary line . . . Having collided, these two currents will form a third, which will deviate from the channel of current history and, according to some calculations, will move perpendicularly to it, but according to others, at an angle that has yet to be established."

"I have become convinced," August said, "that the butcher and the victim are at one only in death. But in life there is a clear distinction ... From the moment of birth ... Entire families, entire nations, peoples, states ... That's where the greatest abomination lies ... A victim who breathes, consumes food, and reproduces, ready to die at any moment and living on into deep old age ... An ancestor-victim, a breeding victim, he begets individuals who know full well how sharp and pitiless their executioner's blades are, but are absolutely unaware of how frail and easily broken the executioner's spine is ... What a pleasure it is to snap it ... How easily it disintegrates into the separate vertebrae ... And how nonferal, glistening, aware and even intelligent, filled with philosophical musings, the eyes of the butcher become in those brief moments ... So let the butchers die now, professor, for each blow struck on their spines transforms them for those brief moments before death into serene, good souls ... Your biblical number will start increasing with immense speed and approach the sacred limit."

"If you enter Sverdlovsk University after the army," the professor said, "I'll give you a note to someone there ... A highly respected man ... He'll help you ... Would you like me to write the note now ... Only deliver it personally ... In private."

"Don't bother," August said quietly. "I'm preparing for a different career ..."

"A pity," the professor sighed and suddenly looked at August intently, straight in the eyes. "People like you ... and perhaps, like me ... should have gills alongside their lungs ... When it becomes difficult to extract oxygen from the air, we could extract it from water ... An absurd image, poetic, not scientific ... I do a bit of translating, after all ... Even a bad poet hits the bullseye at least once, unlike a bad scholar ... There are some interesting words from a certain forgotten author ... Deservedly forgotten, basically ... Sexual appetite is akin to cruelty ... Everything born of woman must die. These words may be polemical and sloppy from the viewpoint of our Central European morality, but they do express the beauty of the ancient Greek worldview, capable of admiring the poetry of tragedy, for instance the poetry of incest, so that one forgets about the essence of the matter and thereby overcomes one's suffering . . ."

The professor would have carried on talking for a long time, but just then someone tapped on the kitchen window that looked out onto the landing of the stairs, and a face was pressed up against the glass.

"It's the culture worker," Sashenka said in annoyance, "Uncle Fyodor . . . What does he want?"

She got up and opened the door.

"Did you get the note?" Uncle Fyodor asked, breathing heavily; he had evidently hurried, jumping up the stairs two steps at a time, despite his lameness. "They're bringing your mother on the morning train . . . Get your coat on."

"I can't," Sashenka said, "I'll come to see her tomorrow . . . Or whenever they allow visits, that is . . . I'll come on Thursday . . ."

"Your mother will be badly disappointed," said Uncle Fyodor, almost imploring. "Her heart is acting up . . . She needs to be taken care of . . ."

"And my husband is ill," Sashenka said firmly in front of everyone, "I can't leave him alone . . ."

She walked over and put her arms around August, and pressed her cheek against his prickly cheek, overgrown with stubble.

Uncle Fyodor looked confused for a moment, then he smiled, stepped across, and held out his hand to August.

"Pleased to meet you," he said, with a broad smile. "Please accept my congratulations . . . And Katerina, Sasha's mother, will be glad. It's a surprise, of course . . . But in these times . . . People don't ask for advice nowadays, and that's all for the best . . . Sasha's heart isn't exactly tough, it's more principled . . . her father was a Party commissar. She takes after him regarding the interests of the state, even

if the violation comes from her own flesh and blood . . . I don't con-
demn her for it . . . And I told Katerina: It's for the best . . . You made
a mistake in terms of helping yourself to the people's property; you
have to atone for it . . . She understood . . . And we spilt our blood on
the front for the interests of the state and the people's property . . .
So don't you have any concerns, Sasha, about your mother being
offended with you," he said, turning to Sashenka now. "She loves
you a lot and she'll love your husband too . . . And accept my per-
sonal congratulations, too . . ." At this point he became totally con-
fused and fell silent.

"What train is it?" August suddenly asked, moving away from
Sashenka and getting up. "The Lvov train?"

"That's the one," said Uncle Fyodor.

"Then I have to hurry," August said hastily, "to get ready and pay
people . . . My things are in the hotel . . ."

After that everything happened quickly, feverishly, awkwardly.
Sashenka started bustling too, rather mechanically, not thinking
about anything apart from how to help her beloved, who was in such
a hurry that he couldn't get his arm into the sleeve of his greatcoat.
She remembered that they ran to the hotel together, but whether it
was still night as they did it or already getting light, and whether the
full moon was blazing away with all its might or the timid celestial
body was lost in a blizzard, and what other phenomena were agitat-
ing the sky—Sashenka paid no attention to all of that but, once she
found herself on the platform at the station, she stopped and looked
around, as if she had suddenly run into something with her chest.
Her chest really was hurting, like after a hard bump, and all around
her, in the sky, and on the railroad tracks, there was trepidation,
lights glowed faintly, illuminating the sleepers; there was a smell of
coal, and the clouds, the stars, and the moon—not full and round,
but still quite massive—continuously created various, different
freakish pictures, swapping places, disappearing and reappearing

again, and each picture had its own meaning and order; Sashenka guessed that, but because each picture on the sky was so short-lived, it was impossible to grasp that order, and so everything seemed like haphazard chaos. And it was this imperfect vision that produced the sense of alarm growing stronger and stronger in Sashenka's heart.

"Why don't you look at me?" August asked. "Are you offended? Do you despise me?"

"I don't want you to leave alone," Sashenka said, "I want to go with you . . ."

"I'll write to you," August said, "and you'll come to me as soon as the matter of my demobilization has been settled . . . I'll go to university, and you'll study too . . ."

The station was located in one of the surviving railroad buildings, which used to house the railroad technical college. Passengers with bundles and suitcases were now streaming out of it, attempting to occupy a convenient position on the platform in advance, in preparation for a difficult boarding, since the train had only a short waiting time. The previous station building, destroyed by bombs during an air raid in 1944, was now fenced off with barbed wire and lit up by floodlights on towers. The captured Romanians and convicts were working there. The convicts were already busily doing something in the ruins, but the Romanians had obviously only been brought recently, and they were still taking a roll call.

Uncle Fyodor ran to-and-fro along the platform with his wounded leg skidding on the slippery snow, trying to find out where exactly the prison car was attached—at the front or the back of the train—and in his hands he had a little sack of presents that he was hoping to hand on to Sashenka's mother. He ran up to Sashenka and August several times, to pass on new and more precise information about the prison car, but every time, when he saw their strange, incomprehensible faces, his courage failed him and he walked off to one side.

A wind started blowing and tearing at the station trees, tousling the forest plantations in the distance beyond the lines, swirling the clouds, the stars, and the moon around the sky in a carousel, scattering the celestial pictures about. The sudden drop in atmospheric pressure, resulting from the thickening of the air in some layers of the atmosphere and its attenuation in others, frightened the passengers ahead of time, so that they started running to-and-fro with their bundles and suitcases ten minutes before the train's arrival, striking people coming toward them dangerous blows—especially when the blow came from the corner of a plywood suitcase or a trunk bound with sheet metal. Uncle Fyodor had started running about even earlier, when nature was still relatively calm, because his aorta, weakened by his injury, had already sensed the approach of the squally snowstorm when it was still far distant. In fact, some others also sensed it, but the general mass of people only became agitated under the direct influence of the blizzard. The blizzard, however, had a strange effect on Sashenka and August. Sashenka moved close to August and looked up at him, her pupils moved upward and inward, closer to the bridge of her nose, as happens with the approach of sleep, or a fainting fit, or death, and her eyes were filled with awe combined with fear. She saw only her beloved's head and the agitated heavens above it, and he seemed to be looking down at her from those agitated heavens.

"The train," shouted Uncle Fyodor. "Your mother . . . she's waving to you, Sashenka . . . Look . . . They've brought her . . . She's here . . ." He choked and spluttered in his joy . . .

"My love," Sashenka said to August, without looking back, although Uncle Fyodor was tugging at her, trying to make her notice her mother, who was calling to Sashenka over the heads of the escorts and straining to get to her. "You, my love forever . . ."

Uncle Fyodor, skidding and stumbling on his injured leg, ran over to get a look at Sashenka's mother and tried to hand her the presents, since the prisoners were already being loaded into a tarpaulin-covered truck, but Sashenka's mother, who had managed to squeeze into the final row and so had gained an extra minute or two, immediately dispatched Uncle Fyodor back to Sashenka, to tell her daughter to run over to the cordon of escorts and show her mother what she looked like and tell her in a couple of words how she was getting on, and if she couldn't manage that, then at least to look around.

"Your mother asked," Uncle Fyodor shouted, panting for breath from running and wincing at the pain in his injured leg, "your mother's calling you . . . Or at least glance around . . . She misses you . . ."

However, Sashenka probably didn't even hear him, and perhaps she didn't even see him, for, as the physiologist Charles Bell said: "When feeling consumes us completely, external impressions no longer exist for us, we turn our eyes upward, making a movement that we have not learned and have not acquired."

"Always only you . . ." Sashenka said joyfully.

"Yes," said August, and his face sank down from the heavens onto Sashenka's breast.

Beside the railroad cars, passengers grabbed and pummeled each other, temporarily transformed into the bitterest of enemies by the briefness of the train's halt. They swarmed, trying to squeeze their bundles and bodies through to the front of the line, forgetting about the love of mankind, since the train had already sounded its whistle to depart, and the next train wouldn't arrive for another twenty-four hours, which would be spent on the floor or on the benches at the station.

"I'll write," August shouted from the steps of the last car as it departed into the space illuminated by the low railroad lamps.

Uncle Fyodor carried on running from Sashenka, standing at the far end of the platform, to the mail sheds, beside which the prisoners were getting into the trucks; he wanted very badly to take a look at Katerina, to cheer her up, to pass on the presents if he could manage it, and to have the joy of her presence, standing close by and exchanging a word or two, because he had been pining badly without her; but the moment Fyodor appeared at the cordon, Katerina immediately heartlessly drove him back to her daughter, refusing to listen to anything and demanding that he bring her daughter back with him.

"Your mother's asking," Fyodor shouted, covered in perspiration, whistling as he breathed and feeling pain in his kidneys now— he had an old wound there, from 1941, that had been well patched up in a regular hospital and rarely bothered him, except when he was very tired and agitated.

"Come on, your mother's feeling anxious," Fyodor shouted. "You've seen your husband off now . . . What else . . . They'll take your mother away . . . Maybe they'll only keep her here for the night . . . I heard they're sending her to the next region . . . Not to the district center, but to the next region . . . Well, look at her at least . . . She's your mother, after all . . ."

But Sashenka didn't look back to where her mother, standing in the rumbling truck, was straining toward her, but at the snow-covered tracks, where Sashenka's beloved had been lost to view amid the low railroad track lights . . .

Five minutes had already gone by, the train had obviously already crossed the bridge, and beyond the bridge a long climb began; the trains always moved slowly and heavily there, rounding the city in a wide arc, and if her beloved was standing at the window, then by the light of the moon anyone who was now walking along Zagrebelnaya Street, which ran right up close to the railroad embankment, could easily see his face; and from the Zagrebelnaya hill beside the little church it was quite possible to see him for a long, long time, and, if it was a sunny day, for even longer, until the engine rounded the hill and pulled the entire train into the tunnel beside the Raiki Forest.

Meanwhile, life on the platform was settling down. Those who had not managed to squeeze into the cars had gone away, dragging the bundles and suitcases that were heavier now, jostling and hurrying as before in order to grab the benches in the station and not spend a day lying on the floor.

"They took your mother away," Fyodor said quietly. His face was weary and pained. "I didn't manage to give her the presents after all, it was too awkward . . . and she needed them, from the look of things, oh she really needed some nourishment . . . There's a kilogram of fatback here, and dried plums, you can easily drink hot water with them, instead of candy or sugar . . . And did you settle things with your husband? Will you go to him, then?"

"We haven't decided yet," Sashenka replied, smiling pensively, because it was pleasant to talk about her beloved. "He's going to write to me . . . If he's demobilized, we'll move to a big city, maybe to Moscow, because August needs to carry on with his studies . . . He wants me to study too, but I'll get a job for the time being; after all, we have to have clothes, and food, and they'll probably give me a place to live at the factory . . . I just have to master a good trade. I'd like to learn to be a seamstress, work my time at the factory, and then work in the quiet at home . . . And earn lots of money; people are really short of decent clothes now."

Sashenka explained all of this in thorough detail, and speaking the words gave her a good, calm feeling.

"Your mother will help," said Fyodor. "And I'll help too . . . After all, we're almost family. I'll get a job at the Chemapparat factory . . . They won't give your mother much time—the widow of a frontline veteran. I had a talk with the general . . . She'll be back home by autumn . . . So, if you have a child, of course, things will be a bit more difficult . . . But don't you hang back, we'll get by all right, we'll survive . . ."

He put his arm round Sashenka's shoulders and they set off from the station along the hard-trampled, slippery road. And while they walked together like that, all the way through the frozen city, they had time to forgive each other in their hearts for all the bad things, both the old ones and the not so old, and even to become friends.

What happens to people, why they act one way and not another toward someone else, is still hard to understand after all, no matter how well it might all have been studied, how primitively easy it is to explain and how thoroughly the answer has been learned. There is always a little "but" about liking and disliking, running throughout that infinitely unclear world that is called human relationships, in a world full of fleeting mirages and chain reactions, in a world where living organs—blood, lymph, nerve fibers, seminal fluid, bile— interact in a mysterious sequence with the phenomena of the earth's magnetism, the sun's emanations, and the phases of the moon. The human ocean is the most amazing, fathomless, and unknowable. Some assert that this is precisely what Job was writing about in his book, in exhorting people not to be deluded by the simplicity that is perceptible to the naked eye, and exhorting them never to cease feeling amazement at the mysteries of existence. And there are three main mysteries of existence. The greatest mystery of the universe is life. The greatest mystery of life is man. The greatest mystery of man is creativity. And on this matter the very greatest wisdom, the most accessible to the human soul has been spoken: "Mark me, and be astonished, and lay your hand upon your mouth" (Job 21:5).

12

I n late September, Sashenka gave birth to a little girl. Sash-
enka's mother had returned from imprisonment long before
then; she had been sentenced to six months, but the sentence
had been commuted because she was pregnant. She had given birth
in summer, three months before Sashenka, and also had a little girl.
Olga had also given birth, in March, and her daughter was already
sitting up and crawling about, and she could give a painful pinch.
Sashenka and Oksanka lived in the small room, and Sashenka's
mother and Fyodor and Sashenka's sister Verochka lived in the
dining room. Vasya and Olga were back in the kitchen, but now they
had cordoned off a rather large area for themselves, and not with
a screen, but with a brick partition that they had hired workers to
build, so that in place of a spacious kitchen, a small room had been
formed,with a narrow passage, barely large enough for the stove to
fit into. Nadenka, Olga's daughter, was big for her age, she still didn't
know how to ask for the potty, so she always had a sour smell, but she
had realized exceptionally early that those who eat are the ones who
live and grow strong, and no matter who sat down at the table and
no matter what they ate—lenten gruel made of rye flour; or soup
made of fodder beets; or potatoes in their jackets, improved with
yellowish, poor-quality fat that caused heartburn—no matter what
they ate, Nadenka reached out her hand with the same rapturous

delight toward the steam billowing out of the saucepan, and it wasn't even possible to say that she was begging, it was simply that she was delighted by the sight and smell of food, as other children are delighted by a rattle. One day Vasya, who now worked in a carpentry workshop and earned quite good money, allowed Nadenka to lick a piece of fatback. Nadenka went into such raptures that Olga wrapped the piece of fatback in a clean piece of cloth that was folded over double, tied it on a string, so that Nadenka wouldn't swallow it, and gave it to her to suck on, like a soother, until Katerina saw it and gave Olga a good piece of her mind for doing that.

Olga and Vasya sat there, large and good-natured, in their little room carved out of the kitchen, loving each other without any words or explanations, with nothing but caresses, and Nadenka, with Vasya's meek eyes, crawled about on Olga's knees, releasing bubbles from her little mouth and bumping into Olga's protruding stomach, because Olga was pregnant again.

Sashenka's sister Verochka had only been walking for three months, but she also reiterated in some ways the people who had given her life. She liked to laugh, and when she did, tiny little dimples appeared on her cheeks, as they did on Katerina's, but when she did something bad—for instance, threw a cup off the table or when she once pee-peed straight into her father Fyodor's face, with a pure, childish little squirt, not yellow, but white, like warm water, not yet saturated with acrid salts of uric acid—when she pee-peed on her father, she knitted her brows and wrinkled up her little forehead so sincerely that one could sense her absolute repentance and honest, but not stupid, good-heartedness. Fyodor laughed, wiped his wet lips and said:

"What does she eat . . . Her waste output is still as pure as tears."

Sashenka called her daughter after her late grandma Oksana. At first, she wouldn't let anyone else near her and always changed her daughter's diapers and bathed her herself. Sashenka wouldn't even let her own mother take Oksana, and when Katerina did take her, because Sashenka hadn't always put the child's nappy on the right way and she was crying and jerking her head - when Sashenka's mother did take the child, Sashenka felt terribly anxious and hovered around them, like a cat whose kitten has been taken from her. Oksanka's eyes were tiny, and so were her little fingers, and her little hands, and her little snub nose, but Oksana's irises were huge and blue, taking up all of the eyeball, completely grown-up, restless and nervous like her father's, and at the same time curious, not merely looking, but examining. Now Sashenka loved the nights when she could be alone with Oksanka and no one threatened their seclusion. If the little girl woke up and jerked her head anxiously, getting ready to cry, Sashenka carefully jingled grandma Oksana's old necklace of Turkish and Polish coins above her, and the granddaughter of the dentist Leopold Lvovich, killed by a blow from a brick to the back of his head, stared with her big, strong, quite un-babylike eyes at this Cossack trophy, her great-grandmother's coin necklace, as if she was guessing at some secret meaning and contradiction in it and was exhausted by a level of concentration that was still beyond her.

"Oh, loolay, loolay, loolay," Sashenka sang, "Nothing for the other people's children, but bread rings for Oksanochka, so she can sleep at night. When daddy writes, we'll go to Moscow . . . He's going to study at the university . . . And you'll grow up . . . You'll wear little marquisette blouses, and little lisle thread stockings on your legs . . . And your mummy will get old . . ."

The tears flowed down Sashenka's cheeks, but her heart was filled with a gratifying, sweet yearning that was reminiscent in some ways of her old yearning as a girl, only this yearning was calm and gentle, without any audacity, hate, or rebellion. Especially when there were warm autumn nights with train whistles, with a brief rustling of rain, greenish flashes of light from some unknown source in the distance and an immense sky, not like September, but more like August, so alive, so diamond-bright, so infinitely varied, that it was simply impossible to believe that all this was indifferent and blind toward her and the life around her.

One day Fyodor called into the military commissariat, to which he had already written an inquiry on his own initiative, and when he came back he took a long time trying to gather his strength, avoiding answering questions directly, and then he couldn't hold out any longer and in the middle of the night, lying in bed on the linen sheets that had been intended for Sashenka's dowry, although now, thanks to Olga, they had become simple household items and were already washed out, lying there on those sheets with his arms around Sashenka's mother, he spoke into her ear, telling her that the military commissariat had answered vaguely about the lieutenant, in indefinite hints.

"Who can tell," Fyodor said with a sigh, "even in peacetime these airmen get knocked off like flies . . ."

Fortunately, Sashenka didn't hear this conversation, since it was held in very low voices; of course, she heard her mother start sobbing on the other side of the wall, but since her time in prison Sashenka's mother sobbed quite often; she had become exceptionally weepy, and often cried, not over some serious matter, when tears are a soothing solace to the soul, but over any petty nonsense, and Sashenka took no notice. She rocked Oksanka, and lifted her own head up from time to time, staring out the night-dark window and thinking her own thoughts . . .

One sultry autumn day, Sashenka was walking along the avenue with Oksanka. It was the drought-ridden, hungry autumn of 1946, which followed a hot summer with a failed harvest. The temperature was higher than any of the old folk could remember at that time of year, and this was obviously connected with the atmospheric phenomena that had been agitating nature all year long. Exceptionally severe famine had broken out, especially in regions far from the center, and in a number of cases it had even surpassed the hunger of wartime; in addition the strength engendered by hopes of the enemy's imminent rout and a happy, peacetime life, had been exhausted now, the stamina of people's bodies had been reduced, and the death rate had risen to an extraordinary level. War invalids, whose bodies had been shot to pieces at the front, were dying; chronically ill people, whose bleeding ulcers, tuberculosis, and other disease processes, temporarily suppressed by powerful emotions, had become more acute after the five-year break and started taking their revenge, were dying; children, their living organisms deprived of essential vitamins and their bones, deprived of phosphorus, as brittle as old men's, were dying; widows, who had shattered their endurance with unwomanly labor and womanly grief, were dying; and also, as they did at all times, old people were dying, and they were pitied least of all, except by their very nearest and dearest, for there was at least something decent and natural about their deaths.

The muscles that raise the shoulders are sometime referred to by anatomists as "the endurance muscles." In many people these muscles are exceptionally well developed, but unlike mythical Atlantes, supporting the sky on their shoulders, in people these muscles require nourishment from fresh, rich blood, full of digested vitamins, proteins, fats, and carbohydrates, derived from food, and the nerve fibers of these muscles also possess reserves of strength, which, though substantial, are not inexhaustible. And the moment comes when the endurance muscles stop functioning, the shoulders slump, the spine curves, and the heart starts working irregularly. It can be hard to recognize a person like that, and so, when three people—two men and a woman—overtook Sashenka on the avenue, and one of the men called her by name, Sashenka looked at him in amazement. But in fact he was Professor Pavel Danilovich, the former prisoner, who had been released thanks to a petition from a certain Moscow celebrity, and thanks to the honesty of the orderly, who was now deceased, having been killed that spring by bandits in the Raiki forest, and also thanks to the good-heartedness of the colonel, the head of the local security forces, to whom the orderly had presented the petition. And so, as a consequence of these three factors, Pavel Danilovich was now at liberty. However, to judge from their appearance, Pavel Danilovich and his wife were living at the extreme stage of poverty, having sold off all their property and items of value during his imprisonment. Pavel Danilovich was scruffy, louse-ridden, unshaved and also, for some reason, on crutches; his right leg was a swollen log, sealed into gray, badly soiled plaster. His wife had somehow lengthened out and would no longer have dared to flirt with the deceased orderly, for every woman knows her own value, and her value at the moment was the very lowest, with her dusty, mouse-gray, plain wool dress, which robbed her of her final strength in this heat, and her breasts that no longer stood out firm and pointed, but drooped like empty army ration bags. This pitiful appearance was completed by a skinny mesh shopping bag, which did, however, have a bunch of green onions protruding from it, although the stems had wilted and buckled, and the heads were not slim and supple as they would be in spring, but swollen and flabby to match the autumn season.

That is how quickly a woman's appearance is affected by external events, nutrition, and her inner, intimate life. The impoverished couple were accompanied by a youth with a skinny neck and inflamed eyes. The youth's hollow chest, afflicted by sicknesses since his childhood, could easily have provoked revulsion, even loathing, and perhaps it did provoke them in certain physically healthy tillers of the land, with rounded chests, inflated by the air of the fields and the forests, and muscles acquired from agricultural labor and natural selection. That was probably why Sashenka could sense that the professor's wife, despite her present appearance, instinctively took a very dim view of the youth and only tolerated him as yet another of her husband's whims, for she came from a line of hereditary tillers of the land, in which all the men were two meters tall and could smash a plank with a blow of their fist. And the youth had a rather strange name too—Liusik.

"Liusik," Pavel Danilovich shouted, clearly delighted at this meeting, "remember, I told you about a student... He and I became acquainted in strange and tragic circumstances... A highly interesting individual... Yes... He made highly interesting observations concerning the problems of the biblical number... Concerning the mystery of the biblical limit... This is his wife... I have been looking for you," he said, turning toward Sashenka. "It's awkward to call into your home, but I was hoping to meet you..."

"Quiet," Sashenka said angrily, "you'll wake the child..."

"I beg your pardon," Pavel Danilovich said almost in a whisper, embarrassed. "Is this his son?"

"His daughter," said Sashenka, really angry now, moving back and shielding Oksanka with her body, as if afraid that such dirty, unpleasant people would do something bad to her daughter.

"I would like to have a talk with you," said the professor.

"I don't have any time," Sashenka replied impatiently, "I have to feed the child soon... And in any case what's the point of these conversations..."

"It concerns your husband," said the professor.

"Do you know something?" Sashenka shrieked, and her heart started pounding heavily.

"Not here," said the professor. "We live not far away... Let's go, it won't take long..."

The professor really did live not far away. The room was rather spacious and sunny, although it was almost empty and extremely neglected. There was a rather fine mahogany table with mismatched legs, an egg-shaped mirror hanging on the wall, and two iron bedsteads, sloppily made up. And piles of books on the floor. The books were the only thing in which there was any sense of order; the piles were arranged neatly in a chessboard pattern, and an oilcloth, obviously removed from the table, had been laid out under them.

"Would you like some tea?" the professor asked, "Liusik, warm up the tea. . . ."

Liusik, who kept well away from Sashenka and was obviously afraid of her and blushed when he accidentally met her gaze - Liusik was the one who took the kettle and went out.

"Your husband left me his notebook," the professor said, "his notes . . . Or rather, until recently my wife kept them . . . But when I returned, I familiarized myself . . . Interesting, extremely interesting . . . But there's a lot I don't understand . . . Do you happen to have anything else . . . Possibly it could cast light . . ."

"No," said Sashenka, perplexed, "I don't know anything. He didn't tell me . . . We didn't have time . . . And I've never heard about that notebook before . . ."

"An interesting notebook, a darling notebook," said Professor Danilovich, stroking the calico cover in jubilation, like a child with a toy. "Liusik quite independently . . . There's something similar . . . In his work . . . Or rather, they complement each other . . . And that's what . . ."

"Your Liusik's insane," his wife shouted angrily, "he's a cybernetician . . . And it says in every textbook, every child knows, that cybernetics is a bourgeois pseudoscience . . ."

"Now, who told you that he's a cybernetician?" the professor said peaceably, refusing to be provoked into a quarrel. "The little kitten isn't a cybernetician; he attempts, from the absolutely real positions of dialectical materialism, to employ vector algebra as an instrument for analyzing the laws of history . . . A mathematical analysis of the quantity and direction of events in history."

"It's all Liusik," the professor's wife shouted, almost crying, turning to Sashenka and suddenly looking for support from her, "he's a cybernetician, I can definitely sense it . . . You can't fool me . . . And this gray-haired man isn't ashamed to consort with him . . . With this madman . . . Or perhaps he's a cunning fraudster . . . He's not ashamed . . . A well-known scholar, the hope of literary scholarship, the translator of Lord Byron . . . I sacrificed everything for him . . . I was well provided for, my husband was a Soviet functionary . . . He loved me, he would have done anything for me . . . But I believed *him*."

She reached out her hand toward Pavel Danilovich, who sat there with his face wrinkled up, as if he had eaten something sour, since he was afraid that the scene and his wife's tears would go on for a long time, and that would prevent him from concentrating, and meanwhile something new, which had been striving to break out for a long time, but had so far remained elusive, was now stirring in his brain.

"I believed him," the professor's wife shouted, breaking into floods of tears, "I considered it my duty to save him for Russia, for the future . . . And he's taken up with a cybernetician who is alien to our values, who is quite simply physically incapable of understanding our people or its aspirations . . ."

She stopped talking, because Liusik had brought the kettle.

"It would be good to have wine," the professor said. "Days like today should be celebrated with wine . . . Today is not just any day . . ."—Pavel Danilovich turned toward Sashenka—" . . . a long chain of deliberations and calculations has been terminated . . . A result has been achieved . . . Naturally, only a preliminary result as yet . . . Yes, a result is like an abyss . . . Herein lies the price of every discovery, every achievement . . . The road leads no further . . . Wait, the Lord says to the victims in the Bible, until your number shall become such that my tolerance of the executioners shall be exhausted . . . Yes, I don't remember the Biblical text precisely now . . . This number will be reached in 1979 . . . That is precisely the number and the date that is spoken of in the Bible ... The date from which a new history shall begin ..."

"I cannot agree with you," said Liusik, setting the kettle on a metal stand, "even though we have worked together. That conclusion is too hasty, and the result is contingent. Certainly, it is elegant and beguiling in its definiteness, but I have no doubt that you have committed elementary mathematical errors ... That happens even with great mathematicians ..."

"That's Yurkievich," Pavel Danilovich shouted angrily. "I'm sure you've been associating with that crackpot old dotard again ..."

"Sigmund Antonovich taught me to love mathematics," said Liusik.

"But he's an anti-Semite," Pavel Danilovich shouted. "How can you associate with that individual ... For shame, for shame ..."

"Ah, Pavel Danilovich," said Liusik, sitting down and pensively resting his chin on his hand, "there are places, apart from the iron ore mines, where even housewives suffer from silicosis ... Koch's tubercle bacillus infiltrates the organism independently of the individual, and in some localities the process is ongoing in every individual ... Sometimes unperceived even by him ... It is not the individual who must be restored to health, but the locality ... I've thought about this a lot ... And in a healthy locality, healthy children will be born, who will not be in danger of becoming infected ... Therefore, I will not take the hand of a Czech, Frenchman, Englishman, Belgian or Dane, for example, if I observe in him even the slightest indications of anti-Semitism ... A different locality, a different climate, the demands on him are different ... But I can quite well be friends with a Pole, for instance, even if this 'Koch bacillus' is present in him, and even if he regards it affectionately, provided, of course, that he does not overstep a certain line ..."

"You're a difficult man, Liusik," Pavel Danilovich said, "a terrible man, but it's a pity that you didn't know this student ... A pity that you and he will probably never meet in this world ..."

"He's alive," Sashenka shouted in a strangled voice that made Oksanka wake up and start crying. "You're lying, lying . . . You're the one who's mad . . ."

"Yes," the professor said absentmindedly, "actually, I imagined it to myself . . . Don't you worry . . . I have an imagination, and dreams . . . For instance, I dreamed that I would die at forty seven . . . On March seventh . . . Even the date . . . And in a prison infirmary, moreover . . . That dream is actually quite optimistic . . . Two and a half years of life still ahead of me . . ."

"You shouldn't have been let out of jail," Sashenka shouted. The tears were streaming down her face, and Oksanka couldn't calm down either.

The professor and his wife whispered together, while Liusik stood beside the mirror, facing the wall, and his ears and neck were red from embarrassment and confusion.

"I'm going," Sashenka said. Her heart was hurting, aching from the suffering inflicted on it in this house, suffering that had affrighted her very soul, for in any case she already thought about her beloved the whole night long, pining for him, dreaming of his clumsy kisses and wanting to show him his daughter. And now, after what the professor had said, for the first time during their separation, she had suddenly thought that her beloved might die, and recalled the way he had lain on that terrible night, with his arm bent, pressing his iron hand to his temple. Sashenka couldn't forgive these people for all this.

"I'm going," Sashenka said bitterly. "All of you here are enemies of the people . . . You said anti-Soviet things here . . . You think I'm a little fool and I don't understand . . . My father died for the motherland . . . And here you . . . You bastards . . . You've got lice creeping about over there . . . Creeping across the pillow." She took particular satisfaction in saying that, because she saw the professor's wife blush . . .

There really was a gray clothes louse creeping across the pillow, cutting across it diagonally, and Sashenka felt better, even though her heart still hurt as badly as ever; she pushed the door with her foot, darted out onto the landing and loitered for a moment, listening to the professor's wife shouting.

"That's your Liusik," the professor's wife shouted. "I'll tell him so to his face . . . He's dirty, he smells . . . We've never had any parasites . . . He scratches himself at the table . . . I don't want him to come here . . . It's either him or me."

The professor's wife broke into hysterical sobbing, and Sashenka walked down the stairs and out into the street.

Before Sashenka had even reached the end of the side street, the professor's wife overtook her. The professor's wife was wearing a man's jacket, thrown on over her robe, and very beautiful house slippers trimmed with fur, the only things that maintained her respectable appearance, serving as a reminder of her former well-provided life.

"Bear in mind that all his comments, his notes, his papers, I'll destroy them all . . . He's mistaken, but he's not an enemy of the people . . . He's muddleheaded . . . And three of my brothers were killed in this war, and my father in the civil war . . . So there now . . . And if you notify the security forces. Distorting the situation . . . Then your husband will be held accountable . . . All his notes are up there . . . Don't you think I won't say anything . . . So there now . . ."

She turned around and set off back home at a trot, and Sashenka walked on. Sasha's heart was sad and troubled, but Oksanka started wiggling her eyebrows strangely and wrinkling up her nose, and then she sneezed and sighed exactly like a grown-up, so that Sashenka laughed and pressed her daughter's sweet-smelling little face against her own.

At home, everything was in a jolly mess; they were bathing the little girls. Since three families lived here and that created a crush in the little scrap of space that was left of the kitchen, Sashenka's mother Katerina had suggested bathing all the children together, on the same day, in order not to obstruct the stove all the time. On her way back, Sashenka had already noticed that the windows in the three-story house on the corner were bright with electricity. That meant they had electricity too, since they were on the same line as that house. And the electric light really was on, and the kerosene lamps were standing there extinguished and unnecessary, looking comical. Every time they were given power for one or two days a week, it lifted Sasha's mood, although it might seem like such a little thing, but even so, it made everything different, and she could believe that soon her life would become really good, and a letter would arrive from August, who hadn't been able to write sooner for military reasons, but Sashenka never allowed herself to think of what would happen after that, because after that things could become so good that her heart would have started aching from the joy of it, the tears would have come pouring down and her temples would have clenched up tight. That was why Sashenka always thought only as far as the letter, and after that she simply felt glad and was affectionate with everyone, trying to oblige her mother, and Olga, and Fyodor, and even Vasya, who still had a bad chest, but his condition seemed to be improving, and during the day he coughed less often, since he drank the potion recommended by the woman in the choir.

Now the apartment illuminated with electricity was filled with a calm, merry peace. Little Nadya and little Vera, already bathed and swaddled in fluffy towels, were sitting side by side on the sofa, pink and warm, smelling delicious, looking extremely like each other today, even more than they looked like their parents.

"Get Oksana undressed quickly," said Sashenka's mother. "They suddenly put on the power, that's why we decided to make today bath day . . ."

Bathed and steamed, Oksanka also turned pink and started look-
ing a bit like little Nadya and Vera, as if they were her sisters.

They organized a joint supper. Fyodor opened a jar of stewed
pork that was left over from the abundance of winter, Sashenka's
mother made lots of rye-flour pancakes, and Olga set on the table a
bowl of hard dumplings, stale doughnuts and poppyseed crumpets
of various different shapes and sorts. Although Vasya earned quite
good money, clothes and shoes still had to be bought, and little
Nadya had to be fed, and now Olga couldn't go out to do work by
the day, whitewashing walls and washing floors, because she was
pregnant, and so every Sunday she went to the church porch and
they gave her quite a lot, for she took little Nadya with her, and she
had a big stomach, since she was preparing to give birth again. All
this softened people's hearts, especially the peasant women's, and
so Olga could even afford to keep some of the alms she received as
a reserve, and now she set out part of that reserve on the common
table. When everyone was seated at the table, Fyodor suddenly
started fidgeting, whispered something to Katerina, jumped up
and walked out, but very quickly returned with a bottle of murky
moonshine; he obviously hadn't gone very far, only to Franya's lit-
tle room under the stairs. Everyone drank, even Sashenka took just
a tiny sip, and started feeling very jolly, she wanted to kiss everyone
and cry. Her mother actually hugged her, gave her a kiss and sud-
denly said:

"Forgive me, Sashenka, forgive me, my daughter, that things are
so cheerless for you in this world . . ."

There was a slight commotion at the table, but all three little girls,
well steamed and calm after their baths, carried on sleeping side by
side on the sofa, without hearing the commotion, building up their
strength for their future, exhausting lives.

"All right," said Fyodor, "crying's the last thing we want at
a moment like this . . . I want to tell you this story . . . During a

bombing raid one night I spent the whole night sheltering behind something or other, and when it got light, I realized that I'd been sheltering from the shrapnel behind a wooden trellis, overgrown with Virginia creeper, but I didn't know that during the night, so I was calm, and perhaps I was saved by not running across open ground in search of cover . . ."

He wrinkled up his forehead for a moment, perhaps wishing to draw conclusions of some kind from this story told out of context, but he wasn't able to add anything, and only laughed. But Vasya and Olga dozed off shoulder to shoulder, good-natured and big-boned, looking like brother and sister, and not missing a chance to cosset each other, even at the common table.

Meanwhile it was a superb evening, with no drop in pressure or red clouds with a ponderous sun setting into them, or any other unpleasant signs to be observed, everything in nature was gentle and lyrical, in halftones, there was no increase in the magnetic charge of the upper layers of the atmosphere affecting the blood vessels, or any of the various loud sounds that can set a sick heart fluttering. But even so, Professor Pavel Danilovich had suddenly died only half an hour earlier. And one couldn't say that he had been particularly upset by the quarrel and the conversations; on the contrary, after Sashenka left, the quarrel had rapidly exhausted itself, and they had all sat down to drink tea with dry biscuits bought at competitive-market prices. True, Pavel Danilovich did have a bad habit that was harmful for the health, the habit of taking a book when he drank tea and sipping while he read. On this occasion, it was Spinoza, a thinker in whom materialism is diluted with an admixture of "theological blood." The book had been read a great deal, it was frayed and tattered, and Pavel Danilovich had written in the margins in his own skittering, almost illegible handwriting.

"Cognition is a form of struggle for the biological stability of the human species," Pavel Danilovich had written, "a form that replaces millions of years of evolutionary selection. In the evolutionary selection that is necessary for the existence of a species, it is the mass that participates, and the individual is a fleeting element. Cognition is the anchoring of the stability of the individual, hence the biological hatred of the depersonalized mass for the individual, insofar as the quality of the mass is reduced. Moreover, especial hatred is not aroused by external, scientific, cognition that is visible to the eye, from which it is possible to defend oneself by ignorance or indifference, but by the cognition of simple moral truths, an inner, fixed cognition, or rather, almost fixed, invisible to the eye, in which changes are not measured in years, centuries and millennia, but in civilizations, and against which there is no defense. We deny, Spinoza writes, that God could not do that which He does: in other words, Spinoza's topic is predetermination. God is not free in his actions and is subject to strict rules ... This extremely important definition concerns the perfection of God. All things accomplished by Him are so perfect that they could not be accomplished by Him more perfectly. Everything is necessary and predetermined, otherwise He would be inconstant, which would be a great imperfection ... No one knows all the causes of things so that they can judge concerning them as to whether there is truly any disorder in nature."

Further on in the margins, in Pavel Danilovich's skittering hand: "The question of questions is whether the world is fortuitous, whether life is fortuitous, whether events are fortuitous, or everything conforms to laws, and, consequently, is predetermined. It seems to me that the law-governed will always encompass the fortuitous, forming a system, so to speak. Within the system, its own imperfect, fortuitous laws operate, but the entire system as a whole is perfect and its movement is predetermined, that is to say, the higher laws predominate over the entire system as a whole, but do not dominate its individual parts. And such is the arrangement for everything capable of movement. Within the system movement is fortuitous, external to it everything is strictly law-governed and moves in a predetermined direction. However, this predetermined direction is itself fortuitous from the viewpoint of a different, greater system, which includes in itself a multitude of such systems, moving in different, fortuitous directions, and this entire encompassing system as a whole moves in a fashion that is law-governed and predetermined, and cannot change its direction, which is equally fortuitous from the viewpoint of a still greater system ... And so on to infinity. Human destinies, and the events associated with them, including both the most vast and the most commonplace, are subject to this same law. Movements are predetermined for each individual, but fortuitous from the viewpoint of a greater system. However, a thinking, living system is distinguished by the fact that it is capable of expanding the sphere of the fortuitous, of expanding, through the power of imagination, the cramped prison confines of perfection and conformity to laws, of delighting in the unknown, in whim and desire, of forgetting about predetermination and experiencing happiness, melancholy, hatred, honor, shame and greatness, no matter how comical these may be from the viewpoint of the great system. Hence Spinoza's definition: 'Honor and shame are not only useless, but fatal, they are based on vanity and the error that man is the cause of all things and therefore deserving of praise or censure' is only true from the viewpoint of the highest system for the entire cycle of the development of mankind as a whole, but false for the internal stages of that cycle. Universal chaos is the mingling together of the fortuitous and the law-governed, and the question is: What is it that crowns the whole, that is ultimate in the incalculable sequence of countless systems called the universe?—and this will evidently never be comprehensible to a finite brain. To torment oneself over defining the true meaning of human life is preposterous, for in order to understand this, one has to cease being human, to move beyond the bounds of the system and lose oneself. For someone who has succeeded in doing this, in becoming nonhuman, this question ceases to have any meaning. It becomes petty, ludicrous, and unnecessary. Weakness and fortuitousness are valuable qualities of everything living, and man, in defiance of the absolutely essential reason and cognition that render life more secure and more impersonal, man will cling to this ability to feel that he is himself and is unique, distinct from everything and from those of his own kind. Perhaps our invented little earthly meaning of life consists precisely in that. For millions of years biological natural selection has been striving toward stability, simplicity, unification and law-governed consistency, and perhaps it coincides with the genuine meaning of life, a meaning that is non-earthly but known to man, while the invented, little, human meaning strives toward anarchy, toward unsociability, toward rebellion, toward dissimilitude, in order to maintain a taste for life, in order not to lose the appetite for life through small, comical, personal suffering and the pacification following this little suffering, which protects man like a screen from the big, non-earthly horror, making man become bogged down in his little suffering so that he only reaches the edge of the precipice at the end of his life. Woe to him who has attained unto non-earthly wisdom prematurely and has succeeded in rising above his suffering and laughing at it. Earthly suffering is like a blindfold on the eyes that protects man, concealing from him his brief instant and the great NOTHING that follows it."

After reading these lines, Pavel Danilovich looked up and saw Liusik, who was dunking a dry biscuit in his tea. He half rose, about to say something, but suddenly burst into laughter. It was not hysterics, it was the healthy, full-blooded laughter of a man who had realized the reason for his failures and was delighting in the new life that should, accordingly, have come to him. However, Pavel Danilovich did not laugh for long, for he suddenly fell and lost consciousness. Since Pavel Danilovich had previously suffered a blockage (thrombosis) of the cerebral blood vessels, the professor's wife was frightened, but not completely at a loss. She and Liusik quickly undressed the sick man, trying not to disturb the leg sealed in plaster, and put him to bed, as is essential in such cases, with his head slightly raised by thrusting three pillows under it. Liusik ran to the post office to call for an ambulance. The ambulance did not arrive immediately, but the doctor told the professor's wife that this had not changed matters, since her husband had not suffered a simple thrombosis, but an acute hemorrhage, in other words, a cerebral stroke, and he had been dead for a long time. After that the doctor left and the professor's wife pulled the two superfluous pillows out from under the deceased's head, and the professor assumed a natural, calm pose, without a kink in his neck, but with his neck smoothly extended and the head, forever silenced now, lowered right down.

"Is it possible to feel with one's hand this essential reality enclosed in the head under the skull?" the German philosopher Herder wrote. "The deity himself, say I, has covered it with a forest, a symbol of the sacred groves where mysteries were once consummated. I am gripped by a religious thrill at the thought of this shady mount, concealing within itself lightning bolts, each of which, emerging from chaos, is capable of illuminating, adorning or devastating the whole world."

And now the professor's gray-haired head rested motionless on the pillow, preserving in its cooling depths his final discoveries, which had not been recorded on paper in his skittering hand, but had flashed like bolts of lightning and laid waste his blood vessels. There was life only on the professor's lips: curled sarcastically, they mocked at mysticism, idealism, and the prophetic dreams that had foretold two more years of life for the professor and death in a prison hospital.

The grief of the professor's wife was so great that she did not scream or cry, and made very few movements in general; as people who do not understand physiological processes sometimes say, her heart had turned to stone.

If the bodily pain is not excessive or completely absent, but the mental pain is great, this leads to depression. In anticipation of suffering a person experiences anxiety, but if there is no hope, then that anxiety develops into despair. And indeed, the blood circulation of the professor's wife slowed, her face turned pale, her muscles became feeble, her eyelids sank lower, her head sank down onto her constricted breast, her lips, cheeks, and lower jaw sagged under their own weight, her eyes became dull and were frequently moistened by tears, her eyebrows assumed an inclined position, and the corners of her mouth turned downward.

The professor's wife sat on a chair by Pavel Danilovich's head, but Liusik sat at the feet of the deceased, and now his face was the same as the face of the professor's wife, who did not like him. Certainly, since Liusik's organism was younger and less experienced, every now and then he made an effort at active self-expression, which manifested itself in sighs so deep that they induced spasms of the muscles of respiration and a hard lump stirred in his throat, his eyes and the wings of his nose twitched spasmodically, and the folds on his forehead crept upward, and this fractured the line of his eyebrows, as always occurs during deep, honest suffering. It is no accident that anatomists sometimes refer to this complex of muscles as "the muscles of grief."

Liusik and the professor's wife sat like this all night long by the light of a candle, having draped sheets over the mirror and switched off the lights, which had suddenly flashed on and actually frightened them at first. The two of them also spoke to each other frugally, only when necessary, as they saw Pavel Danilovich off on his final journey on a jolting municipal services cart. A certain confusion arose in this connection: the professor's wife insisted that before her husband was put in the coffin, the plaster must be removed from his bad leg. But this only took place in the early evening of the following day. However, while the night of rare beauty continued, full-mooned, starry and windless, it agitated those whose hearts were free, it was a sweet night for caresses, good for the conception of large, heavy infants.

For the first time in many months, Sashenka fell asleep calmly on that night, beside Oksanka, who was sleeping, pink from her bath; and for the first time, Sashenka dreamed calmly and clearly of her beloved. Everything was good for them and everything was the same as it had been then: sweet torture, blissful torment, in which her strength gratifyingly dissolved away, joyful moans burst forth from her chest and, at the last, there came the disappearance, the fusion, the drunken challenge to destiny, which had divided them into two separate lives. And then came calm, weariness, and deep, sound sleep. The second half of the night arrived and everything all around also began sinking into impetuous, irresistible sleep, and those whose hearts were downcast slept sitting, with their eyes open, and were lost to themselves until the first sounds of morning. But the night kept growing lovelier, and the moment came when its beauty began to inspire terror. Countless swarms of stars teemed, the brightest of them blazed with unbearable brightness, and those that were concealed in cosmic darkness began gradually showing through, assuming form, and there was no end to them. And the moon took on a savagely blinding appearance, unlike its every-night one.

Terror differs from fear in that a large part is played in it by poetic imagination. This is why terror is also akin to beauty. Precisely such a beautiful night is described by the biblical Job in his fourth book: "In thoughts from the visions of the night, when deep sleep falleth on men, fear came upon me, and trembling, which made all my bones to shake. Then a spirit passed before my face; the hair of my flesh stood up: it stood still, but I could not discern the form thereof: an image was before mine eyes, there was silence, and I heard a voice, saying: Shall mortal man be more just than God? Shall a man be more pure than his maker?"

But everything living slept on that night, and this vision, with no human eyes to behold it, dissolved away uselessly and without trace before the dawn. Only the unfortunate Job, the most keen-eyed among men, was awake on an exactly similar night two thousand years before. Incidentally, a leading specialist in the area of geotectonics, the German scientist Stille, asserted that our planet's prolonged period of tectonic calm was coming to an end, and he did not exclude the danger of the earth's crust fracturing, as occurred at the end of the Cambrian geological period. In this regard attempts, admittedly tentative and now forgotten, were made to use this geotectonic hypothesis to explain the ludicrously barbarous and bloody history of mankind. We know, for instance, of one attempt made, not by a philosopher or a geophysicist, but by a failed writer, a Jew who adopted the Lutheran faith and died at the age of twenty-five. Turmoil, travails, wars, instability, the triumph of ignorance, the blood of innocent victims, the groans of the weak, provoking in response only the voluptuous laughter of the butchers—he attempts to explain all this by the reflection, admittedly in vague and complex terms, that is experienced, without their being aware of it, by living things—the reflection of those catastrophic processes, which, according to Stille, threaten to break open the earth's crust. Naturally, one should not give any weight to extreme forms such as this, since even if the utmost effort has been made to be objective and all-encompassing, they must be regarded with great caution. At the same time, however, it should be noted that many authoritative materialists regard Stille's works with great respect: once they are liberated from their cataclysmic husk, there is much that is just and true to be found in the ideas embedded in them. Indeed, the end of the Cambrian period, when there were massive cataclysms, when eruptions occurred, mountains were built, new continents were formed, oceans evaporated, lava and magma fell as rain, destroying all living things, and the Neogene Quaternary period, in which modern man lives, represent the most important revolutionary eras in the development of our planet.

A mosquito born in July is in no danger from the snowy blizzards and hard frosts of December of the same year, and likewise man is in no danger from Stille's geotectonic cataclysms, although they could possibly occur during our Quaternary period. According to the mathematical law of the similarity of systems, in which the law-governed encompasses the fortuitous, life will quite naturally be extinguished long before the ambient environmental conditions cease to be suitable for it. Nonetheless, unlike the mosquito, man subconsciously senses the breath of these cataclysms with his intellect and his imagination, he worries, becomes agitated and feels frightened by a danger that is nonexistent for him. Perhaps it is in order to kill the apocalyptic fear flowing in his blood of the death of the planet, which holds no danger for man, that man aspires so absurdly to an artificial death. Psychologists have determined that many suicides are panic-struck and terrified by their inescapable future death, and so they kill themselves to kill the fear.

"Oh, loolay-loolay-loolay," Sashenka whispered quietly, because Oksana had tumbled away from her mother's side and started cooing anxiously: "Oh, loolay-loolay-loolay, nothing for the other people's children, but bread rings for Oksanochka, so she will sleep at night."

A naive, unpretentious, human dawn was beginning, and God's agonizingly wise, soul-crucifying night was ending.

1967